CHINESE MEDICINE MEN

SHERMAN COCHRAN

CHINESE MEDICINE MEN

Consumer Culture in
China and Southeast Asia

HARVARD UNIVERSITY PRESS

Cambridge, Massachusetts, and London, England • 2006

For Macu, Colly, Bill, and June

Library of Congress Cataloging-in-Publication Data

Cochran, Sherman, 1940–
    Chinese medicine men: consumer culture in China and Southeast Asia /
  Sherman Cochran.
      p. cm.
    Includes bibliographical references and index.
    ISBN 0-674-02161-4
    1. Consumer behavior—China—History. 2. Consumer behavior—Southeast
  Asia—History. 3. Popular culture—China—History. 4. Popular culture—
  Southeast Asia—History. 5. Drugs—Marketing. I. Title.

HF5415.33.C6C63 2006
306.30951—dc22   2005043546

ACKNOWLEDGMENTS

"Can I use advertisements in my research?" I asked my academic adviser, Jonathan Spence, when I was a graduate student more than thirty years ago. He agreed that it was worth a try, and since then I have asked many other people the same question in various forms as I have sought help with a series of projects, especially this one. The people on the receiving end of this question have given thoughtful and helpful answers even when my topic seemed remote from their fields of specialization. My thanks go to all of them, including the ones whose names are not included here.

For comments on the original manuscript for this book, I am grateful to Beatrice Bartlett, Michael Hunt, Michael Kammen, Peter Katzenstein, Thomas Lyons, Robert J. Smith, Jonathan Spence, and two anonymous readers for Harvard University Press. For comments on parts of it, I wish to thank Robert Culp, Sara Friedman, Takeshi Hamashita, Gail Henderson, Andrew Hsieh, Ping-chen Hsiung, Susan Naquin, and Sidney Tarrow. For the making of the maps, I owe a debt to Thomas Lyons and Eric Singer, and in trying to see what the illustrations signify, I was fortunate to be able to consult Jeffrey Cody, Kerry Fan, Johnathan Farris, Lai Delin, and Martie Young. These friends and colleagues have challenged me to rise to their high standards, and I take the blame for the places where I have fallen short.

Without archives this book would not have been possible. In Hong Kong, Sally Aw and Sharon Tsang kindly gave me access to the Aw Boon-haw Archives. In Singapore, Lily Tan introduced me to the Singapore National Archives. At the Shanghai Municipal Archives, Feng Shoucai and Ma Changlin have served faithfully, while access to their institution's collections has broadened spectacularly. Since the founding of the Shanghai Municipal History Museum, Pan Junxiang has been my guide there. At the Center for Research on Chinese Business History in the Shanghai Academy of Social Sciences, my close colleagues Cheng Linsun, Huang Hanmin, Lu Xinglong, Shen Zuwei, Zhang Zhongli, and Zhang Zhongmin have provided me with the most crucial help of all. They have put in my hands valuable unpublished source materials that have come from outside as well as within their own center, and they have repeatedly opened doors that would otherwise have been closed to me.

My research in these archives and elsewhere would not have been feasible without financial support. For a grant that covered the costs of research in East Asia, I want to thank the Henry Luce Foundation for Asian Studies in New York. For fellowships that gave me the opportunity to write this book, I am grateful to the Woodrow Wilson International Center for Scholars, Washington, D.C., and the National Humanities Center, Research Triangle Park, North Carolina. For research assistance, I have had funding from the Department of History and the East Asia Program at Cornell. My research assistants have included Christoph Giebel, Patrick Hess, Xiaojia Hou, Ningkang Jiang, Haiyan Lee, Conny Marquardt, Eric Singer, and Liren Zheng. They have made significant contributions to this book, and Dr. Zheng, a specialist in Southeast Asian as well as Chinese history, has made the greatest contributions of all.

In this project I have benefited from skillful editorial assistance every step of the way. At Cornell, Katie Kristof worked with early drafts of chapters. At the National Humanities Center, Karen Carroll put the manuscript in proper form. For Harvard University Press, Ann Twombly edited the manuscript precisely and constructively—even moreso than is generally expected at a distinguished academic press—and Kathleen McDermott and Susan Abel gracefully presided over the transformation of the manuscript into a book. Operating from her own home, Kathryn Torgeson expertly added the index.

While writing this book, I have depended heavily on my loved ones to see me through a time of personal loss and recovery, and I am grateful for the chance to dedicate it to members of my family: my sister, brother, and sister-in-law for sustaining me through thick and thin, and my wife for opening the way into the future.

CONTENTS

Consumer Culture in Chinese History

> I go to villages in northeastern China to see what the world looks like beyond the frontiers of globalization and I find the teenage girls in go-go boots. . . . Open your borders to globalization's cultural onslaught, without protective filters, and you could go to sleep at night thinking you're an Indian, an Egyptian, an Israeli, a Chinese or a Brazilian and wake up the next morning to find that all your kids look like Ginger Spice and your boys all want to dress like Hulk Hogan.
>
> Thomas L. Friedman, *The Lexus and the Olive Tree* (2000)

> It is clear that consumers are not the automatons many analysts would have us believe. The initial encounter soon begins to fade as McDonald's loses its exotic appeal and gradually gains acceptance (or rejection) as ordinary food for busy consumers. . . .
>
> The process of localization correlates closely with the maturation of a generation of local people who grew up eating at the Golden Arches. By the time the children of the original consumers enter the scene, McDonald's is no longer perceived as a foreign enterprise.
>
> James L. Watson, *Golden Arches East* (1997)

In these passages the journalist Thomas Friedman and the anthropologist James Watson have raised urgent questions for today's world. How has consumer culture reached "beyond the frontiers of globalization"? Have big, Western-based transnational corporations like McDonald's fast-food restaurants imposed themselves from the top down and carried out "globalization's cultural onslaught"? Or have consumers throughout the world responded from the bottom up and subjected these Western corporations to "the process of localization"? Friedman and Watson are only two among many who have taken sides in this debate, which bears on an even bioadei question. Have Western-based transnational corporations been homogenizing the world's cultures, or have individual consumers in local cultures been diversifying the world's cultures?[1]

In this book I hope to contribute to the debate over homogenization and localization by shifting its focus and setting it in a new historical context. Friedman and Watson have aligned themselves against each other (implicitly in the above quotations and explicitly elsewhere), and they and others have argued on the basis of fundamentally different definitions of consumer culture and its agents.[2] Some have defined it as a culture in which goods as material objects are widely diffused, and they have specified institutions (especially Western-based corporations) as the primary agents that have carried out the process of diffusion. Others have conceived of consumer culture as a culture in which goods are interpreted as representations, and they have identified individuals (especially local consumers of goods) as the primary agents that interpret these representations.[3] In the epigraph Friedman seems inclined toward the "diffusion" definition, and Watson seems more in line with the "representations" definition. And yet, despite these differences, antagonists on both sides of the debate have all tended to adopt the same point of departure: the point at which a Western-based corporation touches individual consumers in a non-Western local culture.

At first I was inclined to follow their lead. In researching earlier books, I had found that big, Western-based corporations, such as John D. Rockefeller's Standard Oil Company and James B. Duke's British-American Tobacco Company, came to dominate China's market for their goods in the early twentieth century.[4] But in research for this book I discovered that in the pharmaceutical industry big, Western-owned corporations played a different role in China.

In Chinese history, as in the history of the United States, England, Canada, Japan, and undoubtedly other countries, the purveyors of patent medicines and pharmaceutical products were among the first to make use of print media in promoting consumer culture.[5] In light of this seemingly worldwide pattern, I was not surprised to find that in China these pioneers included some of the world's biggest Western-based pharmaceutical companies; by 1920 American-owned Eli Lilly and Parke, Davis, German-owned Bayer, British-owned Burroughs Wellcome, and Canadian-owned Williams Medicine Company all had opened offices in Shanghai.

But I was surprised to find that during the first half of the twentieth century these Western-based global giants did not build as many branch stores or distribute goods and advertisements as widely in China as Chinese-owned pharmaceutical businesses did.[6]

This case of local businesses surpassing their Western rivals and dominating the market of a non-Western country presents an opportunity to take a different point of departure from the one adopted by Friedman, Watson, and others in the debate over the spread of consumer culture. Instead of concentrating on the point where Western-based corporations have touched non-Western local cultures, I have shifted the focus to the numerous points where Chinese-owned businesses have touched local cultures in China (Chapters 2–5) and Southeast Asia (Chapter 6). I have not assumed that the agents of consumer culture have been confined either to corporations based in the West (at the "core" of the world capitalist system) or to consumers residing in non-Western local cultures (on the "periphery" of the world capitalist system). I have searched within Chinese and Southeast Asian history for additional institutions (besides Western-based corporations) and other individuals (besides local consumers of goods) that became agents of consumer culture. To keep my focus sharp, I have limited it to direct agents that manufactured, distributed, or consumed specific medical products, thereby excluding agents that had indirect influence on consumer culture.[7]

In my search for direct agents of consumer culture, I have investigated both institutions and individuals because I do not consider the "diffusion" definition and the "representations" definition of consumer culture to be wholly incompatible. The two can be combined in an encompassing and historically useful definition of consumer culture as a culture in which institutions (diffusing goods) and individuals (producing representations of goods) interact with each other over time. Adopting this broad definition, I have not been concerned with determining whether Western-based corporations were the primary agents of consumer culture and individual consumers were secondary agents or vice versa. Instead, I have sought to identify previously ignored or unappreciated direct agents of consumer culture, and I have been impressed by the reach and effectiveness of such agents originating within China and Southeast Asia—that is, on the non-Western "periphery." My findings on these Chinese agents call into question the assumption that Western-based corporations have been the sole initiators of the spread of consumer culture and that they have invariably introduced it from the West into non-Western markets. Up to now debaters on both sides of the issue seem to have shared this ethnocentric assumption, and I hope to go beyond it.

If phrased in the terms used by Friedman and Watson, the argument in this book is that during the late nineteenth and early twentieth centuries Chinese agents of consumer culture reached "beyond the frontiers of globalization," arranged for "the evasion of political boundaries," carried out "the process of localization," and increased "cultural homogenization." These four themes are developed and documented in the following chapters, but before considering the evidence in support of them, it is important to recognize that they raise questions about existing interpretations of Chinese and Southeast Asian history.

The Frontiers of Long-Distance Trade

By all accounts, Chinese businesses did not distribute goods throughout the entire world in the nineteenth and early twentieth centuries. The question pursued in this book is how far they reached beyond the frontiers of Western-led globalization in China and Southeast Asia. The controversial nature of this question is evident in a debate over the extent of Chinese long-distance trade in the nineteenth century.

Among specialists on the nineteenth century, G. William Skinner has led the way in establishing the framework for a lively debate about the frontiers of long-distance trade. In a series of influential studies, he has analyzed China's marketing structure at all levels of the urban hierarchy, from villages and market towns at the rural base to the largest cities at the urban cores of what he calls macroregions. In nineteenth-century China he has delineated eight macroregions: North, Northwest, Lower Yangzi, Middle Yangzi, Upper Yangzi, Southeast, South (Lingnan), and Southwest (Yun-Gui), as well as one macroregion, Northeast (Manchuria), that did not become fully formed until the twentieth century (Map 1.1). In all these macroregions, topographical features such as mountain ranges set formidable boundaries for long-distance trade.[8]

According to Skinner, Chinese entrepreneurs succeeded in traversing these macroregional boundaries within China only by forming big and far-flung social networks. Like members of family firms in almost all parts of the world, they based these networks on kinship. In addition, as Skin-

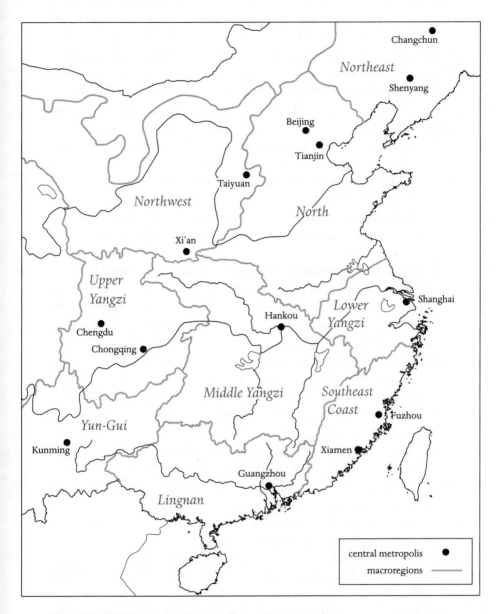

Map 1.1. China's macroregions and central metropolises.
Map by Thomas Lyons, based on macroregions from Skinner,
"Regional Urbanization," 214, map 1.

ner has pointed out, they were able to recruit and bind together trustworthy nonrelatives in their large-scale networks because of "a special feature": the members of each network "shared a common origin (that is,
t'ung-hsiang, same-native-place ties)." These native-place ties differed from
hometown ties or ties based on place of birth. All Chinese inherit their
native places from their fathers, whether or not they or their fathers have
ever been to their native places. Taking advantage of this legacy, they
make use of native-place ties in forming social networks for many reasons, including shared spoken language, familiarity with each other's families or lineages, and the prospect of returning to retire in their native
places. In Skinner's words, the basis for these entrepreneurial alliances in
Chinese social networks "came down to a matter of trust and accountabil-
ity, on the one hand, and of reliable business competence, on the other . . .
and theirs was a vital role in the articulation of China's semiclosed
regional economies."[9]

Building on Skinner's insights, William T. Rowe has reaffirmed the vital
role that these Chinese networks played in China's long-distance trade in
the nineteenth century and has gone a step further, to suggest that the
country's regional economies were not as semiclosed as Skinner supposed. In a study of Hankou, a city nicknamed "the Chicago of China"
because of its commercially strategic location on waterways near the center of the country, Rowe has argued that Chinese social networks based
on native-place ties managed nothing less than "a truly integrated national
market" in the latter half of the eighteenth century and the entire nineteenth century. According to his findings, Chinese trading groups overcame barriers of distance and preindustrial technology and successfully
circulated not only luxury goods but also low-priced bulk commodities
such as grain and raw cotton throughout the country. Although Rowe has
candidly acknowledged that "meaningful statistics" on this nationwide
trade are not currently available, he has cited considerable nonquantita-
tive evidence that is very convincing.[10]

While Skinner and Rowe have confined themselves to China, Takeshi
Hamashita has shown the reach of Chinese networks outside China.
Reappraising China's imperial tributary system, he has discovered that it
served the purposes of "intra-Asian trade" as well as interstate foreign
relations, and he has renamed it "the tributary trade system." He has
acknowledged that Western powers linked this trading system with international markets, which led to "the closer integration of the Southeast

Asian and southern Chinese economies and their extension into the Indian Ocean trade zone" in the nineteenth century. But he has insisted that these Western initiatives did not give Westerners control over intra-Asian trade even in Western colonies—much less the uncolonized states of China and Japan. Remaining under Asian management, "the marketing structure in the European colonies [as well as non-colonies] in Asia continued to display the characteristics of the traditional intra-Asian trade associated with the tributary system."[11] Hamashita has emphasized the longevity of the China-centered tributary trade system and suggests that it "functioned from the Tang through Qing dynasties, from the seventh century to 1911."[12] After the fall of the Qing, China's last imperial dynasty, the tributary trade system ceased to function because China's political leaders at the capital in Beijing no longer played their crucial role in determining trade as well as tribute in East Asia.

As my summaries imply, these scholars have challenged each other. Skinner's notion of semiclosed macroregions (which he published in the 1970s) was challenged by Rowe's characterization of a national market (which he published in the 1980s). Similarly, Hamashita's mapping of intra-Asian trade (which he began publishing in the 1980s and is still elaborating) has challenged Skinner's and Rowe's confinement of their schemes within China's national borders. Their disagreements leave unresolved the question of how the frontiers of long-distance trade in nineteenth-century China and East Asia should be mapped.

At a theoretical level the very terms of the debate, as framed by Skinner, have been challenged. In a recent sophisticated critique Carolyn Cartier has argued that Skinner's macroregional model is untenable because central-place theory has become outmoded. She claims that Skinner has discouraged historians from investigating long-distance trade by setting seemingly fixed macroregional boundaries. As an alternative, she calls for an "unbounded regional geography" that would focus on human agency and "the social construction of regional meaning." Her aim, she says, is to put "emphasis on social processes over spatial patterns."[13]

Although not convincing on all her points, Cartier has raised issues that deserve serious attention and are addressed in this book. On the one hand, she overstates her case when she goes so far as to say that "the structural embeddedness in the macroregion perspectives discourages investigation into . . . long-distance and maritime trade."[14] In reply, one might plausibly argue that Skinner's macroregional model has actually stimulated Rowe's investigation of long-distance trade and Hamashita's research on maritime trade. I have found that Skinner's work has encouraged me to investigate long-distance trade, and despite Cartier's objections to his macroregional scheme, I have retained it as the basis for several maps in this book.

On the other hand, Cartier is very perceptive in her call for more attention to human agency. How can the frontiers of long-distance trade be mapped unless the roles played on the ground by Chinese entrepreneurs, distributors, merchants, and other long-distance traders are more fully understood? Besides tracing impersonal flows of goods up and down urban hierarchies and within and between macroregions (as Skinner has done), it is important to investigate the highly personal processes of negotiating trade agreements across macroregional boundaries (see Chapters 2 and 4), across enemy lines in wartime (Chapter 5), and across national borders (Chapter 6).[15] Besides analyzing guilds, tributary trade systems, and other institutional arrangements (as Rowe and Hamashita have done), it is worth paying attention to brokers making transactions and translating ideas at all levels of businesses' distribution systems.

In addition, it is worth asking whether human agency has shaped space on the frontiers of long-distance trade differently in the twentieth century from the way it did in the nineteenth century. Skinner, Rowe, Hamashita, and others have provided nineteenth-century baselines for addressing this question, but up to now specialists on twentieth-century China and Southeast Asia have not followed their lead.

The Evasion of Political Barriers

Ironically, although the mapping of China's and Southeast Asia's trading frontiers has generated a lively debate among nineteenth-century specialists, it has not had the same effect on twentieth-century specialists. While Skinner, Rowe, and Hamashita have shown that Chinese merchants succeeded in extending trade over long distances in the nineteenth century, Lloyd Eastman, Parks Coble, Marie-Claire Bergère, and William Kirby have argued that Chinese capitalists fell under tight political control, which severely restricted them in the early twentieth century.

Eastman, Coble, and Bergère have noted that Chiang Kai-shek's Nationalist government cracked down on Chinese capitalists and extracted forced "donations" in Shanghai as early as the spring of 1927, shortly after Chiang completed the Northern Expedition and founded a new national capital at Nanjing. On the basis of that and other official actions, they have concluded that the Nationalist government proceeded to limit the growth of Chinese businesses by imposing state capitalism on China during the "Nanjing decade" (1927–1937). In Bergère's concise summary of this thesis, the Chinese bourgeoisie became "subordinated to, and integrated into, the State apparatus."[16]

Subsequently the Nationalist government dominated Chinese capitalists even more fully during the Sino-Japanese War (1937–1945) and the Chinese Civil War (1946–1949), according to Kirby. Subtly distinguishing his interpretation from earlier ones of the Nanjing decade, Kirby has noted that the Nationalist government gave priority to heavy industry over light industry, and he has acknowledged that light industry was "largely outside government control before 1937."[17] Nonetheless, like Coble, Eastman, and Bergère, he has observed that the Nationalist government began to formulate industrial plans before the Sino-Japanese War. In addition, he has, more than the other historians, emphasized that following the war it "continued in the direction of increased economic control and expanded the state sector and the planned economy at a rapid rate."[18]

Meanwhile, foreign governments also made official interventions and imposed economic controls on Chinese businesses during the early twentieth century, according to historians of China and Southeast Asia. In a recent book Parks Coble has documented the Japanese seizure of Chinese-owned factories immediately after Japan's military invasion of China in 1937. This imposition of Japanese authority, he has concluded, set tight limitations on Chinese capitalists and sharply reduced their marketing of goods. In his words, "From an economic standpoint, as it was actually implemented, the [Japanese] New Order was nothing more than a colonial regime over China. The Japanese imposed controls over the economy of the lower Yangzi, confiscated factories and gave them to Japanese companies, and severely restricted market activity." Reacting against Japanese rule, "the vast majority [of Chinese businesses] made every effort to escape Japanese control and domination."[19] Not until the last years of the war (1943–1945), he claims, did they begin to cooperate with the Japanese, and by then it was too late to market goods successfully because hyperinflation was raging and China's economy was collapsing.

In Southeast Asia, Western as well as Japanese colonial regimes set similar restrictions, according to the Southeast Asian historian Carl Trocki. In his chronology Western colonial governments completed "the absorption of Chinese settlements in Southeast Asia by European colonies (1830–80) . . . and the integration of the overseas Chinese into the global capitalist system (1880–1910)." While citing Singapore as his principal case, Trocki has asserted that the "Chinese history of Singapore is a microcosm of this process of [Western] envelopment of Chinese economic activity [throughout Southeast Asia]."[20] Although Japan did not occupy Southeast Asian countries as long as it did China, it ousted Western colonial governments after it bombed Pearl Harbor and imposed its own military rule in Southeast Asia between 1942 and 1945.

In sum, political historians have reached a consensus that Chinese, Western, and Japanese governments subordinated, integrated, restricted, and enveloped Chinese capitalists and businesses in the early twentieth century. This interpretation provides a convincing analysis of government-business relations if evaluated strictly from the standpoint of governments, but it is not fully convincing if evaluated from the standpoint of the businesses that are described in this book. The following chapters show how Chinese-owned businesses used various strategies to evade government policies, overcome political barriers, and reach national and international markets. In Chapter 2 I discuss Chinese owners of a drugstore who widely distributed traditional Chinese medicines in the nineteenth century and introduced a nationwide network of new branch stores in the twentieth century. In Chapters 3 and 4 I describe Chinese owners of Western-style drugstores who made use of new print media to advertise nationwide and to control nationwide distribution through locally owned franchises as well as their own branch stores. In Chapters 5 and 6 I portray Chinese owners of Western-style drugstores who built up businesses that not only survived but grew steadily or even spectacularly both in China under Nationalist rule and Japanese occupation and in Southeast Asia under Western colonial governments and Japanese occupation.

These examples suggest that political historians have overestimated the capacity of Chinese, Japanese, and Western governments to control and limit Chinese capitalists and businesses in the early twentieth century. Despite governments' official interventions, the Chinese businesses that are described here captured national and international markets more successfully than their Western rivals were able to do in China and Southeast Asia. Moreover, they arguably retained these markets more fully and more enduringly than businesses anywhere else in the world were able to do at the time.

If this is true, how were these Chinese business networks able to overcome topographical and official barriers in peacetime, cross enemy lines in wartime, and manage markets for medicine under politically unstable conditions? A key feature of their business strategies was their use of print media to promote consumer culture, which, in the process, became localized.

The Process of Localization

In the field of Chinese history many have discussed the process of localization, often using a synonym for it that applies specifically to China, Sinicization. They have debated the relevance of the concept of Sinicization in more than one historical context—including the dealings of Han Chinese with Manchus and other non-Han peoples—and most commonly they have applied it to the history of Chinese relations with the West.[21] In analyzing localization, historians (unlike the anthropologist James Watson, who is quoted at the beginning of this chapter) have generally focused on highly educated, cosmopolitan, Westernized Chinese thinkers, and they have shown how these figures translated, transformed, and thus localized what was learned from the West. They have adopted varied and creative approaches to this subject that range from intellectual biographies to collective portraits to cultural studies, but they have generally shared one assumption: that this process of localization was carried out exclusively by China's intellectuals.[22] In her contribution to this literature, Tani Barlow has made this assumption explicit. In her words, China's educated elite "monopolized the appropriation of Western ideas, forms, signs, and discourses [in early twentieth-century China]."[23]

This sharp focus on elite intellectuals has by no means precluded investigations into the transmission of ideas from one Chinese person to another over time. For example, one historian, Paul Cohen, has suggested that the Chinese localization of Western ideas can be traced through two phases. In phase one, Chinese "pioneers" learned about the West abroad or along the margins of Chinese society in treaty ports and transformed "what was once totally strange into something a little less strange, gradually desensitizing people to the newness of the new, making it less conspicuous, more palatable." Then, in phase two, Chinese "legitimizers" achieved "broad acceptance" in China for "changes that a short time before would have been acceptable only on the acculturated fringes." In this two-phase process, pioneers from treaty ports assaulted China's hinterlands, and legitimizers in the hinterlands "legitimize[d] the assaults through Sinicization."[24]

Cohen has formulated this two-phase sequence, with its distinction between pioneers and legitimizers, to make analytical connections between prominent reformers and their intellectual heirs (such as pioneers in the Taiping Rebellion of the 1850s and 1860s and legitimizers in the Hundred Days Reforms of 1898). He has also used it to show linkages between revolutionary leaders and their intellectual heirs (such as the pioneer Sun Yat-sen in the early twentieth century and the legitimizer Mao Zedong later in that century). Like other intellectual historians, Cohen has concentrated exclusively on the role of elite intellectuals in the process of localization.

The work of intellectual historians is indispensable for understanding the initial phases of localization—intellectual pioneering and the beginnings of intellectual legitimization—but the process of localization did not stop there. Who were the cultural mediators in subsequent phases and how did they reformulate, invent, and otherwise legitimize Western ideas, forms, signs, and discourses to make them acceptable or even appealing to wider Chinese audiences? In Chapters 3–6, I show that Chinese entrepreneurs and their staff members and affiliates have acted as cultural mediators between China's intellectual elite and its consumers. The entrepreneurs employed members of China's intellectual elite as commercial artists and architects, localized the ideas and images of these and other intellectuals as part of their marketing strategies, and used print media to distribute their versions of "the West" more widely than Chinese intellectuals' publications were able to do.

As the portraits in the following chapters show, these Chinese entrepreneurs were by no means all identical, but by comparison with China's intellectual elite, they were far less cosmopolitan and Westernized. They were not educated in the West or at Western-sponsored schools in China, did not serve as compradors or employees in Western-owned businesses, and did not learn Western languages or spend time in Western countries. Typically, they had little formal education of any kind and were not very literate in Chinese or any other language. The characterizations of them here show that uncosmopolitan and un-Westernized figures played prominent roles in the localization of Western ideas and images in China. Their participation in this process raises questions about how they perceived "the West" (after it was filtered through layers of Chinese intellectual pioneers and legitimizers) and whether their own creations of "Western" culture had homogenizing effects on Chinese culture.

The Extent of Homogenization

Cultural homogenization is notoriously difficult to define. Fortunately, historians have formulated general concepts of Chinese mass culture and specific concepts of Chinese medical culture that help to clarify the issues surrounding it. They have viewed Chinese culture from more than one angle, but their interpretations generally point to the seemingly unqualified conclusion that Chinese culture remained impervious to cultural homogenization until China's government imposed it after the founding of the People's Republic in 1949.

In their article on the beginnings of mass culture in China, Leo Lee and Andrew Nathan have described the introduction of mass media dating from the late nineteenth century, and they have found no evidence that these media had homogenizing effects before 1949. Defining mass culture as "culture that is nationwide, universal to all classes, and consciously engineered and controlled from above," they have concluded that in China "it was not until after 1949 that a truly mass audience was created."[25]

While Lee and Nathan have evaluated the effects of mass media from the top down, Nathan Sivin has reached a similar conclusion in his interpretation of Chinese consumers' views of medicine from the bottom up. Before 1949, according to Sivin, Chinese consumers had a multiplicity of medical options, which they did not homogenize into either a closed monolithic system of "Chinese medicine" or a dualistic choice between "Chinese medicine" and "Western medicine." He characterizes Chinese consumers' eclectic range of possible therapies and treatments as "medical pluralism," and he concludes that "the abiding problem of medical pluralism" is central to any understanding of Chinese medical practice before and throughout the first half of the twentieth century. In his view, "Chinese chose freely throughout history—as freely as their social and financial circumstances permitted—among priests, spirit mediums, magicians, itinerant herbalists and acupuncturists, classical physicians, and other healers." Writing in 1987, Sivin noted that this wide variety of choices was then still available in some Chinese communities on the periphery of the mainland. In China these choices were present until the

1980s, when the government of the People's Republic "eradicated [most of them] as superstitious, and the pluralism of the past has given way to the dualism of traditional and modern medicine."[26]

These influential interpretations raise important analytical and chronological questions that I pursue in this book. Lee and Nathan's definition of mass culture as "culture that is nationwide, universal to all classes, and consciously . . . controlled from above" is not adopted wholesale here because it is problematic. If taken literally, this definition sets unrealistic standards for assessing mass culture in Chinese history. In a country so large and diverse, it is doubtful whether any cultural medium even up to the present has become nationwide and universal to all classes; and in any country it is questionable whether culture is ever engineered and controlled entirely from above. Nonetheless, this definition has the advantage of specifying three criteria—reach across space, infiltration of classes, and control over cultural media—that are worth retaining. By these three criteria, how successful were the Chinese entrepreneurs who marketed medicine in early twentieth-century China? The following chapters (especially 3, 4, and 6) describe and evaluate attempts to reach nationwide, touch various classes, and homogenize Chinese consumers into "a truly mass audience."

Similarly, Nathan Sivin's thesis that Chinese "medical pluralism" gave way to Sino-Western or traditional-modern "dualism" only under official pressures in the People's Republic needs to be adjusted before it can be adopted here. Sivin formulated it to interpret Chinese consumers' attitudes toward medical practices, whereas this book discusses their attitudes toward medical products. But the question that he has raised is no less relevant to Chinese consumers' choices between "Chinese medicine" *(Zhong yao)* and "Western medicine" *(Xi yao)* as types of pharmaceutical goods than it is to their choices between "Chinese medicine" *(Zhong yi)* and "Western medicine" *(Xi yi)* as forms of medical practice.

As I show in the following chapters, Chinese entrepreneurs vigorously campaigned to promote Sino-Western dualism. They did not merely leave it to consumers to differentiate between traditional Chinese medicines, which were inherited from the past, and modern Western medicines, which were imported in the present. Instead, they painstakingly invented Chinese "traditions," and they elaborately constructed and aggressively promoted their own (Chinese) images of seemingly Western "new medicine" *(xin yao)*.

How effective were Chinese entrepreneurs in their efforts to homogenize Chinese consumers' medical pluralism into their versions of Sino-

Western dualism? The following chapters raise the possibility that Lee and Nathan and Sivin have drawn the line too sharply at 1949 as the sole turning point in the history of China's cultural homogenization. If these chapters are any indication, Chinese entrepreneurs contributed to the process of homogenizing Chinese consumers' tastes through advertising campaigns in the first half of the twentieth century before the government of the People's Republic redirected it in official campaigns during the second half of the century. By taking into account the effects of advertising on Chinese consumers before 1949, the following chapters identify earlier phases in the process of cultural homogenization and propose refinements of its chronology in Chinese history.

These four themes—the frontiers of long-distance trade, the evasion of political barriers, the process of localization, and the extent of homogenization—are developed in the following chapters, but each chapter is about a different entrepreneur and a different business. Moreover, each of Chapters 3–6 highlights the use of different print media: in Chapter 3, posters and calendars; in Chapter 4, shop signs, storefronts, and architectural designs; in Chapter 5, magazines and medical journals; in Chapter 6, newspapers and outdoor advertisements such as billboards, parades, and amusement parks. These four chapters illustrate the fact that Chinese entrepreneurs selling Western-style drugs were the ones in the medicine business who exploited the new media. By contrast, Chinese entrepreneurs selling traditional Chinese medicines tended not to make use of these media during the nineteenth and early twentieth centuries.

And yet it would be wrong to assume that traditional Chinese drugstores played no role in consumer culture at this time. Like big Chinese Western-style drugstores, they also pushed out the frontiers of long-distance trade, evaded political barriers, carried out localization, and contributed to homogenization. Their promotional techniques differed from those of Western-style drugstores. Nonetheless, even as Chinese sellers of Western-style medicines introduced Chinese consumers to their newly invented images of "the modern West," so too did Chinese sellers of Chinese-style medicines introduce Chinese consumers to their newly invented images of "traditional China."

2

Inventing Imperial Traditions and Building Olde Shoppes

> [Tongren Tang] today is perhaps the most unostentatious of all the old drug stores in this city [Beijing]. It has no old drug store sign hanging above its door and there is nothing at all attractive about its exterior or interior and yet it is possibly one of the busiest drug stores in China. . . .

> Like other pharmacies throughout the world, old Chinese drug stores become famous on account of some special preparation or compound which can be had only by them, and the Tung Jen T'ang [Tongren Tang] is no exception. They prepare special pills, probably twenty different kinds for as many ailments, and people come from all over the country to purchase these pills.

> John Cameron, "Some Sidelights on Pharmacy in Peking, China" (1925)

In this description of China's most famous traditional medicine store, a British pharmacologist attributed its success to the ability of its pills to sell themselves. By the time he wrote these words in 1925, John Cameron had been a member of the Department of Pharmacy at Peking Union Medical College for four years, and on the basis of his travels and surveys in China, he noted the contrast between marketing by "old fashioned Chinese drug stores" (like Tongren Tang) and marketing by "new patent medicine shops" (like the ones described in later chapters of this book).[1] Each old-fashioned Chinese drugstore, he observed, marketed its medicines by simply making them available in its own shop. He dated the origin of this kind of shop from at least as early as the Song dynasty (960–1279), and he reported that he had seen examples of it in rural as well as urban China. "In almost every village of this vast republic," Cameron noted, "one may find at least one old fashioned Chinese drug shop—and in Peking, there are hundreds of them." Nearly devoid of promotional devices, these shops featured at most a shop sign on the outside and a "dark and dismal appearance" on the inside, and they were "all very much alike—in fact they all seem to have been built on the same plan."[2] In all these respects Tongren Tang and other old-fashioned Chinese drugstores contrasted sharply with Western-style drugstores, which, he said, had not reached China until the early twentieth century, had remained confined to a few of its larger cities, and had resorted to sensational advertising from shops that "are usually brilliantly lit, and have a large supply of showcases."[3]

Did Tongren Tang successfully market its goods by steadfastly refusing to promote them and by relying solely on its "special preparation or compound" to attract customers "from all over the country"? It is true, as Cameron noted, that Tongren Tang was only one of many old-style drugstores in China and that these stores were located in cities, towns, and villages throughout the country by the early twentieth century.[4] It is also true that Tongren Tang was an old drugstore, that its shop in Beijing remained unostentatious even as recently as the early twentieth century, and that it and other sellers of traditional Chinese medicines did not generally give their goods and their shops a Western appearance or run pictorial advertisements in print media. To this extent, traditional drugstores contrasted with modern ones in Chinese history.

At the same time, it is not true that Tongren Tang's pills made this store famous without any efforts at promotion by its owners. Tongren Tang was founded by a family named Yue whose promotion of the sale of Chinese medicine can be traced back through no fewer than ten generations. As early as the fifteenth century, Yue Liangcai became the first family member on record to engage in this trade. Having no shop, he was derisively called a bell doctor *(lingyi)* because he was an itinerant vendor who jingled a bell on a walking stick as he hawked medicines.[5] From these humble beginnings the Yue family eventually acquired wealth and status, and its members became particularly adept at inventing elite traditions as devices for marketing medicine. To illustrate their marketing strategies, two members of the family are described here: Yue Pingquan (1810–1880), who turned a well-established business-government relationship to new commercial advantage; and Yue Daren (1875–1934), who introduced a new vehicle for distribution, the nationwide chain store, under the guise of Olde Yue Family Shoppes.

Yue Pingquan and Tongren Tang

In 1843, when Yue Pingquan became manager of Tongren Tang, he inherited family burdens as well as family benefits. His ancestors had founded Tongren Tang in the seventeenth century, but by 1843 the Yues had not controlled the business for ninety years (since a disastrous fire in 1753), and his immediate predecessors had witnessed a steady decline of revenue at Tongren Tang. Yue Pingquan reversed this trend, and thirty-seven years later, by the time of his death in 1880, he had brought Tongren Tang wholly under his family's ownership and management and had spread its reputation throughout the country. The key to his success lay in his commercial exploitation of the political institutions of the Qing dynasty (1644–1912); he was able to take advantage of these institutions only because he was heir to his family's earlier achievements, especially his ancestors' success at securing Tongren Tang's appointment as official supplier of medicine to the Qing imperial court.

ACQUIRING OFFICIAL STATUS

In 1669 Yue Pingquan's great-great-great-great-grandfather Yue Xianyang founded Tongren Tang and from the beginning sought official favor. Even Yue Xianyang's choice of the name for his business implied a connection with official life: Tongren Tang invoked Confucianism, the philosophy that was used to legitimize imperial authority. The name's first character, *tong,* means "shared," or part of a unity; the middle character, *ren,* means "humaneness," the very first of the five Confucian virtues (humaneness, righteousness, propriety, wisdom, and faithfulness); and the last character, *tang,* means "hall," which was the last character in the names of almost all traditional medicine stores. So the name Tongren Tang can be translated as the Hall of Shared Humaneness.[6]

Before opening Tongren Tang, Yue Xianyang had already begun his quest for official status. He had prepared for and taken the Qing dynasty's official civil service examinations, and, having failed, he had used his contacts to land an appointment as a doctor in the Imperial Hospital (Taiyi yuan) which served the Qing court through the Imperial Household Agency (Neiwufu), a large and well-endowed organization that was independent of the regular bureaucracy.[7] According to some accounts, he then capitalized on his access to the Imperial Hospital's library by stealing secret recipes for medicines from its files.[8]

In 1702, with recipes in hand, Yue Xianyang's son, Yue Fengming, opened Tongren Tang's first store. Between 1669 and his death in 1688, Yue Xianyang had operated his business as nothing more than a small workshop—literally a "medicine room" *(yao shi)*. Now Yue Fengming built a full-fledged medicine store *(yao pu)* on a site in Beijing's most elite commercial district, Dashalan.[9] Like all merchants, he was officially prohibited from selecting a location in the walled Inner City (Neicheng), which the Manchu-led Qing had reserved for the imperial court and its banner people since the founding of the dynasty in 1644. Yue Fengming built Tongren Tang near the Front Gate (Qianmen), one of the three great gates connecting the Inner City to the Outer City, thereby placing it as close to the imperial court as it could officially be (Figure 2.1). In opening Tongren Tang on Dashalan, a narrow alley filled with well-established shops, he also positioned it in Beijing's most prestigious commercial district, where it would be accessible to all manner of consumers.[10]

Once Tongren Tang was open, Yue Fengming won greater favor at court. Like his father, Yue Fengming became a medical official at the Imperial Hospital, and he secured official permission for the publication of catalogues of Tongren Tang's medicines. In 1706 he issued two of these catalogues, *Pills, Powders, Ointments, Tonics, and Other Compounds Passed Down through Generations of the Yue Family (Yueshi shidai zuchuan wan san gao dan xialiao peifang)*, which identified 362 medicines, and *A List of Tongren Tang's Medicines (Tongren tang yaomu)*.[11] Thereafter he and his successors regularly enlarged, republished, and recirculated these catalogues of Tongren Tang's medicines—always identifying the medicines but never revealing their secret recipes or instructions for preparation.[12] The version published in 1889 contained 495 medicines (Figure 2.2).

Yue Fengming and his family also gained influence at court through family and native-place ties. His key contact was Zhang Shiji, the head of the Imperial Pharmacy (Yuyao fang), which, like the Imperial Hospital, served the imperial family through the Imperial Household Agency. He and Zhang had distant relatives in common, and both of them traced their ancestries back to Shaoxing, a prefecture in the Lower Yangzi region seven hundred miles southeast of Beijing, whose natives had migrated in large numbers to the capital and had come to dominate the lower level of the government's bureaucracy by the eighteenth century. To solidify this native-place connection, the Yues married one of their sons to Zhang Shiji's daughter.[13]

By all these means—their preparations for the civil service examinations, their naming of their store, their placement of it in a prominent location, their pursuit of positions in the Imperial Hospital, their publications of lists of their medicines, their use of family and native-place ties with the head of the Imperial Pharmacy—the Yues sought a coveted designation as supplier of medicine to the imperial court, and after half a century they finally achieved the desired result in 1723. Once Tongren Tang was appointed an official supplier of medicine, the Yues made the most of this opportunity. Every three months they replenished the stocks of the Imperial Pharmacy, which served the needs of a thousand residents in the imperial palace. In addition, they were on call to fill prescriptions at any time for the Imperial Hospital's staff, which included approximately one hundred doctors and pharmacists.[14] With the Imperial Pharmacist Zhang Shiji as the Yues' ally, Tongren Tang became the sole medicine supplier that had the privilege of receiving payments in advance from the Qing court.[15]

During the next thirty years, 1723–1753, the Yue family greatly benefited from imperial patronage. From the Yongzheng emperor (r. 1723–1735) Tongren Tang received one payment in advance amounting to forty thousand ounces of silver *(liang),* and from Yongzheng's successor, the Qianlong emperor (r. 1736–1796), Tongren Tang's payment in advance was three thousand ounces of silver per year.[16] In addition, the appointment meant that Tongren Tang's name was placed on the imperial household's list of goods, which showed commodities that had received the imperial endorsement, "Made for the Emperor" *(yu zhi).* As Gary Hamilton and Chi-kong Lai have pointed out in their study of the lists of famous products circulating in late imperial China, this one "was by far the most important. . . . To have a product on this list assured success and prosperity for its manufacturer, as it did for those manufacturers in England who could place upon their products the words, 'by special appointment to H. M. the King.'"[17]

Then suddenly in 1753 the Yue family's climb to imperial prominence and financial success at Tongren Tang was cut off by a fire that burned down the store, took the lives of some of the Yues, and substantially diminished the family's fortune. Tongren Tang retained its official status as supplier to the imperial court and was rebuilt by the Yues' ally Zhang Shiji, the head of the Imperial Pharmacy, who convinced the Qing court to allocate twenty thousand ounces of silver for this purpose, but the store and the Yue family suffered a long-term setback.[18] When the store reopened, the members of the Yue family held only 20 percent of its shares, and within a few decades they lost almost all control over the store, retaining by 1818 a mere .5 of its 46.5 shares (which were then held by a total of twenty-one shareholders). In the early nineteenth century, under the Daoguang emperor (r. 1821–1851), Tongren Tang's advance payments fell to only two thousand ounces of silver per year (compared to three thousand in the late eighteenth century).[19] In 1834, already in decline, Tongren Tang was brought down by another fire, which burned the store to the ground.

USING OFFICIAL CONNECTIONS FOR PROMOTIONAL PURPOSES

In 1843, less than a decade after this last fire, Yue Pingquan took over as Tongren Tang's new manager and began revitalizing it by deriving new commercial benefits from its long-standing relationship with the Qing court. Like earlier Yues, he made contacts with Qing officials, and in the course of his career he built up an extensive network of personal connections. Near the beginning of his career in 1854, at age forty-four, he bought a fourth-class imperial degree to give himself greater access to officials (as many merchants did at the time), and near the end of his life in 1878, at age sixty-eight, he purchased a second-class imperial degree. By the latter date, if not earlier, his influence must have been extensive, since such high-level degrees were not commonly sold by the Qing.[20]

Yue Pingquan aggressively exploited these official connections to protect Tongren Tang's reputation in ways that other Chinese merchants apparently did not do. Like other merchants, he was not able to bring lawsuits against rivals' trademark infringements in the Western sense of the term because Qing China had no provision in its legal code concerning violations of intellectual property rights and imitations of trademarks or shop signs. According to William Alford's history of intellectual property law in China, Chinese merchants under the Qing dynasty almost invariably found that this lack of legal sanction left them powerless. As a result, they seldom called on officials to protect their stores' reputations, and in the rare cases when they did so, they had little success.[21]

If Alford is right about this pattern of merchants' legal passivity, then Yue Pingquan proved to be a striking exception to it because he repeatedly called on the police to protect Tongren Tang against its rivals' infringements on its name. In 1852, when two brothers named Yu began selling traditional Chinese medicine in Beijing under the name Tongren Tang (using the same three Chinese characters as the Yue family did), Yue Pingquan complained to Beijing's Central Borough Police (zhongcheng chayuan), and his complaint brought swift and decisive action. The police arrested the Yu brothers and made an example of them by parading them through the streets in chains as a warning to anyone inclined to commit the same crime.[22]

In 1869 Yue Pingquan again convinced the police to take action, this time against a similar but not identical infringement on Tongren Tang's name. Another of Yue's rivals opened a new drugstore in Beijing by the name of Tongren Tang, using for *ren* a Chinese character that sounded the same as the one on the sign at the Yue family's store but was written differently and meant "person" or "human." (If the name of the Yue family's store is translated as the Hall of Shared Humaneness, then the very similar name of their rival's store may be translated as the Hall of Shared Humanness. Each of these characters for *ren* is relatively simple; the Yue family's is written in four strokes, the other one in two). Once again Yue Pingquan lodged a complaint, and once again the police closed down his rival. This time, for good measure, the police posted official notices (*gaoshi*) throughout Beijing warning others not to imitate Tongren Tang ever again.[23]

Even as Yue Pingquan used his connections with the police to protect Tongren Tang's reputation, he used his connections with the imperial court to promote the sale of its goods through the Qing's civil service examination system. In his promotional campaigns he shrewdly targeted examination candidates, who were ideally positioned to spread the word about Tongren Tang's products. Three out of every four years, thousands of these young men came to the Qing capital of Beijing—ten thousand at a time to take the examinations for a second-tier degree (*juren*), and five or six thousand to take the examination for the top-tier metropolitan degree (*jinshi*).[24] Those who passed took up official posts in the capital and throughout the provinces, and those who failed returned to their homes in all parts of the country. It is difficult to imagine another elite group of young Chinese with greater potential for exercising wide influence on popular taste in late imperial China.[25]

While these examination candidates were in Beijing for the top-level examinations, Yue Pingquan presented each of them with two gifts: a lantern and a packet of preventative medicines (*ping'anji*), both inscribed

"Tongren Tang" and "Yue" in red characters. The candidates were provided with the lanterns to guide them from their residences to their examination cells, where they had to take their seats before dawn every day. More important for Tongren Tang's purposes, the candidates were expected to take the medicines to their new posts or their hometowns, distribute them as gifts, and build up Tongren Tang's reputation.[26]

Besides identifying Tongren Tang with China's political elite through the imperial examination system, Yue Pingquan also identified his business with China's social elite by making charitable contributions to urban welfare in Beijing. He opened soup kitchens (*zhouchang*—literally porridge booths) for the poor in front of Tongren Tang's store on the coldest winter days and hottest summer days, and he lit Beijing's walkways by installing street lanterns that were all inscribed with the characters "Tongren Tang." In addition, Yue Pingquan formed and financed a firefighting unit. He equipped it with up-to-date fire engines that were imported from Germany, and he named it "The Tongren Tang Charitable Water Brigade" (Tongren Tang pushan shuihui). In the late nineteenth century this was one of several fire brigades that were privately financed and privately run *(min juan min ban)* in Beijing. In 1888 it distinguished itself from the others when its fire engines proved to be the only ones capable of shooting water high enough to put out a fire in a tower of Taihe Gate at the imperial palace—a feat that won public praise from perhaps the most influential figure in the Qing government, the Empress Dowager Cixi.[27]

Yue Pingquan and his wife, Xu Shi, who succeeded him on his death in 1880, relied on their family to make these innovative promotional devices work. They mobilized the Yues' financial resources and bought out all Tongren Tang shareholders who were not members of the family. Refusing to employ any nonrelatives, they hired only Yue men, their wives, and their sons; they excluded all others, even Yue daughters, because all daughters, in accordance with Chinese custom, would eventually marry "out" into other families. Yue Pingquan and Xu Shi adopted these policies to keep the secret recipes of Tongren Tang's medicines within the family and to convert members of the family into a disciplined workforce.[28] In the process, they put in place a durable organization.

After Yue Pingquan's death, Xu Shi (Figure 2.3) added more family regulations, notably a system for paying employees monthly wages at low rates and daily commissions at high rates, a system that remained in effect from the late nineteenth century to the 1950s.[29] Not until she died in 1907,

on the eve of the fall of the Qing dynasty, did her successors begin to rein-
terpret her and Yue Pingquan's legacy.

PRESERVING TONGREN TANG IN A POST-IMPERIAL AGE

In 1911, when the 268-year-old Qing dynasty was overthrown and China's
two-thousand-year-old imperial system came to an end, Tongren Tang
might well have been expected to suffer or even collapse. No longer was
there an official Imperial Pharmacy to buy medicine from Tongren Tang.
No longer was there a police force under imperial rule to protect Tongren
Tang from imitators. No longer was there an official imperial examination
system with candidates spreading the word about Tongren Tang's medicines. And yet, despite Tongren Tang's loss of imperial patronage, it flour-
ished. In 1922, ten years after the Qing had formally abdicated, the
members of the Yue family made a gesture that dramatized the contrast
between the imperial family's vulnerability and Tongren Tang's durabil-
ity: the Yues wrote off the Qing court's accumulated debt to Tongren
Tang in the amount of 187,387 ounces of silver and 235,634 strings of copper coins *(diao)*.[30]

Why did Tongren Tang survive the fall of imperial China and continue
to grow in the early twentieth century? In 1907, following the death of
Yue Pingquan's widow, Xu Shi, the members of the Yue family met and
devised a new formal partnership under a clearly established charter.
They accepted it despite (or perhaps because of) their failure to reach
agreement on who should be the head of Tongren Tang. They divided the
family's assets among the surviving sons in accordance with the Chinese
custom of partible inheritance *(fen jia),* and they placed Tongren Tang
under "the joint management of the [family's] four branches" *(sifang gong
guan)*. Under this arrangement, they formed a joint general office consisting of one representative from each of the four branches, and every year
the joint general office allocated ten thousand ounces of silver to each
branch. Throughout the first half of the twentieth century, they never did
agree on a single permanent head for the business. Eventually they added
the provision that every year each branch would place its own separate
seal on Tongren Tang's account books and would hold its own separate
key to one of the four padlocks on the door to Tongren Tang's medicine
warehouse. Under this arrangement, the door could be opened only in
the presence of representatives of all four branches of the family.[31]

Under this divided and mutually distrustful leadership, the Yue family members agreed in 1907 that they would accept and enforce family traditions as Yue Pingquan had laid them down for Tongren Tang. Following his precedents, they decided that they would retain only one store for Tongren Tang—the one at Dashalan in Beijing—and that they would all refrain from opening another store by this name. They considered Tongren Tang to be the property of the whole family, and they vowed to prevent others from learning its secret recipes or adopting its name and shop sign.[32]

In the early twentieth century the Yue family's joint management remained committed to these policies and overcame almost all challenges to them by individual members of the family. In 1926 one member of the family, Yue Daren, put the family's resolutions of 1907 to the test by building a new medicine store under the name Tongren Tang in the city of Chengdu, which was located in the Upper Yangzi region more than a thousand miles southwest of Beijing. He claimed that a local family named Chen had infringed on Tongren Tang's name by giving its medicine business the same name. Meanwhile, the Chen family accused Yue of being the real interloper, pointing out that the Chen family had been the sole and continuous owner and operator of its Tongren Tang in Chengdu since 1740—longer than the Yue family had been the sole and continuous owner and operator of Tongren Tang in Beijing. As the dispute escalated, the Chen family sued Yue Daren for trademark infringement in Chengdu under laws that had been introduced in the early twentieth century, and Yue Daren fought back, arranging a change of venue from Chengdu to China's highest court at the time, the Daliyuan in Beijing. But in his hometown he failed to win his family's support, lost the case, and had to change the name of the store in Chengdu.[33]

Two years later, in 1928, a member of another branch of the family, Yue Duzhou, succeeded in building a branch of Tongren Tang in the city of Nanjing, along the Lower Yangzi River, six hundred miles south of Beijing. This violation of the clan rules (*jia gui*) set off a storm of criticism against him from the other branches of the Yue family.[34] Yue Duzhou had studied business management in France during the early 1920s and had returned to China with a grand scheme for building a laboratory and subjecting Tongren Tang's medicines to chemical analysis, but his family flatly refused to finance this proposal and sternly reprimanded him for "forgetting our ancestors" *(wang zu)*.[35] Despite his family's opposition, Yue Duzhou financed his new store on his own and came back to the family with a proposal that it could not refuse. Whenever the Nanjing store made money, he would share the profits with the entire Yue family, but whenever the store lost money, he would cover all its debts himself. Only on these terms did he convince the family to give him permission, be-grudgingly, to operate the Nanjing store under the name Tongren Tang.[36]

In 1931 another member of the same branch of the family, Yue You-shen, tried to seize upon this precedent by opening a store in North China at Taiyuan, three hundred miles west of Beijing, under a sign proclaiming that it was a "Branch Store of Beijing's Tongren Tang," but he was unable to do so. When his local rivals raised doubts about the store's relationship to Beijing's Tongren Tang and accused Yue of fraud, the Yue family in Beijing confirmed that it had not given its approval for this branch of Tongren Tang. Lacking his family's support, Yue Youshen ultimately backed down and dropped the name Tongren Tang from the store.[37]

Thereafter, in the 1930s and 1940s, the Yues opened no other branches named Tongren Tang, and so it had only two stores, one in Beijing and one in Nanjing.[38] And yet, despite this seemingly self-limiting business strategy, Tongren Tang's reputation spread widely. In the 1920s its sales revenue at the Beijing store reached three thousand yuan per day, and its medicines were distributed in every province of China and among over-seas Chinese in Southeast Asia, Europe, and the United States.[39]

If Tongren Tang had only two stores and if it lost its ties to imperial institutions with the fall of the Qing dynasty, how did the Yues popularize its goods so widely in the early twentieth century? At the same time that the Yues tenaciously clung to family traditions in limiting the construction of stores under Tongren Tang's name, they invented new traditions by opening "olde" drugstores under other names.

Yue Daren and Olde Yue Family Shoppes

In 1907, at the same meeting where the Yue family's joint management barred family members from opening new stores under the name Tong-ren Tang, there was no objection to their plans for opening medicine stores under other names. In fact, the family rules that were laid down allowed all family members to borrow from Tongren Tang the character *ren* ("humaneness") for use on their shop signs and permitted them to add elsewhere (usually painted on their storefronts) the designation "Olde Yue Family Shoppe" (Yuejia lao pu). While this agreement reserved the name Tongren Tang for the "main store" *(zong dian)* at Dashalan in Beijing, it cleared the way for family members to open new stores that were indirectly identified as descendants of the old one.[40]

Thus unleashed, various members of the Yue family proceeded to open chain stores on a national scale—thirty-four Olde Yue Family Shoppes selling traditional Chinese medicine opened in twenty-four cities between 1907 and 1949.[41] The founders of these stores came from all four branches of the Yue family, and one of them, Yue Daren, had the greatest success. In 1914, when he opened his first store, he was able to draw its initial capital from a total of 60,000 yuan (40,000 ounces of silver) that he and his younger brothers had inherited on the death of their father (Yue Pingquan's son) in 1912.[42] During the next two decades, he steadily built up this business, and by the time of his death in 1934, he had raised its capital to 1 million yuan and was generating sales revenue valued at 1–1.25 million yuan per year.[43] Yue Daren's management of Daren Tang, the biggest of the Yue family's chains of medicine shops, illustrates how the Yues adapted as members of a merchant family in post-imperial China and used "tradition" to appeal to consumers.

BUILDING OSTENTATIOUSLY TRADITIONAL NEW STORES
Yue Daren, like several of his relatives from all branches of the Yue family, spent time in the West.[44] Born in 1875 and raised in Beijing, he traveled as a young man to Europe in the first years of the twentieth century with the Qing dynasty's ambassador to Germany, Lu Haihuan. (In Figure 2.4 he is pictured in Western dress, with his family). He visited Germany and England between 1907 and 1912—precisely the time that chain stores began to spread across England and Germany in significant numbers.[45] On his return to China after the fall of the Qing dynasty, he acquired a reputation as a Western-style capitalist because of his investments in industrial enterprises such as the Daren Iron Foundry (Daren tie gongchang) and the Bohai Chemical Company (Bohai huaxue gongsi). He also created a chain of drugstores, but he did not give his drugstores a Western appearance or advertise them in Western-style media.[46] He called his medicine business Jingdu Daren Tang (The Hall in the Capital for Extending Humaneness), and he did more than name it after himself; he identified it with Tongren Tang by using the characters *ren* and *tang,* and he conveyed

the impression that Daren Tang would "extend" (*da*) its reach far beyond "the Capital," Beijing.

From the beginning Yue Daren carefully selected for his headquarters a site from which he could supply branch stores. Despite the reference in his business's name to Beijing, he never attempted to set up his headquarters there. Initially he tried to locate Daren Tang's headquarters and factory in Shanghai, which conducted more interurban trade than any other city in China at the time, but his medicine plant there soon failed because the weather conditions in the Lower Yangzi region around Shanghai proved to be too humid for storing and processing his medicinal herbs (which were grown in North China). So in 1914 he moved from Shanghai to Tianjin, which conducted more interurban trade than any other city in North China, and set up his headquarters and factory in Tianjin's Hongqiao District at Shenjia zhalan.[47] During the next twenty years, he proceeded to add eighteen branch stores in twelve additional cities, which were located at the cores of eight of China's nine macroregions: the Northeast (at Dalian and Changchun), North (at Qingdao, Kaifeng, and Zhengzhou), and Northwest (at Xi'an); the Lower Yangzi (at Shanghai), Middle Yangzi (at Hankou and Changsha), and Upper Yangzi (at Chengdu); and the Southeast (at Fuzhou) and South (at Hong Kong), leaving the Southwest as the only region of China in which he had no branch store (Map 2.1).[48]

In these cities throughout China, Yue Daren built stores that were designed to catch the consumer's eye. As such, they contrasted sharply with Tongren Tang. At the time, although Tongren Tang's store was on a prestigious site at Dashalan in Beijing, it occupied a very unpretentious building that featured post-and-beam construction, a facade in understated wooden latticework, a roof of standard tiles, and an open front with wooden shutters and no glass windows (Figure 2.5). This store dated from 1900; yet another fire—this one set during the Boxer uprising—had burned down the previous building.[49] As John Cameron noted in 1925, Tongren Tang "is perhaps the most unostentatious of all the old drug stores in this city [Beijing]."[50]

If Tongren Tang was unostentatious, the same could not be said for Daren Tang. In contrast with Tongren Tang's unadorned store in Beijing, Daren Tang's main store in Tianjin was elaborately decorated. It had post-and-beam construction that resembled the basic design of Tongren Tang, but its entrance was much grander, featuring stone steps, big, heavy doors in the shape of a Chinese-style scepter (*ruyishi menlou*), a carving of drag-

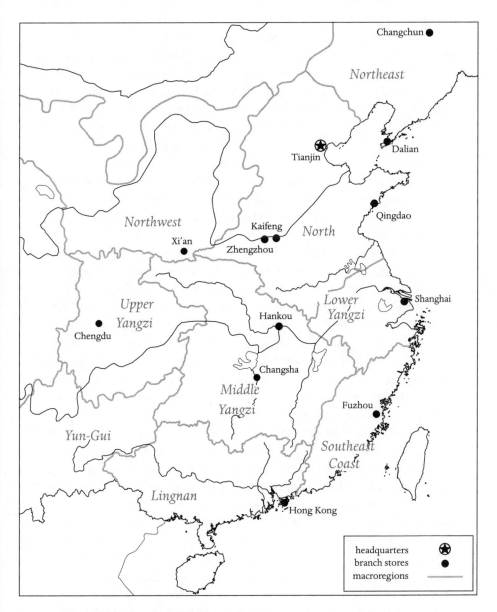

Map 2.1. Daren Tang's drugstores, 1930s.
Map by Thomas Lyons, based on macroregions from Skinner,
"Regional Urbanization," 214, map 1.

30 *Chinese Medicine Men*

ons, phoenixes, and flowers over the doors, a shop sign over the carving, and a pair of inscriptions running down either side of the doors (Figure 2.6). The massive front doors opened into a courtyard building *(siheyuan)* and led past a courtyard where a rock garden and other Daoist symbols of nature, longevity, and good health could be seen as one made one's way to the sales and consulting rooms. Over the middle counter in the salesroom hung a shop sign; written in black against a white background were the words "Daren Tang, Ye Olde Yue Family Shoppe from the Capital" (Jingdu Daren Tang Yuejia Laopu), in the same calligraphy that the Qianlong emperor had used in the eighteenth century to inscribe Tongren Tang's sign. Although this design and decor conveyed China's greatness before extensive contact with the West, Yue Daren showed no reluctance to make use of imported Western building materials, notably plate-glass windows that were mounted on either side of the front doors.[51]

Daren Tang's branch stores throughout China were modeled after its main store in Tianjin. At their entrances they all had stone steps, scepter-shaped doors, carved decorations over the doors, outdoor and indoor shop signs, pairs of inscriptions, courtyards, and plate-glass display windows. To the rear of their salesrooms they all had storage space, just as Daren Tang's main store in Tianjin did. Only in size did the branch stores differ from the main one. Whereas the main store covered thirteen thousand square feet (with three hundred square feet devoted to the salesroom), the largest of the branch stores (the one at Hankou) occupied a two-hundred-square-foot lot.[52]

If Daren Tang was ostentatiously traditional on the outside, it was equally so on the inside. Like Tongren Tang and almost all traditional drugstores in China during the early twentieth century, each of Daren Tang's stores had a high counter that was U-shaped, with the left side for prepared medicines, the right side for prescribed medicines, and the middle for settling accounts.[53] To this conventional interior Yue Daren added an unconventional feature: a ten-foot-long set of abacuses embedded in the middle counter. Whenever his cashiers slammed the sandalwood beads against the brass frame of the abacuses, they sent a loud clacking sound reverberating down the counter and throughout the store—the sound of sales racking up. Thus did Yue Daren break the sedate silence that was expected in traditional medicine stores and loudly appeal to consumers by stirring up excitement like that found in the hubbub of outdoor markets.[54] By their sound as well as their appearance, his stores lured in consumers.

GIVING CONSUMERS TRADITIONAL TREATMENT

Once consumers crossed Daren Tang's threshold, Yue Daren expected them to be treated in a traditional manner, and he trained his staff members accordingly. As we saw, Yue Pingquan had relied exclusively on members of the Yue family to staff Tongren Tang's one store in Beijing. Following his grandfather's example, Yue Daren confined his staff to Yue family members at Daren Tang's headquarters in Tianjin, where all the company's medicines were made in accordance with secret recipes.[55] Outside Tianjin, as Yue Daren added branch stores, he replicated the pattern by having a local family manage each one. His family, not the local families, owned the branch stores, but he attempted to link the other families to his own by bringing young men from the local families to Tianjin, forming fictive kinship relations with them, and training them as apprentices before sending them back to work at Daren Tang's branch stores in their hometowns.

At Daren Tang's headquarters in Tianjin, Yue Daren cast himself in the role of the traditional patriarch with ultimate authority over apprentices. He personally bestowed a special name or style *(hao)* on each of Daren Tang's teachers or masters *(xiansheng),* and each of these masters tutored and lived with a group of eight or ten apprentices. Under each master's supervision, the apprentices worked eight hours a day and studied in the evening. They spent three years learning about traditional Chinese medical theory, calligraphy, and the use of the abacus, and they ultimately memorized four hundred basic rules governing the preparation of Chinese herbal remedies. Once they successfully completed their apprenticeships, Yue Daren elevated them to the status of masters, gave them names, and assigned them to positions on the staffs of Daren Tang's stores in their hometowns.[56]

Yue Daren continued to treat his store managers as family members once they were on the job. He tried to bind them to him through master-disciple bonds and fictive kinship ties, and he expected them to follow the rules that he had laid down in his manual for managers, *Sayings and Laws to Be Followed (Yanchu fasui),* and to submit reports to him on a regular basis for an in-house publication, *Store News (Haoxun).*[57] Ultimately he provided confirmation of his familial relationships with his staff members by promising that those who gave Daren Tang long years of faithful service could count on appointments and training for their sons as their successors, and he fulfilled this promise.[58]

By all these means Yue Daren trained managers to give consumers the impression that each of Daren Tang's stores was local, like other "traditional" Chinese drugstores, which generally used similar master-disciple systems for training apprentices at the time.[59] In actual fact, his stores were part of a nationwide chain, but his staff members were recruited and trained to present each one as "family"-operated.

PROMOTING THE TRADITIONAL

In promoting Daren Tang, Yue Daren was unmodern in the sense that he did not advertise through colorful posters, billboards, and other pictorial media, and he adopted promotional techniques similar to those used at Tongren Tang. Like Tongren Tang, Daren Tang placed advertisements in only one of the print media, newspapers, and even in these advertisements both stores distinguished themselves from Western-style Chinese drugstores by featuring no pictures and by printing their names in cursive traditional Chinese calligraphy *(shufa);* Western-style Chinese drugstores, in contrast, gave their names in modern Chinese calligraphy *(meishu).*[60] In general, Daren Tang promoted itself in the same cultural media as Tongren Tang did, although its appeal to consumers was somewhat more direct and less subtle than Tongren Tang's.

In presenting goods to consumers, Daren Tang closely followed Tongren Tang's example. Whereas some traditional Chinese medicine shops sold raw herbs that consumers had to prepare at home, Daren Tang and Tongren Tang generally produced more convenient ready-to-use traditional Chinese medicines *(cheng yao).* Also like Tongren Tang, Daren Tang frequently dispensed its medicines in the form of "big pills" *(da wan),* which were about the size of walnuts and were usually coated in white wax; the consumer had only to open one to find fifty to one hundred small pills inside.[61]

Daren Tang distinguished its goods from Tongren Tang's mainly by making its pricing policies more explicit. Throughout Tongren Tang's long history, it had built up a reputation for giving no discounts and carrying only the highest-quality herbal medicines, and in the twentieth century it maintained this standard by dominating the purchasing of medicinal herbs in North China. Whereas many traditional medicine stores and trade associations from all regions of China periodically sent delegations to North China's biggest medicine fairs, only Tongren Tang and its trade association permanently maintained their own brokers, purchasing offices, and private residences at these rural locations year-round.[62] Daren Tang also purchased high-quality raw herbs at the same medicine fairs, but, while Tongren Tang discreetly made no mention of

Table 2.1. Tongren Tang's and Daren Tang's Principal Products

Name of product	Purpose	Targeted consumers
Tortoise Shell and Deer Antler Ginseng Pills (Shengui lurong wan)	Increase energy and sexual potency	Men
Black Chicken and White Chicken Pills (Wuji baifeng wan)	Prevent irregular menstruation	Women
Women's Golden Pills (Nujin dan)	Increase fertility	Women
Nine-Prescriptions Pills (Jiufang zhibao dan)	Treat vomiting and stomach aches	Children
Children's Revival Pills (Xiao'er huichun dan)	Stop fevers and convulsions	Children
Tiger Bone Wine (Hugu jiu)	Relieve arthritis	Elderly
Ox's Gallstone Pills for Heart Pain (Niuhuang qingxin wan)	Self-explanatory	All
Ox's Gallstone Pills to Calm Nerves (Angong niuhuang dan)	Self-explanatory	All
Dog Skin Plasters (Goupi gaoyao)	Remedy muscle strains	All
Big Pills for Flexibility (Da huoluo dan)	Restore motion after palsy or paralysis	All

Sources: Hou Shiheng, "Tongren Tang," in *Beijing laozihao,* ed. Hou Shiheng (Beijing: Zhongguo huanjing kexue, 1991), 401; He Bei, "Tianjin Daren Tang," in *Jinmen laozihao,* ed. Tianjin wenshi ziliao yanjiuhui (Tianjin: Baihua wenyi, 1992), 261–262; Beijing Zhongyiyao laonian baojian yanjiusuo, ed., "Tongren Tang jianshi," in *Beijing Tongren Tang mingya,* (Beijing: Zhongyi guji, 1986), 1–11.

prices on its goods, Yue Daren adopted the policy of appealing to consumers by marketing Daren Tang's goods at "good prices" *(shan jia)*.[63]

Similarly, in his decisions about what to carry in his stores, Yue Daren began by drawing heavily on Tongren Tang's goods and supplemented these with products from his own company. At their peak, Daren Tang's stores had on their shelves as many as one thousand medicines—all made by Tongren Tang or Daren Tang—including separate specialty items for men, women, children, and the elderly (Table 2.1).

In promoting the sale of his goods, Yue Daren updated Tongren Tang's techniques to fit his own time. For example, he became a philanthropist like his grandfather, but he sponsored institutions that had not been fashionable in his grandfather's day. In 1921, at Tianjin, Yue Daren founded Daren Girls' School (Daren nu xiao), with himself as chairman of the school's board of directors and with Ma Qianli, a widely known educator, as headmaster. Until the school closed in 1926, Yue generated favorable publicity through it and attracted progressive teachers, including Deng Yingchao, the wife of Zhou Enlai. In 1924 Yue Daren opened another charitable institution, a free eye clinic in Tianjin, which was run by a respected eye doctor, Li Zongyao.[64]

On traditional holidays Yue Daren celebrated as his grandfather might have done, but he often added his own consumer-oriented touch. Every year he staged Beijing operas and hosted banquets for local dignitaries on the birthday of Sun Simiao, a Daoist healer who had compiled a thirty-volume pharmacological classic, *Essential Recipes for One Thousand Cases (Qian jin yao fang)*, during the Tang dynasty (618–907) and had later become canonized as the King of Medicine (yao wang), and these banquets were probably comparable to those that his grandfather had hosted. Similarly, on the second day of the Chinese New Year Yue Daren held a ceremony to worship the God of Wealth (cai shen) at Daren Tang. To make explicit the commercial purpose of such cultural events, Yue Daren added his own payoff: a silver coin worth twenty cents for everyone in attendance. Another of his crowd-pleasers was a band that gave free concerts. He recruited the band's conductor from outside the company, and he retained the musicians—all outfitted in colorful uniforms—as full-time employees at Daren Tang.[65]

PRESERVING THE TRADITIONAL?

Under the management of Yue Daren and other members of the Yue family, Tongren Tang and the Olde Yue Family Shoppes showed extraordinary resiliency. In the 1920s and 1930s the Yues educated several of their sons and daughters in Europe and the United States. Subsequently these returning students were appointed to managerial positions in the family's traditional medicine businesses in China, and some of them have continued to serve as managers of Tongren Tang ever since, even after the founding of the People's Republic in 1949.[66]

In the early 1950s Yue Songsheng, a nephew of Yue Daren and the only son of the former Beijing police chief Yue Dayi, took the lead in making contributions to the newly founded People's Republic. He readily endorsed the government's policies, especially the transformation of capitalist enterprises like Tongren Tang and Daren Tang into "joint public and private enterprises" *(gongsi heying qiye)*. In 1955 Mao Zedong, Zhou Enlai, and other political leaders met with Yue Songsheng, declared that he was their most important capitalist ally in North China, and appointed him vice mayor of the city of Beijing.[67] Under state control since then, Tongren Tang has been renovated and has opened branch stores. In 1991 Tongren Tang was designated as a first-class state-run enterprise and was registered in more than forty countries. And yet Tongren Tang's main store is still tucked away on the narrow alley of Dashalan, south of Front Gate in Beijing, and it is still celebrated for appealing to Chinese consumers not through Western-style media but as "an olde established shoppe" *(laoshanghao)*.[68]

This characterization of Tongren Tang might well leave the impression that the Yues preserved it and their other medicine stores by stubbornly and unwaveringly clinging to an unchanging tradition. If so, then this impression is misleading. As I have shown here, the Yues of the late nineteenth and early twentieth centuries did not cling to tradition so much as give new meanings to it.

Giving New Meanings to Tradition

John Cameron in 1925 asserted that Tongren Tang's pills made the store famous, and this chapter has not refuted his point. Surely Tongren Tang's and Daren Tang's successes were at least partially attributable to the efficacy of their traditional medicines, which favorably impressed Western as well as Chinese pharmacologists at the time. In fact, one of Daren Tang's Western admirers, German-owned Bayer, the world's biggest manufacturer of modern pharmaceutical goods at the time, was so impressed with Daren Tang's products that it approached Yue Daren in the 1930s with a proposal to form a joint venture (which did not come into existence for logistical reasons).[69] But Cameron's implication that Tongren Tang achieved fame for its medicines without promoting them is not borne out by its history. Yue Pingquan and Yue Daren actively marketed their medicines, and in the process they substantially transformed their family's business.

In the late nineteenth and early twentieth centuries, the Yues were not traditional in the conventional sense of the term as it was then applied to Chinese merchants. That is, they did not passively retain from the past all "gentlemanly customs of doing business" *(junzi zhi feng de maimai)* as some old-fashioned Beijing shopkeepers did, according to Lao She, a leading writer and commentator on Beijing at the time.[70] They fit this description to the extent that they did not promote the sale of their goods through lithographed posters, billboards, and other pictorial media that reached China from the West in the late nineteenth and early twentieth centuries. But their decision not to adopt these Western-style advertising media seems to have been part of an active marketing strategy rather than a passive acceptance of tradition.

Yue Pingquan made imaginative departures from past practices—inventing numerous new traditions rather than being trapped in a single old tradition—and Yue Daren introduced even more radical innovations in the name of tradition, especially in his construction and design of chain stores for managing the interregional distribution of goods throughout China. As a cosmopolitan traveler in the West, Yue Daren had observed Western business practices and seems to have drawn a sophisticated distinction between Western businesses' organizational forms (such as chain stores) and their advertising (especially through print media). Since his principal marketing problem in China was how to supply a market, he readily embraced the Western idea of the chain store. But, since he did not need to reshape Chinese consumers' preferences or create a demand for his type of products (which had become familiar in China long before Yue Pingquan and remained so long after Yue Daren), he categorically rejected Western-style advertising through print media and found other ways to project an image of his shops and goods as traditional.

As later chapters show, Yue Daren bore a close resemblance to Chinese owners of Western-style drugstores in his adoption of the chain store as an organizational form and in his design of Daren Tang's eye-catching new "traditional" shops, which complemented Western-style drugstores' eye-catching "modern" shops. But Chinese owners of Western-style drug-stores formulated different advertising strategies because they faced different marketing problems. Unlike Yue Daren, they entered a market in which Chinese consumers were generally not familiar with their products, and they made use of Western-style pictorial media to heighten or create demand for their goods.

Ironically, in contrast with Yue Daren, the Chinese purveyors of Western-style goods lacked experience in the West and with Westerners. They generally did not travel to the West or receive training in Western-sponsored schools, Western-owned businesses, or other Western organizations in the West or China. Like the Yues, these Chinese entrepreneurs sold medicines made in China, but they packaged their medicines, decorated their drugstores, and designed their advertising all in what they regarded as a Western style. Generally illiterate in Western languages and lacking direct exposure to Western countries, Chinese owners of Western-style drugstores imagined and produced advertising to identify their goods as "Western" without consulting Westerners, and the one who produced perhaps the most imaginative "Western" advertising of all was China's King of Advertising, Huang Chujiu.

3

Advertising Dreams

> Today . . . calendar posters are popular with ordinary people in Chinese society. The women in calendar posters are sick. Not only are calendar painters unskilled but the subjects of their paintings are disgusting and depraved. China has lots of women who are strong and healthy, but calendar painters only draw sickly ladies so weak that they could be knocked down by a gust of wind. This kind of sickness does not come from society. It comes from the painters.
>
> Lu Xun, "Lu Xun zai Zhonghua yishu daxue yanjiang jilu" (1930)

Was Lu Xun, a leading Chinese writer and critic, right? Was advertising wholly an expression of commercial artists' "sick" fantasies and not at all a reflection of society at large? If so, then why did calendar posters and other advertisements become, in Lu Xun's words, "popular with ordinary people in Chinese society"?[1]

Lu Xun was undoubtedly right not to adopt the common and untrustworthy assumption that advertising directly reflects social reality or simply expresses popular attitudes. While it is tempting to imagine that advertising is a mirror that reflects a true image of society and popular thought, specialists on advertising in Western history have convincingly shown that at most it has been, in the words of the American historian Roland Marchand, "not a true mirror but a Zerrspiegel, a distorting mirror . . . a fun-house mirror [that] not only distorted, it also selected."[2]

If Lu Xun was right not to attribute advertising simply to society, he was wrong, I think, to attribute it solely to commercial artists. As we shall see later in this chapter, certain Chinese commercial artists did play crucial roles as creators of advertising images, especially images of women, but they were not the only, or even the principal, historical figures responsible for making and popularizing advertisements in China during the first half of the twentieth century. More pivotal in the process were Chinese entrepreneurs. To illustrate their role, the focus here is on Huang Chujiu (1872–1931), a manufacturer and distributor of "new medicine," who was known in early twentieth-century China as the King of Advertising *(guanggao da wang).*[3]

The Dream of Western Solutions to Chinese Problems

Huang Chujiu (Figure 3.1) based his first major advertising campaign on the premise that, at the beginning of the twentieth century, Chinese yearned for Western solutions to their medical problems. He tested the popularity of this belief by introducing China's first Chinese-made drug that appeared to be Western. He distributed the drug in bottles under a Chinese name, Ailuo bunaozhi (Ailuo Brain Tonic), which sounded like a Chinese transliteration of a Western name. He also had China's biggest publishing house, the Commercial Press, print on the label and the outer paper wrapper, in English, that the product was invented by Dr. T. C. Yale (Figure 3.2). Thus, on the outside, this medicine gave the impression that it was Western.[4]

CHINESE ORIGINS OF A "WESTERN" ALTERNATIVE
Huang presented Ailuo Brain Tonic as Western even though he had no Western partner or Western financial backing, had never been to the West, and had never studied Western pharmacology or received any Western education. Born in 1872 in Taoyuan village, Yuyao county, Shaoxing prefecture, Zhejiang Province, seventy miles south of Shanghai, he had grown up as the son of a Chinese herbal doctor and had learned about Chinese medicine as an apprentice in his father's clinic. In his home village he had until the age of fifteen attended a "private" school *(sishu)* of the kind that rejected Western educational reforms in favor of traditional Chinese learning.[5] Only once had he been exposed to a Western-oriented institution—he had enrolled briefly at the Qingxin Academy (Qingxin shuyuan) in 1887 after his father's death had prompted him and his mother to move to Shanghai. But in Shanghai he had soon discovered opportunities to make money selling medicine as a street peddler, so he had begun skipping classes and then dropped out of school, ending his formal education altogether. From then on he had gradually built up a business selling Chinese medicines, first as a hawker in teahouses and wine shops around the Temple of the City God (Chenghuang miao) and

then as the proprietor of a small, traditional drugstore that he and his mother had opened in Shanghai's old walled city.[6]

In 1890, when Huang moved his business into Shanghai's French Concession, he took his first step toward identifying it with Western medicine by converting his shop from an old-style drugstore into a new-style one. He dropped its original traditional-sounding name, the Hall of Long Life (Yishou tang), which ended in *tang* (hall), as did the names of Tongren Tang, Daren Tang, and many other old-style Chinese drugstores. In its place he adopted an explicitly foreign-sounding name that was appropriate for Shanghai's French Concession, the Great China-France Drugstore (Zhongfa da yaofang), which ended in a new Chinese term, *yaofang* (drugstore). He also gave his new drugstore a name in English, the Great Eastern Dispensary, which he included along with its Chinese name on his letterhead and his shop sign (Figure 3.3). Later he moved his Shanghai drugstore one last time from the French Concession into the International Settlement.[7]

Huang's drugstore and the label on his Ailuo Brain Tonic might have appeared to be Western, but there was in fact nothing Western about the contents of this medicine. He bought its recipe from a Chinese pharmacist, Wu Kunrong, who had intended that it be used as a sedative. Huang employed forty Chinese workers to produce and bottle it, and he distributed it through his and other Chinese-owned new-style drugstores. He promoted it in advertising campaigns exclusively through Chinese-language media—newspapers, handbills, and posters—and he concentrated in this advertising on promoting his "Western" medicine by locating it in a Chinese medical context.[8] (Because Huang's drugstore and the other stores in this book all concentrated their advertising in Chinese-language media and achieved recognition from consumers for their names in Chinese, not English, I have referred to them by English translations of their Chinese names rather than by their English names—in this case calling Huang's business Great China-France Drugstores rather than the Great Eastern Dispensary).

Huang's advertising urged Chinese to try his "Western" brain tonic to make up for the deficiencies of Chinese medicine. He traced these deficiencies to the traditional Chinese medical theory of the Five Yin Orbs and Six Yang Orbs *(wu zang liu fu)* and found fault with it for focusing too sharply on relations or functions in the body and not enough on relations or functions in the brain *(naozhi)*. From Western medical theory he had learned, he said, that the brain was a Sixth Yin Orb, and, on the basis of this discovery, he claimed to have formulated a new synthesis—the theory of the *Six* Yin Orbs and Six Yang Orbs *(liu zang liu fu)*.[9]

In his advertising Huang thus invoked Western medical theory as the basis for his product, Ailuo Brain Tonic, but he delivered this message in terminology and logic that remained firmly embedded in Chinese medical theory. Whereas Huang claimed to be adopting a Western medical perspective, he described the body entirely in terms of orbs *(zang)*, not organs, even though, as the medical historian Manfred Porkert has pointed out, "statements bearing on a certain orb can under no circumstances be made to agree completely with statements bearing on the corresponding organ in Western thought. . . . [It is fallacious to assume] that congruence may be achieved between the description of a Chinese orb and the characteristics that Western medicine postulates for its substratum."[10] Huang made no comment on the differences between Chinese and Western modes of thinking about orbs and organs, or, for that matter, about health and disease in general. Instead, keeping his advertisements strictly in Chinese terms, he boasted that he had discovered the "Western" theory of the Sixth Yin Orb and that it revealed the Chinese need for "brain health" *(jiannao)*—precisely the need that his product would satisfy.[11]

OVERCOMING OBJECTIONS TO CLAIMS OF WESTERNNESS

Huang's product had barely hit the market before he faced two challenges to the claims in his advertising. In 1907, less than a year after Huang introduced Ailuo Brain Tonic, he was approached by "a little American bum" *(Meiguo xiao wulai*—to quote the characterization given in the Huang family's version of the story) who demanded royalties because he claimed to be the son of T. C. Yale, the inventor identified on the label of Ailuo Brain Tonic. Recognizing this as a minor threat, Huang disposed of it by quietly paying off this Mr. Yale in exchange for his signature on a legal document granting all rights over Ailuo Brain Tonic to Huang's Great China-France Drugstore.[12]

Later in 1907 another complaint was lodged by a Portuguese physician named Yale. This doctor, an established medical practitioner in Shanghai's International Settlement, sued Huang for using his name to promote a drug without his permission and filed charges in the Mixed Court of the International Settlement. This time, unable to settle quietly out of court,

Huang confronted his Western accuser and used the occasion to generate publicity for himself and his business.

Pleading innocent, Huang claimed that he had used the name T. C. Yale on the label because it was the Western equivalent of his own name. He explained that his name, Huang, meant yellow, and since Yellow was not a common Western surname, he chose a common Western surname that sounds like Yellow: Yale. As for the initials T. C., these were the first letters of his two given names, Chu and Jiu, as romanized to represent the sounds of these two characters when pronounced in his native dialect.[13]

Huang's performance in the courtroom was mesmerizing. The judge found in his favor and dismissed the charges, and newspaper reporters described his victory in sensational stories. As a result, Huang's reputation as a slippery character *(huatou)* spread widely.[14] Even among Shanghainese (who have often been stereotyped by Chinese from elsewhere as "wily"), he became known jokingly as "one of the two and a half slipperiest characters in town."[15]

This publicity certainly did not hurt Huang's promotion of Ailuo Brain Tonic, and if sales and profits are any indication, it gave the product a big boost. Following the trial, Huang quickly earned high profits on Ailuo Brain Tonic. He produced it at an average variable cost of .40 yuan per 168-cc bottle and sold it at two yuan per bottle, a profit of 400 percent. As the profits rolled in, Huang used them to buy a fancy automobile, renovate a three-story building made of reinforced concrete, and begin distributing his goods in China outside Shanghai. By 1911 he had reinvested enough profits in the Great China-France Drugstore to make it the second largest new-style Chinese drugstore in Shanghai, with capital of 68,000 yuan, annual sales revenue of 250,000 yuan, and annual profits of 50,000 yuan. At that time he made his business officially Western. By paying several hundred yuan to the Portuguese consul in Shanghai, he bought the citizenship of a deceased Portuguese resident of Shanghai, and he registered the Great China-France Drugstore as a Portuguese enterprise. From then on, the company's letterhead proclaimed in Chinese as well as English that it was a Portuguese business.[16]

By successfully introducing Ailuo Brain Tonic and defending it in court, Huang set precedents that opened the way for the sale in China of Chinese-made "new medicine" that appeared to have foreign origins. Impressed by his high profit rates, several Chinese drugstores began making their own new-style medicines, which became known as "goods under local trademarks" *(benpai chanpin).* By the mid-1930s the Great China-France Drugstore manufactured more than five hundred such drugs under its local trademark, and it was by no means unique. Several other Chinese-owned new-style drugstores each made a comparable number of drugs under their local trademarks (see Chapter 4).[17]

POPULARIZING WESTERN SOLUTIONS TO CHINESE MEDICAL PROBLEMS

Why did Huang Chujiu's advertising for Ailuo Brain Tonic become popular? Huang personally played the leading role in devising specific advertising campaigns for merchandising his goods, but how did he make his advertising effective? Was it (in Lu Xun's terms) because Huang's advertising ideas and images came from society or from the advertiser?

In this particular case, such questions are difficult to answer because scholars are still debating the history of Chinese popular attitudes toward medicine, a field worthy of future research. On the basis of work done thus far, it seems that Huang's emphasis on a Western solution as a viable alternative to Chinese medicine was an idea espoused at the time only by a segment of China's educated elite and was not representative of popular thought in Chinese society as a whole. Intellectual and political historians have shown that advocates of modern Western medical practice *(Xi yi)* and defenders of traditional Chinese medicine *(Zhong yi)* battled fiercely and mobilized substantial organizations against each other during the first half of the twentieth century, but these scholars have concentrated exclusively on the educated elite—intellectuals, political leaders, physicians—leaving open the question of whether other Chinese thought of medicine in these dualistic Sino-Western terms.[18]

As I noted in Chapter 1, Nathan Sivin and other scholars have postulated that in medical practice "pluralism" did not give way to Sino-Western or traditional-modern "dualism" before the founding of the People's Republic in 1949. As we will see in later chapters, this thesis is questionable as it applies to the first half of the twentieth century, but it seems valid as a description of China in the 1890s and at the turn of the century, when Huang first broke into the market. At that time he apparently advertised in a society where most Chinese consumers thought of their medical options not dualistically, in Sino-Western terms, but eclectically, in a framework of medical pluralism.

Huang thus initially popularized his medicine as "Western" in a society where Western medicine had strong support from a small segment of the

Chinese elite but had not become widely popular. Faced with this market-ing challenge, he devised a strategy for promoting Western medicine that differed from the one adopted by members of China's intellectual elite. He advertised using familiar Chinese medical terms (body orbs) rather than unfamiliar Western scientific ones (body organs), and he thereby made his product seem intelligible and unthreatening to Chinese con-sumers even while it retained its appeal as an (apparent) import from the exotic Occident. In Lu Xun's terms, one might say that Huang's advertis-ing came from both himself (through his selective adaptation of Chinese intellectuals' advocacy of Western medicine) and society (through his accommodation to popular unfamiliarity with Western medicine).

The Dream of the Triumph of Economic Nationalism

In 1911, emboldened by his success with "Western" Ailuo Brain Tonic, Huang Chujiu began to produce an imitation of a Japanese-made medi-cine that was called Humane Elixir (a two-character name pronounced Jintan in Japanese and Rendan in Mandarin). Eventually, during an anti-Japanese boycott in China four years later, Huang began to compete with the Japanese manufacturer of this medicine by introducing nationalistic "buy-Chinese" advertising, but initially he viewed it as a model for his own business.

HUANG'S JAPANESE MODEL: HUMANE ELIXIR

From Huang's point of view, Japanese-made Humane Elixir was the obvi-ous choice as a model for his own product because it was by far the most popular foreign-made medicine in China. According to the American con-sul general in Shanghai at the time, Humane Elixir's sales in China were nearly equal to those of all other foreign-made pharmaceutical products combined.[19] Its popularity was not traceable to its therapeutic efficacy, at least not according to an analysis done at the time by the American Med-ical Association, which concluded that Humane Elixir "possessed no material potency" because it lacked "potent alkaloids" and consisted mostly of sugars that were "highly aromatized, suggesting 'breath per-fumes' like 'sen sen.'"[20] But if the medical efficacy of Humane Elixir was open to doubt, the commercial potency of the company that marketed it in China was undeniable.

The company's Japanese founder, Morishita Hiroshi, had an eye on

China even before he began to produce Humane Elixir at Osaka in 1893. Throughout his life he had been interested in "Chinese medicine" (*kanpo* in Japanese), and while serving with the Japanese army in Taiwan, he had conceived the idea of making Humane Elixir.[21] After consulting a Japanese Sinologist and a Japanese journalist specializing in China, he chose for the product a name that was probably borrowed in part from Tongren Tang. The first character, Humane (pronounced *jin* in Japanese and *ren* in Chinese) was the same as the second character in Tongren Tang. The second character in the Japanese product's name, Elixir, was the term long used to describe Daoist potions and other traditional Chinese tonics.[22]

Within a decade after formulating Humane Elixir, Morishita extended his distribution system from Japan to China. By 1908 it maintained sales offices in three Chinese cities (Shanghai in the Lower Yangzi, Hankou in the Middle Yangzi, Tianjin in North China) and made each of these offices responsible for a sales territory encompassing five or six of China's provinces. At the Shanghai office he established Toa and Company, capitalized at five hundred thousand yen, to serve as his headquarters in China. Toa recruited Chinese-owned businesses as distributors and convinced them to sell Humane Elixir to the exclusion of Western pharmaceutical products by granting them seven to ten months' credit (compared with only three months' credit from Western companies) and by protecting them from fluctuations in market prices. Whenever the market rose above the agreed-upon price, it allowed them to keep surplus profits, and whenever the market fell below the agreed-upon price, it allowed them to pass their losses along to the company.[23] By using this strategy, it distributed Humane Elixir throughout China before Huang Chujiu entered the market at Shanghai. As the American consul general at Shanghai remarked about Humane Elixir at the time, "This company has spared no pains, either in canvassing or publicity campaigns, to exploit thoroughly and systematically the whole of China, so that even in remoter interior sections it is difficult to escape the familiar poster extolling the virtues of 'Jintan' [Humane Elixir]."[24]

As these references to Humane Elixir's "publicity campaigns" and its "familiar poster" suggest, the Japanese company armed its large-scale distribution system with a full arsenal of advertising weapons. By 1910 it was already the number one advertiser in Japan, and it set its sights on the same goal in China.[25] While sending its message through a wide range of media—newspapers, magazines, billboards, posters, handbills, calendars, parades—Humane Elixir's management focused attention sharply on a single image: its trademark. This trademark was well designed to reach illiterate as well as literate Chinese consumers, according to an American advertising analyst who was sent by the U.S. Department of Commerce to spend eighteen months surveying advertising in China, Japan, and the Philippines during the late 1910s. "The best 'chop' is nearly always pictorial, supplemented in most cases with a few easily read Chinese characters," he observed in his report on advertising in China, and he cited Humane Elixir as his prime example: "One of the very best chops is that used by the Japanese 'Jintan' . . . which is advertised and used all over China. The chop consists of nothing but the head and shoulders of a man wearing a distinctive kind of hat, together with two simple Chinese characters that even the most illiterate coolie can read and remember."[26] This description of the two characters as "simple" is no exaggeration. Each is written in only four strokes.

In the 1910s Humane Elixir made its trademark familiar to illiterate as well as literate Chinese by featuring it in outdoor advertisements over and over again, especially on billboards and in parades of sandwich board carriers (Figures 3.4 and 3.5).[27] In fact, it eventually made the Humane Elixir man's face on its trademark so familiar that he had an effect on men's fashions in China. Adopting his heavy black mustache as their model, many Chinese men grew similar mustaches and were seen wearing them in China's cities (including Beijing, as the novelist Lin Yutang noted) and in China's countryside (as portrayed in Wu Zuxiang's short story "Fan Village").[28] Even today, long after the image of the Humane Elixir man has ceased to occupy a prominent place in China's landscape, the term "Humane Elixir mustache" (Rendan *huzi*) continues to be used to describe mustaches worn by Chinese men in China.

IMITATING THE JAPANESE MODEL

Favorably impressed by this Japanese company's success, Huang Chujiu tried to make a new medicine indistinguishable from Humane Elixir. He named his new medicine Human Elixir, which was written slightly differently (Figure 3.6) but was pronounced exactly the same as Humane Elixir—even with the same intonation. He thus took advantage of the same homophone, Ren (Humane) and Ren (Human), that Tongren Tang's imitators had exploited forty years earlier. To make Human Elixir,

Huang founded the first Chinese-owned foreign-style mechanized pharmaceutical manufacturer, the Dragon and Tiger Company (Long hu gongsi) and assigned it the task of duplicating Humane Elixir. According to the Dragon and Tiger Company's analysis, Humane Elixir turned out to contain peppermint, borneol, cloves, and catechu, which were all readily available in China. So Huang used these ingredients in his effort to make Human Elixir resemble Humane Elixir as closely as possible.[29]

In advertising, as in manufacturing, Huang initially made his product appear to be similar to its Japanese counterpart. On July 26, 1911, Human Elixir's first day on the market, he advertised it in Shanghai's leading newspaper, *Shenbao*, as "a miraculous cure for all diseases . . . a panacea that in an emergency relieves any physical pain." During the next four years he made no effort in advertising campaigns to differentiate his product from Japanese-made Humane Elixir, no mention of his product's Chinese origins, and no appeal to his Chinese customers' patriotism. In fact (following the example of his own Ailuo Brain Tonic), Huang's advertising included un-Chinese, Western images, such as an orchestra that featured brass horns and a bass drum (known in Chinese as "foreign instruments," *yanghao* and *yanggu*).[30]

Using this strategy of imitation, Huang made a poor start with Human Elixir. Initially he was unable to sell more than one hundred cases per year.[31] Nonetheless, he stayed with the same strategy until 1915, when Japan imposed on the Chinese government the Twenty-one Demands—a wide-ranging set of economic rights and privileges for Japanese in China—which provoked Chinese protests, including a boycott against Japanese-made goods.

SELLING "NATIONAL GOODS"

On March 23, 1915, less than two months after Japan's Twenty-one Demands were made public, Chinese leaders of Shanghai's twenty major guilds formed the Society for the Use of National Goods (Quan yong guohuo hui) and started boycotting Japanese-made goods and promoting Chinese-made substitutes. Though officially banned by the Chinese government in Beijing, this organization quickly extended its reach, opening offices at seventy locations in China by May 1915.[32] As the boycott spread, Huang Chujiu tried to capitalize on it by advertising Human Elixir as one of China's "national goods."

Between May and August 1915 Huang filled his newspaper advertisements with nationalistic slogans in support of Human Elixir. These advertisements exhorted Chinese consumers to "Stop the Economic Drain [Abroad]" *(louzhi)*, "Restore Economic Rights [to Chinese]" *(wanhui liquan)*, and "Buy 100 Percent National Goods" *(mai wanquan guohuo)*.[33] Conceding that Huang's Human Elixir had once not tasted as good as his foreign rival's product, his advertising insisted that it had been worth buying even then because it had always been an effective medicine and had always been a 100 percent national product. Besides, as of 1915, Human Elixir tasted "not a bit inferior to foreign goods [*waihuo*]," his advertising claimed, because he had improved it by combining raw materials from China with "the most up-to-date manufacturing techniques from the West." To enhance their visual appeal, Huang's newspaper advertisements contained nationalistic drawings along with nationalistic slogans. One advertisement from 1915, for example, employed the emotionally charged imagery of the flag and flagpole: the Chinese character for country *(guo)* formed the flagpole's base; the character for China *(Zhong)* was the pole; and a flag emblazoned with "Human Elixir" flew from the top of the pole.[34]

While adopting the rhetoric of modern nationalistic competition, Huang did not abandon the imagery of traditional Chinese harmony. Instead, he blended the two. In 1915 he revised Human Elixir's trademark, for example, so that it contained representations of both nationalistic competitiveness and traditional harmony. To signify nationalism he highlighted in circles Chinese characters meaning "Chinese National Goods" *(Zhonghua guohuo)*. To invoke tradition, he pictured a dragon and a tiger: according to traditional Daoist symbolism, a divine elixir is produced when yang (the dragon) and yin (the tiger) are brought together in a harmonization of opposites (Figure 3.6).[35] This trademark gave the impression that Human Elixir was an official product as well as a nationalistic and traditional one by declaring that it had received special recognition from three government agencies: approval from the Ministry of Health, tax exempt status from the Ministry of Finance, and official registration from the Trademark Bureau.[36] To reinforce this impression, Huang bought for himself honorific official titles, including Presidential Adviser *(da zong-tongfu ziyi)* to Yuan Shikai, who presided over China's republican government in 1915.[37]

Even while Huang used nationalistic and traditional imagery to differentiate his product from his Japanese rival's, he adopted that rival's financial and promotional techniques to strengthen his company's distribution system. In 1915 he converted his business to a limited liability company and recruited several Chinese investors to help him raise its capital to one hundred thousand yuan. With this backing he began offering exactly the same credit to Chinese distributors as his Japanese rival had offered, allowing them to hold goods up to ten months before they were required to make any payment. To supply these distributors with advertising, he followed step-by-step in his Japanese rival's tracks, sending out advertising teams to put up posters wherever Humane Elixir's advertising appeared in Shanghai and dispatching another four or five teams to do the same in other cities, towns, and villages outside Shanghai. These teams hired local children to parade around in tall hats and white gowns while marching to the beat of drums and handing out leaflets.[38]

And yet, despite all this fanfare, Huang did not earn high profits. At the end of the boycott against Japan's Twenty-one Demands in August 1915, he was so disappointed in the sales of Human Elixir that he sold the company for forty thousand yuan to two Chinese publishers, Lufei Bohong and Shen Zhifang, the president and vice president of the Zhonghua Book Company. A year later, after these new owners fared even worse and lost all sixty thousand yuan that they had invested to improve Human Elixir, Huang bought it back from them for twenty thousand yuan, half what they had originally paid him for it.[39]

Between the 1910s and the 1930s Huang continued to sell Human Elixir, with results ranging from poor to mediocre. In an average year he sold 200–300 cases. He regularly underpriced Humane Elixir by 20 percent and at times by as much as 80 percent and, as a result, he frequently suffered losses on Human Elixir and covered them by dipping into profits from Ailuo Brain Tonic. He recorded his highest sales, 1,000–1,260 cases per year, in conjunction with two anti-Japanese boycotts, one during the May Fourth Movement of 1919 and the other during the National Salvation Movement of 1931. But, even selling at these levels, Human Elixir was no match for its Japanese rival. During the boycott of 1919 it yielded profits of twenty thousand yuan—less than half the average annual profits on Huang's Ailuo Brain Tonic at that time—and during the boycott of 1931 its sales amounted to no more than one-thirtieth of Humane Elixir's sales in China (1,260 cases compared with 37,800 cases).[40]

POPULARIZING ECONOMIC NATIONALISM

Why was Huang's advertising for Human Elixir not as effective as his advertising for other products? For it, as for Ailuo Brain Tonic, Huang devised an advertising campaign using ideas and images that had been introduced by members of China's intellectual elite. Since the turn of the century Liang Qichao and other Chinese thinkers had advocated nationalist causes, and during the first third of the century Chinese intellectuals and students led an extraordinary number of antiforeign boycotts—each sparked by a political or diplomatic incident—which were directed primarily against Japan (in 1908, 1909, 1915, 1919–1921, 1923, 1925–1926, 1927, 1928–1929, 1931–1932) and secondarily against Britain (in 1909, 1925–1926, and 1927). Undoubtedly Huang adopted and continued to use "national goods" slogans because some of these boycotts were effective. As C. F. Remer has shown, when one of these boycotts spread widely and lasted more than a year in China, it reduced the sale of foreign-made goods by as much as 25–40 percent in the Lower Yangzi region and South China and by 10 percent in North China.[41] Citing this evidence, the economic historian Hou Chi-ming has gone so far as to conclude that economic nationalism gave Chinese-owned businesses a major advantage over foreign-owned rivals in their battles for China's market.[42] But perhaps this conclusion focuses too sharply on the ideology of nationalism without taking into account businesses' organizational capacities for marketing their goods.

If Huang's rivalry with Japanese-owned Humane Elixir is viewed strictly in ideological terms, it is difficult to explain why he was not more successful. Using nationalistic advertising and benefiting from anti-Japanese boycotts almost every year between 1915 and 1932, he and other participants in the national goods movement made Japanese Humane Elixir their prime target and systematically prevented Chinese consumers from mistaking it for a Chinese-owned business. Even though Humane Elixir's name consisted of Confucian and Daoist terms that were familiar to Chinese consumers, and even though it tried to promote its goods as vaguely "Eastern" (*dongyang*), rather than unambiguously Japanese, it had no way to prevent Huang and anti-Japanese demonstrators from identifying it and denouncing it as Japanese again and again between the 1910s and the 1930s.[43]

If Huang's rivalry with Japanese Humane Elixir is viewed in organizational rather than purely ideological terms, then the explanation for his failure to provide serious competition becomes apparent. Before Huang had even entered the market, Humane Elixir had already instituted an interregional distribution system in China (which was an extension of its national distribution system in Japan), and it continued to market its goods through this system for half a century, not withdrawing until the end of World War II, in 1945. It did not have the biggest distribution system for marketing medicine in China at the time (see Chapter 4), but it had a bigger one than Huang did, and its Japanese staff members and Chinese sales representatives conducted long-distance trade on a much grander scale in China than Huang's Chinese organization was able to do. As a result, while Huang achieved high sales and profits with Ailuo Brain Tonic (in a market where he faced no comparable rival), he failed to do the same with Human Elixir.

The Dream of Women's Bodies

While Huang Chujiu used exotic images of the West to advertise Ailuo Brain Tonic and nationalistic images of China to advertise Human Elixir, these were not the most common images to appear in his advertisements. By far the most common images in advertisements for these and all his other products were of beautiful women.[44] To produce these images, Huang recruited two Chinese commercial artists, Zheng Mantuo (1888–1961) and Hang Zhiying (1900–1947), who eventually became widely known in early twentieth-century China for their calendar posters of women, especially nudes.

UNVEILING NUDES

In 1914 Huang took his first and perhaps biggest step toward successfully commodifying women when he discovered Zheng, then an unknown twenty-six-year-old portrait painter. At the time Zheng was painting portraits of classical Chinese beauties *(shinu hua),* and, after migrating to Shanghai from Hangzhou only a few months earlier, he was hoping to sell his paintings by putting them on display at Zhang Garden, in the heart of Shanghai's commercial district on Nanjing Road.[45]

When Huang saw Zheng's paintings, he immediately recognized potential for advertising. He was particularly impressed by Zheng's rendering of classical Chinese beauties through the use of a painting technique known as rub-and-paint *(cabi dancai),* which made his female subjects "lifelike" and comely—"seemingly available at a viewer's beck and call," as the art critic Zhang Yanfeng has recently observed.[46] Although Zheng had not invented this technique, he was the first to use it in portraits of women.[47]

Huang hired Zheng on the spot and put him to work transforming the image of Chinese women in advertisements. Almost immediately Zheng's advertising images became widely recognized because of their new technique and their subject: women's bodies, including nudes. At the time Chinese artists tended not to paint nudes or even show the shapes of women's figures. In the 1910s a few Chinese artists painted nude models in private, but not until the mid-1920s did they begin to display paintings of nudes in public exhibitions.[48] Nor did photographers publish pictures of Chinese nudes at the time. As Perry Link noticed while surveying literature published in popular Chinese magazines, "Beauties in magazine photographs of the 1910s are always heavily clothed from the neck down."[49]

And yet, as early as 1914, while other Chinese artists and photographers obscured women's bodies in heavy clothing, Zheng Mantuo began painting seminudes for Huang Chujiu's business, and Huang wasted no time publishing them in calendar posters advertising his medicine. For Zheng's very first calendar poster he chose a familiar subject, Yang Guifei (719–756), the royal consort to the Xuanzong emperor during the Tang dynasty, who had long been regarded as one of the four leading Chinese classical beauties. Like previous portraiturists painting her in late imperial China, he placed her in a hot-spring setting and revealed the contours of Yang Guifei's body by showing her wearing a transparent silk bathrobe. Under the title *Yang Guifei Emerging from Her Bath (Guifei chuyu)*, this painting appeared on the calendar poster that Huang's business distributed to its wholesalers, retailers, and customers for the year 1915.[50]

With the publication of this and subsequent calendar posters, Zheng Mantuo's work was soon in great demand. Huang Chujiu tried to retain Zheng, and, by the standards of the time, Huang spent heavily on advertising, paying an annual salary of twenty-four hundred yuan each to his leading commercial artist, his best writer of advertising copy, and his advertising manager.[51] Despite Huang's tempting offers, Zheng soon left the Great China-France Drugstores, opened his own studio, and began to accept commissions. His minimum price for a basic design was five hundred yuan. He offered his clients the opportunity to suggest additions and revisions, and he charged one hundred yuan for each change that they required. Even billing at these high rates, Zheng was overwhelmed with orders, receiving so many that he had the luxury of holding over late requests for calendar posters from one year until the next.[52]

KEEPING UP WITH FASHIONS

After Zheng left Huang's business, Huang began to pay commissions to a younger man, Hang Zhiying, who eventually surpassed Zheng as China's most influential painter of women in advertisements. During the 1910s, as a teenager working in the advertising department at the Commercial Press in Shanghai, Hang had learned Zheng's techniques by literally stealing from him—sneaking into Zheng's office at the Commercial Press and making off with his original drawings.[53] Then, in 1925, Hang left this job, founded his own business, and began to introduce innovations. His new techniques were adapted mainly from the work of Walt Disney (whose cartoons were shown in Shanghai's movie theaters beginning in the late 1920s). Like Disney, Hang named his business after himself (calling it Zhiying Studio), trained students there (serving as master for scores of apprentices before his death in 1947), and organized teams of artists to work collectively on each painting. In his business's hierarchy, he held the top position and signed his name (allowing no other) on all the paintings that were done; below him were two immediate subordinates, Li Mubai (1913–1991) and Jin Xuechen (1904–1997); below them were seven or eight other paid artists; and at the bottom of the organizational structure were unpaid apprentices. According to available evidence, all these artists were men. In fact, all identifiable Chinese calendar painters working for Hang or anyone else were men.[54]

Hang differed from Zheng in his portrayals of Chinese women's heads and bodies. On their faces, he put broad smiles—smiles so broad that he bared their teeth. His modern women smiled with pleasure as they attended social occasions and engaged in Western-style sports—bicycling, tennis, golf, archery—and even his classical beauties broke into grins (rather than keeping their mouths closed behind the demure "cherry lips" that past painters had depicted).[55] Interested in women's heads quite apart from their bodies, Hang was the first Chinese to design calendar posters that showed contemporary women only from the neck or shoulders up.

Before that time Chinese artists had avoided painting close-ups of heads apparently because of a popular belief linking pictures of heads with beheadings and bad deaths. Breaking this taboo, Hang deliberately confined himself to heads in numerous paintings that became known as "portraits of great beauties' heads" *(da tou meinu hua).*[56]

In his portraits of women's bodies, Hang also introduced innovations. Initially, he followed Zheng Mantuo's example in showing classical Chinese beauties sometimes draped in traditional costumes that left their figures seemingly formless and sometimes clad in transparent bathrobes that made them appear seminude.[57] But later he showed women in two types of modern fashions, one Western and one Chinese. When dressing them in Western clothes, he exposed their unbound feet and breasts by showing them in tight-fitting shorts, bathing suits, evening gowns, unbuttoned blouses, and untied halters, and he adopted a motif that became known as the "one bare breast" (Figure 3.7).[58]

When dressing women in modern Chinese style, Hang clothed them in the *qipao,* a Chinese adaptation of a Manchu costume that had a high collar, slits up the sides, and buttons running from the neck across the chest, under the right arm, and down the right side. Whereas earlier painters, including Zheng Mantuo, had shown Manchu and Chinese women in *qipao* that were waist-length jackets with long sleeves and were worn with loose-fitting long skirts or pants, Hang pictured Chinese women in sleeveless floor-length *qipao* that clung tightly from the waist up and fell open at the slit, exposing women's legs from the thigh down.[59] Whether dressing women in Western or Chinese costumes, he and his all-male staff of artists apparently painted them for men, placing them almost invariably in frontal positions and alluring poses and showing them gazing out from calendar posters as though eyeing male spectators.

Hang became renowned for his portraits of nudes and seminudes, and he received orders for calendar posters from many entrepreneurs besides Huang Chujiu. These orders came from both foreign- and Chinese-owned businesses that were generally based in Shanghai, South China, and Southeast Asia. Even the British-American Tobacco Company, proud possessor of the biggest advertising department of any business in China, eventually commissioned Hang to supply fully half of all its advertising paintings in China. Each year during the late 1920s and 1930s, Hang's Zhiying Studio produced a total of more than eighty advertising paintings and earned over 240,000 yuan.[60]

POPULARIZING WOMEN'S BODIES

Why were Huang's calendar posters of women's bodies his most popular advertisements of all? As Lu Xun emphasized, Chinese commercial artists played important roles as painters of the images of women in advertisements, but it was the entrepreneur Huang Chujiu who discovered Zheng Mantuo, the first and eventually most influential Chinese commercial artist of his time, and it was Huang who hired Zheng and put him to work constructing the first advertising images of Chinese women. As he had in campaigns for Ailuo Brain Tonic and Human Elixir, Huang thus played the leading role in the creation of advertising images. Once again his actions raise the question of whether his ideas came from himself or society at large, and once again this question is difficult to answer for lack of detailed studies of Chinese popular taste during the first half of the twentieth century.

If the bold analysis by the historian Mark Elvin is to be taken at face value, then Huang had available to him no Chinese conceptions of the human body as an aesthetic object except those discovered by members of the Chinese elite through contact with the West in the early twentieth century. Before the late nineteenth century, Elvin has argued, Chinese elites traditionally viewed the "body-person" *(shen)* as nothing more than "a peg-doll, a carrier of attributes," and, accordingly, they dressed figures in loose-fitting clothes and had "almost nothing corresponding to 'fashion.'" This "overall Chinese syndrome" in pre-twentieth-century attitudes toward the human body is traceable, according to Elvin, to a "fundamental historical difference between Chinese thought and Western thought. Chinese traditionally assumed that there was a deep gulf between the morally proper and the morally improper. . . . There was no accepted dialogue, either philosophical or artistic, between the correct-upright [*zhehng (zheng)*] and the depraved-oblique [*xier (xie)*], or between the public-impartial [*gong*] and the private–personally based [*si*]." Thus, "virtue" remained uncompromising, unrealistic, and sterile, and "vice" remained human and vital but irredeemable; and so there was an unbridgeable gap between virtue and vice that prevented them from enriching each other, as seems to have happened in the classical, medieval, and early-modern West. Only after Chinese accepted this dialogue under Western influence in the early twentieth century, Elvin has asserted, did they begin to view the unclothed human body as an aesthetic object. Only then did Chinese artists begin to depict clothed women in postures that made viewers conscious of bodies beneath the clothing.[61]

Elvin's thesis seems to be in line with a consensus that was accepted uncritically by art historians until recently. According to this consensus, Chinese artists did not paint nudes prior to the twentieth century.[62] But recently James Cahill has uncovered paintings of Chinese "pin-ups" (as he calls them) from the seventeenth and eighteenth centuries, and he has argued that these paintings show how Chinese artists appropriated Western images of women's bodies before the twentieth century. In the seventeenth century Chinese painted pin-ups of women who were heavily draped in robes and were "bodiless"; then, in the eighteenth century, Chinese artists "heated up" pin-ups, portraying women with more fully articulated bodies that were more explicitly erotic. Chinese artists made this transition under the influence of Western artists (especially the Jesuit missionary Giuseppe Castiglione, who was a painter in residence at the court of the eighteenth-century emperor Qianlong), but they did not merely duplicate Western techniques for portraying women. In Cahill's words, Chinese artists incorporated techniques from European pictures "never through slavish copying or imitation" but rather by combining these techniques "with elements of native style that had long fallen into disuse and are now rediscovered."[63]

Whether or not these seventeenth- and eighteenth-century Chinese pin-ups were available to calendar poster painters in the early twentieth century, it is almost certain that nineteenth-century Chinese images of female seminudes were. For example, the art historian Ellen Laing has rejected a Chinese art critic's suggestion that Zheng Mantuo could have painted his first seminude calendar poster of Yang Guifei's unclothed body only by modeling it after a photograph of a nude Western woman.[64] She has pointed out that Zheng might have used any number of Chinese models because in late imperial paintings "the most common rendition of Yang Guifei coming from the bath shows her in a state of soft lassitude, her nakedness hardly hidden by a transparent robe." If Zheng did not have access to these scrolls, then he would have come across woodblock prints of Yang in similar poses. He surely would have seen them in the popular book *Baimei tupu* (*Register of One Hundred Beauties, Illustrated*) because, according to Laing, it "was repeatedly printed and, as a relatively inexpensive item, easily would have been available to Zheng."[65]

In light of Cahill's discoveries and Laing's observations, Cahill's framework seems preferable to Elvin's for interpreting the paintings of women by Huang Chujiu's commercial artists. It is undeniable that these artists studied English and became aware of Western commercial images (even those of Walt Disney), but Elvin seems to have underestimated Chinese artists' capacity for drawing on Chinese models and localizing Western images. Like Chinese artists in the first phase of painting, as Cahill described it, Zheng did not slavishly copy Western pictures. Instead, he took elements of native style (particularly from the tradition of painting classical Chinese beauties) and combined these elements with his own techniques (notably his rub-and-paint brushwork). And like earlier artists in the second phase, Hang did not respond solely to Western paintings; he seized on the images of women as painted by his Chinese predecessor (in this case imitating Zheng) and "heated up" these images so that they became more explicitly erotic. Just as Chinese painters of pin-ups localized Western images of women's bodies in a two-phase sequence during the seventeenth and eighteenth centuries, so too did Zheng and Hang in the early twentieth century.

When distributed in Huang Chujiu's advertising, how would paintings of women's bodies be perceived by Chinese consumers? If Elvin is right about the difference between the elite's and nonelite's attitudes, Huang faced an even more formidable task in popularizing images of women's bodies with nonelite consumers than with elites. In Elvin's view, the Western "dialogue" between the "correct" and the "depraved" appealed only to the elite in China's largest cities and "was felt by most Chinese to be a deadly allurement . . . and also a source of general social anomia, precisely because it weakened the barriers between the 'correct' and the 'depraved' aspects of life. They lacked the cultural resources needed for the easy handling of this powerful, if peculiar, Western aberration."[66]

By looking only at the visual contents of Huang Chujiu's advertising, it is difficult to determine whether "most Chinese . . . lacked the cultural resources" to engage in a Western dialogue about morality and ideas on the subject of women's bodies. But if we take into account Huang's dissemination of advertising, it becomes readily apparent that he did not use images of women's bodies and other images of the West and the Chinese nation to appeal only to elite consumers. After commissioning elite artists like Zheng and Hang to produce advertising images, Huang made these images accessible to members of all social classes, illiterate as well as literate, especially in Shanghai.

Mass Advertising in Shanghai

In the early twentieth century Huang Chujiu and others in the pharmaceutical industry used advertising to increase sales most dramatically in Shanghai, which pulled ahead of its rivals as the city of choice for the headquarters of Chinese-owned businesses marketing "new medicine." As early as 1907–1908 Shanghai became China's print capital and leading exporter of newspapers and advertising, and between 1911 and 1936 Shanghai surpassed Guangzhou as the most popular base for businesses selling and advertising "new medicine." As late as 1911 Shanghai ranked about the same or slightly behind Guangzhou as a center for this trade: each city housed 28 Chinese-owned new-style drugstores, and Shanghai handled 10 percent of China's imported drugs compared to Guangzhou's 12.2 percent. But by 1936 Shanghai far surpassed Guangzhou as the trading center for Chinese sellers and importers of new-style medicine; it served as home to 166 Chinese-owned new-style drugstores, compared with Guangzhou's 84, and received 77 percent of China's imported drugs, compared with Guangzhou's 5.9 percent (and Tianjin's 9.2 percent).[67]

HUANG'S MASS ADVERTISING

Among Chinese entrepreneurs, Huang Chujiu was one of the first to establish formal headquarters at Shanghai, and for this purpose he designed buildings that themselves served as advertisements. In the 1920s he deliberately selected sites for his buildings at busy intersections in Shanghai's Central District so that they would attract attention. He housed his headquarters in his two most prominent office buildings, one at the corner of Beijing Road and Zhifu Road and the other at the corner of Fuzhou Road and Shandong Road. In 1928, when he decided to build them, he formulated "Basic Guidelines for the Design of the New Stores," which he gave the architects and builders to follow. In these guidelines he emphasized the importance of big plate-glass windows to showcase eye-catching displays, and he allowed no steps at the entrances because he wanted the buildings accessible to all, particularly the frail and elderly in search of medicine. Once completed, the buildings were ringed on the ground floor with windows whose design and construction (not counting displays) cost more than 46,500 yuan. Each building, one yellow and the other green, stood five stories tall and was topped with a roof of gleaming ceramic tiles. Even Huang's medicine factory attracted attention because he gilded its sign with twenty ounces of real gold.[68]

Of all Huang's buildings, the one with the greatest advertising value was the Great World (Da shijie), a five-story amusement hall that he opened in 1917 in Shanghai's French Concession, at the corner of Tibet Road and Avenue Edouard VII. At the Great World Huang installed distorting mirrors, staged Chinese regional operas, and supplied other forms of popular entertainment that attracted huge crowds—an average of twenty thousand paying customers per day—and as the pleasure seekers moved from one floor to the next in this rambling building, he exposed them to walls covered with advertisements for his medicines. Outside the building he also used the Great World to spread his advertising. On its facade he affixed billboards, and from its tower he launched advertising stunts, flying a huge kite, for example, that dropped advertising leaflets onto surrounding neighborhoods. Day after day he tied so much advertising to the Great World that people at the time began jokingly calling the place Huang Chujiu's Commercial World (shangpin shijie) (Figure 3.8).[69]

While designing buildings, Huang Chujiu and his staff also designed advertising at his Shanghai headquarters. He established a specialized advertising section *(guanggao ke)* and heavily funded it, allocating to it between 60 and 75 percent of the budget for his most popular medicines (leaving only 25–40 percent for the cost of manufacturing and distributing these goods). Part of this advertising budget covered salaries for painters and writers, who were well paid by the standards of the time. Another part of the advertising budget financed the founding and operation of a radio station, Mainland Radio (Dalu diantai), a wholly owned subsidiary of Huang's business, which broadcast commercials for his medicines that sponsored serialized adaptations of Chinese classics such as *The Story of the West Wing (Xixiangji)* and other programs every day. A third part of the advertising budget covered the cost of making visual commercials—slide shows and short films that were shown preceding feature-length movies at theaters. And a fourth part of the budget was spent on newspaper advertisements, including some of an unprecedented kind. In the 1920s, for example, Huang Chujiu was the first in Shanghai to take out full-page newspaper advertisements—a practice subsequently adopted by several other new-style drugstores. In 1923, when he launched a new medicine

called Machine for Long Life (Bailingji), he ran full-page advertisements
for it in newspapers once or twice every month, and at the same time he
separately published his own magazine, *Long Life Pictorial (Bailing huabao)*,
which was devoted largely to advertisements for this product.[70]

In Shanghai, besides broadcasting commercials over the radio and running advertisements in newspapers, Huang and other sellers of "new
medicine" distributed advertisements through a merchandising hierarchy
of wholesalers and retailers. At the highest level were the sixteen biggest
Chinese-owned drugstore chains, each capitalized at more than one hundred thousand yuan. They made their own advertising and distributed it
through their own chains of drugstores. By 1936 the sixteen biggest drugstore chains together accounted for 68.3 percent of sales of "new medicine"
in Shanghai. At the next level were medium-sized drugstores, capitalized
at an average of fifteen thousand yuan and with sales of thirty thousand
yuan per year. From these medium-sized drugstores Huang's firm and
other big drug companies rented window space for their advertising. Still
lower in the hierarchy were small drugstores, capitalized at an average of
two thousand yuan and with sales of fifteen to thirty thousand yuan per
year. Below them were restaurants, tobacconists, and other commercial
vendors, including itinerant peddlers. Big drugstores supplied advertising
to these retailers either directly or indirectly, through wholesalers.[71]

In the absence of detailed data, it is difficult to assess the effectiveness of
this advertising in Shanghai, but the available evidence suggests that by
1936 it enabled new-style drugstores to achieve greater sales on the basis
of lower investments than old-style sellers of traditional medicine were
able to do. As Table 3.1 shows, even though in 1936 new-style drugstores
in Shanghai were far less numerous, less well capitalized, and less well
staffed than old-style drugstores were, they generated about the same
amount of total sales revenue. Thus, in Shanghai by 1936 Huang and
other manufacturers of Western-style "new medicine" had nearly matched
the sales volume of Yue Daren and other makers of traditional Chinese
medicines, and they had done so by building only one-third as many
stores, investing barely half as much capital, and hiring considerably fewer
than half as many employees. Surely Huang's business and others in his
industry achieved high sales volume at least in part because they advertised through pictorial and aural media, whereas Yue and other purveyors
of traditional medicine did not.[72]

2.1 Tongren Tang's store (circled) in eighteenth-century Beijing

同仁堂藥目

光緒己丑
仲春重刊

同仁堂藥目敍

2.2 A catalogue of Tongren Tang's medicines

2.3 The Yue family in the 1890s

2.4 Yue Daren and his family in the 1930s

2.5 Tongren Tang's store in the 1920s

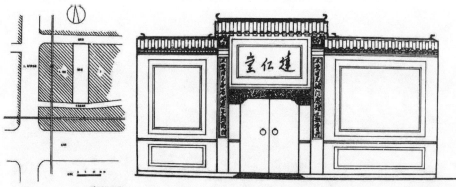

总平面图　　　　　　　　　　　　　　　　大门立面图

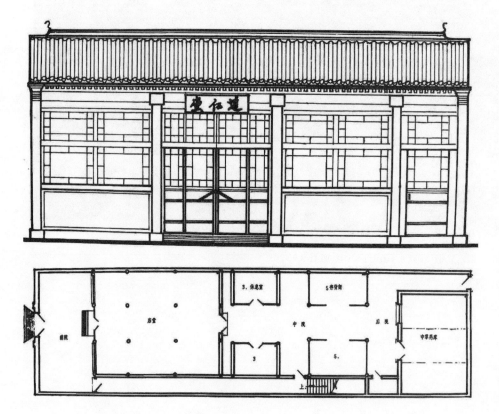

2.6 Daren Tang's main store in Tianjin

3.1 Huang Chujiu

3.6 Human Elixir's trademark with "Chinese National Goods" in the circles and the pairing of the dragon and the tiger

3.7 A calendar poster by Hang Zhiying advertising
Huang Chujiu's medicines

3.8 The Great World amusement hall

Table 3.1. A Comparison of Chinese-Owned New-Style and Old-Style
Drugstores in Shanghai, 1936

	New-style	Old-style
No. of stores	166	498
Capital (in yuan)	7,550,000	13,530,000
No. of employees	2,012	5,400
Sales volume (in yuan)	41,510,000	41,880,000

Source: Shanghai shehui kexue yuan jingji yanjiu suo, *Shanghai jindai xiyao hangye
shi* (Shanghai: Shanghai shehui kexue yuan, 1988), 120, 123.

HUANG'S MASS CONSUMERS

Huang's advertising through various media—calendar posters, newspapers, radio shows, Great World—and his distribution of advertisements
through a marketing hierarchy brought his goods to the attention of
nonelites as well as elites in Shanghai. In this sense, he made his goods
accessible to a mass market. But were nonelites nothing more than window-shoppers or did they become mass consumers?

Without a full breakdown of consumer spending, it is not possible to
analyze precisely how much of Huang's goods were consumed by each
social class. Judging by surveys conducted in Shanghai at the time, however, it is evident that the city's industrial workers had the inclination and
the money to buy his goods. One survey of 230 cotton-mill workers and
their families in 1927–1928 shows that three-quarters of these working-
class families bought medicine, and they gave it high priority, spending
more on it than on toilet articles, entertainment (at theaters and movie
houses), education, religious offerings, or any other item except public
transport, cigarettes, wine, and the essentials of food, housing, and clothing.[73] A later study of 390 families in 1936–1937 also noted workers'
propensity to buy medicine and added nuances to its conclusions by
distinguishing among the spending habits of skilled, semiskilled, and
unskilled workers. According to this report, Shanghai's skilled workers'
expenditures on surplus items (that is, items other than food, housing, and
clothing) amounted to 23.14 percent of their incomes (a figure that is
about the same as the percentage spent on surplus items by American

working class families in the 1930s), semiskilled workers spent 11.52 percent of their incomes on surplus items; and unskilled workers had no income left over for surplus items.[74]

In light of these findings, it seems safe to conclude that a portion of Huang's medicines was consumed by nonelites in the families of skilled industrial workers. It is not likely that the families of semiskilled and unskilled workers bought his medicine, but it is clear that the families of skilled industrial workers in Shanghai during the early twentieth century allocated an average of one to two yuan each year for medicine—enough to buy a product like Huang's Ailuo Brain Tonic (priced at two yuan per bottle).

Poaching and Popularizing

This chapter has shown that Huang Chujiu as a seller of "new medicine" produced images of the West, economic nationalism, and women and distributed these and other images through advertising in Shanghai during the early twentieth century. In appropriating these images Huang coopted some of the Chinese intellectual elite's most cherished causes—advocacy of Western medicine, economic nationalism, and women's liberation—and commodified them to promote his products. In the process he substantially altered the contents of the Chinese intellectual elite's formulations, freely substituting familiar Chinese terms (such as body orbs in Chinese medicine) for unfamiliar foreign ones (such as body organs in Western medicine), loosely mixing old notions (such as traditional harmonization of opposites) with seemingly contradictory new ones (such as competitive economic nationalism), and unabashedly depoliticizing images (such as pictures of liberated women, whom he portrayed as fashionable beauties rather than as serious campaigners for women's rights).

In a word, Huang "poached" on the Chinese intellectual elite's modern discourse. This term, *poach*, has been chosen by the theorist Michel de Certeau to describe a process in which consumers actively use (rather than passively accept) representations, rituals, and laws in any society. By poaching, according to Certeau, consumers defend themselves against whatever culture has been imposed upon them, and their poaching has the effects of subverting and transforming the imposed culture.[75] While Certeau applies this notion of poaching to consumers, it also seems apt as a characterization of what Huang made of the Chinese intellectual elite's ideas and images.

And yet, Certeau's concept of poaching encompasses only part of the process by which Huang's advertising had subversive and transformative effects on Chinese culture during the first half of the twentieth century. Huang did more than defensively poach ideas and images from an intellectual elite. He also aggressively popularized his advertising by distributing it to nonelites as well as elites through a highly structured marketing system in Shanghai. Only with both concepts, poaching and popularizing, is it possible to make a reasonable reply to Lu Xun's criticism of advertising. Huang's popularizing helps to explain why, as Lu Xun acknowledged, advertising became "popular with ordinary people in Chinese society," and Huang's poaching helps to explain why advertisers seemed to Lu Xun, as a member of China's intellectual elite, to be "sick."

As an imaginative poacher of images from Chinese artists and other intellectuals, Huang distinguished himself, but as a popularizer of advertising he by no means had the most far-reaching influence of any Chinese entrepreneur. He marketed medicine intensively in Shanghai, touching consumers in all social classes, and beyond Shanghai he extended his distribution network to other cities and towns—but not to as many as were reached by his Japanese rival, Humane Elixir, and some of his Chinese rivals. To appreciate the full extent of the marketing of medicine, it is necessary to take the measure of the business that had the biggest distribution system of them all in prewar China, Great Five Continents Drugstores.

4

Capturing a National Market

> The International Dispensary, Ltd. [Great Five Continents Drugstores] has two branches in Shanghai and twenty branches throughout China, besides giving its name to 80 agencies in interior cities, which are in reality pharmacies owned by others. [It does] altogether a huge business and in fact [has] an annual turnover of nearly $4,000,000 at the head office. It is the most important unit in the drug trade in Shanghai and China.
>
> C. A. Bacon, "Pharmacy in Shanghai" (1929)

C. A. Bacon, a journalist living and working in China in the 1920s, did not exaggerate when he identified Great Five Continents Drugstores (Wuzhou da yaofang) as "the most important unit in the drug trade in Shanghai and China."[1] He conducted his survey of China's pharmaceutical industry in 1929, and he did not confine it to Chinese-owned businesses. As he implied here and spelled out in his report, Five Continents distributed goods more widely in China than its Western-owned rivals did at the time, and after his report was published, the company's distribution system became much bigger.

How did Five Continents adapt its marketing in China to appeal to consumers nationwide? It did so by creating a hierarchical marketing system and by relying on staff members or other vendors to project an image of its goods as "Western" to consumers at each level. Structurally, its marketing system corresponded with China's urban hierarchy: its headquarters was in Shanghai, which was at the top of China's urban hierarchy as the most populous city and the one conducting the greatest amount of interurban trade; its wholly owned branch stores were in big cities at the cores of China's macroregions; its affiliates (which were not under its ownership) were in smaller cities and towns; and other carriers of its goods and advertising were based in still smaller towns or were itinerant. At each level its marketing was localized or relocalized, in the sense that its staff members or the other purveyors of its products translated or re-translated its advertising messages to consumers in their localities. To appreciate how Five Continents reached consumers, it is worth examining the company's marketing system from top to bottom.

Establishing National Headquarters

Between 1911 and 1932 the man presiding over Five Continents' nation-wide expansion from its headquarters in Shanghai was Xiang Songmao (Figure 4.1), a Chinese entrepreneur who bore a distinct resemblance to Huang Chujiu. Like Huang, Xiang was born in the Lower Yangzi region near Shanghai in the 1870s and died in Shanghai in the early 1930s. Like Huang, he was educated at a "private" school of the kind that rejected Western educational reforms in favor of traditional learning.[2] And like Huang and many other aspiring young Chinese merchants, he left his hometown as a teenager to seek his fortune in a bigger nearby city—first Suzhou and then Shanghai.[3]

Xiang also resembled Huang in his minimal exposure on the job to for-eign companies and business practices. In 1900, through family connections, he landed his first full-fledged job at Chinese-owned Great China-England Drugstores, where he worked his way up from apprentice to accountant in the company's headquarters in Shanghai and eventually to manager of its branch in Hankou.[4] Then in 1911 he left this company to become Five Continents' general manager, a post that he held until his death in 1932.

Throughout this lifelong experience in Chinese schools and businesses, Xiang had only a little more exposure to foreign languages, businesses, and places than Huang Chujiu did. In general he delegated responsibility for making contacts with foreigners. In particular he relied on his brother, Xiang Zailun, who worked for the German-owned drugstore Voelkel and Schroeder. Soon after joining Five Continents, Xiang Songmao traveled with his brother to Japan, where they surveyed the pharmaceutical indus-try and signed a contract with a leading Japanese manufacturer of medical instruments, Noda, which granted to Five Continents the right to be Noda's sole sales agent in China. On his return to Shanghai, Xiang dis-patched two of his young associates at Five Continents on a tour of the United States and Europe, and they signed similar contracts with Ameri-can-, British-, German-, and Austrian-owned pharmaceutical companies. He did not travel to the West himself.[5]

And yet, while Huang Chujiu and Xiang Songmao had a lot in common, they clashed over Xiang's plans for Five Continents' expansion. In 1906 Huang had been one of Five Continents' three cofounders (along with Xie Ruiqing, a pharmacist, and Xia Cuifang, a publisher), and in 1911 he had recruited Xiang to become its general manager. Then in 1916, after Xiang began building branch stores for Five Continents outside Shanghai, the two men came into conflict. Up to that time, Huang had retained the right for his China-France Drugstores to be the sole distributor of Five Continents' goods wherever it had branches outside Shanghai, and he angrily protested and ultimately resigned from Five Continents over Xiang's construction of the company's branch store at Tianjin, where it competed with Huang's branch store. With Huang out of the way, Xiang was free to pursue his plans for expansion; by then Five Continents' other two founders were also gone—one had died and the other had been forced out by Huang—and Xiang was the unrivaled head of the company.[6]

For the next twenty years, 1916–1936, Xiang and Xiang Shengwu, his son, who succeeded him as head of Five Continents in 1932, invested heavily in the company's infrastructure for long-distance trade. By 1936 it had opened twenty-four wholly owned branch drugstores in eighteen cities—sixteen in China and two in Southeast Asia—including branch stores in all of China's nine macroregions except two, the Northwest and Southwest (see Table 4.1). In addition, by 1936 Five Continents became affiliated with independently owned drugstores in another fifty-three Chinese cities and towns located in all nine of China's macroregions, which meant that it had distributors selling medicine under its shop sign in a total of sixty-nine Chinese cities and towns. Every year between 1919 and 1937 Five Continents took advantage of this nationwide distribution system by selling as much as 92 percent, and never less than 63 percent, of its goods outside Shanghai, the city where it was based (Tables 4.2 and 4.3 and Map 4.1).

Table 4.1. Five Continents' Branch Stores in China

Year opened	Location	Macroregion	Capitalization (in yuan), 1921
1912	Jinan	North	6,000
1917	Tianjin	North	10,000
1919	Beijing	North	10,000

Table 4.1. *(continued)*

Year opened	Location	Macroregion	Capitalization (in yuan), 1921
1919	Hankou	Middle Yangzi	10,000
1920	Shanghai (Taihe)	Lower Yangzi	20,000
1920	Yingkou	Northeast	2,400
1920	Bengbu	North	5,000
1920	Wuhu	Lower Yangzi	6,000
1921	Jiujiang	Middle Yangzi	2,000
1925	Xiamen	Southeast	
1926	Shanghai (Hongkou)	Lower Yangzi	
1927	Chongqing	Upper Yangzi	
1928	Hangzhou	Lower Yangzi	2,400[b]
1928	Zhengzhou	North	
1928	Shanghai (North Sichuan Road)	Lower Yangzi	
1930	Shanghai (Penglai Market)	Lower Yangzi	
1930	Shanghai (Dongmen Road)	Lower Yangzi	
1931	Yangzhou	Lower Yangzi	2,500[b]
1931[a]	Bangkok, Thailand	Southeast Asia	
1931[a]	Semarang, Indonesia	Southeast Asia	
1933	Nanchang	Middle Yangzi	
1934	Guangzhou	South	
1935	Shanghai (Jing'an)	Lower Yangzi	
1935	Shanghai (Nanjing Road)	Lower Yangzi	

a. The exact date of the founding of these two overseas branches is not known. They were probably open by 1931 because Five Continents distributed 28 percent of its goods overseas between 1931 and 1937 (see Table 4.5).

b. Investment made as of 1921 in a co-owned drugstore that did not become a branch store until later.

Sources: Wuzhou da yaofang sanshi zhounian jinian kan (Shanghai, 1936), 113–125; Shanghai shehui kexue yuan jingji yanjiu suo, *Shanghai jindai xiyao hangye shi* (Shanghai: Shanghai shehui kexue yuan, 1988), chap. 7; file Q38–37–115, 1920–1921, Wuzhou da yaofang Papers.

Table 4.2. Five Continents' Regional Branches and Local Affiliates, 1936

Macroregion	No. of cities with regional branches	No. of cities and towns with local affiliates
Lower Yangzi	9	19
Middle Yangzi	3	7
Upper Yangzi	1	0
Northeast	1	3
North	5	11
Northwest	0	2
Southeast	1	5
South	1	4
Southwest	0	1
Southeast Asia	2	1
Total	23	53

Note: This table is based on Five Continents' records. In 1929 C. A. Bacon conducted his own survey of China's pharmaceutical industry, and, using data that were presumably less precise than those shown here, he concluded that Five Continents had eighty affiliates. Bacon, "Pharmacy in Shanghai," *Chinese Economic Journal* (August 1929): 658.

Source: Wuzhou da yaofang sanshi zhounian jinian kan (Shanghai, 1936), 126–127.

Table 4.3. Five Continents' Sales in and outside Shanghai

Year	Number of branches outside Shanghai (and no. outside China)	Total volume of sales (in yuan)	Volume of sales outside Shanghai (in yuan)	Percentage of sales outside Shanghai
1915	1	310,000	—	—
1916	1	—[a]	—	—
1917	2	—	—	—
1918	2	—	—	—
1919	4	830,336	640,975	77

Table 4.3 *(continued)*

Year	Number of branches outside Shanghai (and no. outside China)	Total volume of sales (in yuan)	Volume of sales outside Shanghai (in yuan)	Percentage of sales outside Shanghai
1920	10	1,373,831	1,095,998	80
1921	10	1,247,060	915,006	73
1922	10	1,147,993	796,764	69
1923	10	1,282,549	829,135	65
1924	10	1,354,324	856,579	63
1925	11	—	—	—
1926	12	—	—	—
1927	13	—	—	—
1928	15	—	—	—
1929	15	4,000,000	—	—
1930	17	—	—	—
1931	17 (2)	7,642,000	—	92[b]
1932	17 (2)	5,828,989	—	92[b]
1933	18 (2)	6,695,262	—	92[b]
1934	19 (2)	6,822,900	—	92[b]
1935	21 (2)	6,652,167	—	92[b]
1936	21 (2)	11,645,419	—	92[b]
1937	21 (2)	—	—	92[b]

a. Indicates that relevant data are not available.

b. For 1931–1937 the only figure available is the average percentage of sales of one commodity, Man-Made Blood, which was Five Continents' most popular and profitable product.

Sources: Shanghai shehui kexue yuan jingji yanjiu suo, *Shanghai jindai xiyao hangye shi* (Shanghai: Shanghai shehui kexue yuan, 1988), 99, 107–108, 148, 261, 266, 391–392; *Wuzhou da yaofang sanshi zhounian jinian kan* (Shanghai, 1936), 117–125; file Q38-37-115, statistics on profits and capital, 1920–1921, Wuzhou da yaofang Papers.

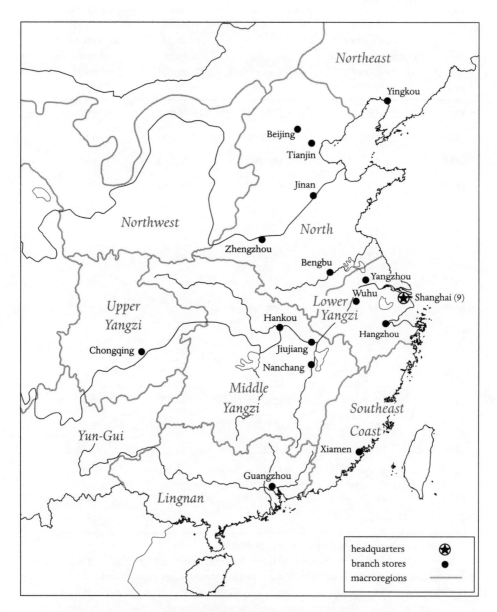

Map 4.1. Five Continents' drugstores, 1930s
Map by Thomas Lyons based on macroregions from Skinner,
"Regional Urbanization," 214, map 1.

Propelled down China's urban hierarchy, Five Continents' goods and advertising also reached outside cities and towns. At the time observers in Chinese villages noted the presence of such advertising in rural households. "In the poorest as well as in the wealthiest homes, are modern posters and illustrated calendars," reported the anthropologist Daniel Kulp on the basis of fieldwork in the villages of South China during the early 1920s. "Usually they contain either advertising materials in color-print or some scene from Chinese history."[7] Five Continents' success and the success of other firms at penetrating rural China can also be inferred from the fact that Chinese peasants were still using pre-1949 calendar posters—including advertisements for Five Continents' goods—to decorate their homes in the early 1990s. In 1992, when the art critic Zhang Yan-feng began searching in China for forms of pre-1949 commercial art, she and her research assistants found little in the cities, where, they were told, such bourgeois remnants had survived until the 1960s but had been destroyed during the Cultural Revolution. So they extended their search into the countryside in four regions—the Lower Yangzi, North China, Northeast China, and South China—where they eventually discovered 586 pre-1949 calendar posters hanging on walls in the homes of peasants.[8]

In Shanghai Xiang Songmao made this vast marketing system possible by raising capital. In 1913, only two years after he joined Five Continents, he converted it from a partnership to a joint-stock limited liability company and immediately expanded its capital base. Whereas it had been initially capitalized at less than 10,000 yuan in 1907, by the end of 1913 (after one year of selling stock) Xiang boosted the figure to 150,000 yuan (Table 4.4). He invested some of this capital in the construction of Five Continents' new headquarters, and he proudly stood in front of it when it was photographed at its opening in 1913 (Figure 4.2).

Meanwhile, Xiang was also attentive to manufacturing and research and development. In 1912, his second year at Five Continents, he opened a medicine workshop, and between 1920 and 1922 he built a pharmaceutical plant and acquired a soap factory and a chemical works.[9] By 1936 Five Continents produced no fewer than 780 Western-style goods under local trademarks—more than any other pharmaceutical company in China at the time—including a few nonmedical products, mostly soaps and cosmetics.[10] Of all these products the most popular and profitable was its oldest, Man-Made Blood (Renzao zilai xue), a tonic that was invented by one of the cofounders of the company, the pharmacist Xie Ruiqing.[11] This

Table 4.4. Five Continents' Capital, Sales, and Profits (in yuan)

Year	Capital	Sales revenue	Profits
1907	10,000	—	—
1913	150,000	310,000	—
1919	—	830,336	31,874
1920	210,000	1,373,831	32,692
1921	—	1,247,060	—
1922	—	1,147,993	—
1923	—	1,282,549	—
1924	—	1,354,324	—
1929	—	4,000,000	143,681
1931	—	7,642,000	—
1932	—	5,828,989	—
1933	—	6,695,262	—
1934	—	6,822,900	—
1935	—	6,652,167	—
1936	2,800,000	11,645,419	3,083,802

Note: No data are available for the years omitted. A dash indicates that relevant data are not available.

Sources: Shanghai shehui kexue yuan jingji yanjiu suo, *Shanghai jindai xiyao hangye shi* (Shanghai: Shanghai shehui kexue yuan, 1988), 99, 148, 261, 266, 391–392; *Wuzhou da yaofang sanshi zhounian jinian kan* (Shanghai, 1936), 117–125; file Q38–37–115, statistics on profits and capital, 1920–1921, Wuzhou da yaofang Papers; Bacon, "Pharmacy in Shanghai," *Chinese Economic Journal* (August 1929): 658.

product was intended to treat anemia, but, like Great China-France Drugstore's Ailuo Brain Tonic, its medicinal efficacy is difficult to evaluate because its ingredients were not disclosed. Also like Ailuo Brain Tonic, Man-Made Blood was given Western-style packaging and promoted in Chinese-language media (Figure 4.3). Producing it in Shanghai, Xiang widely distributed it in all China's macroregions and overseas (Table 4.5).

Xiang's investments in all aspects of Five Continents—manufacturing, research and development, and marketing—brought the desired results. The company's annual sales revenue climbed from one financial plateau to the next—from .3 million yuan in the mid-1910s to 1.3 million in the early 1920s, then to more than 6 million in the early 1930s, and ultimately to a peak of 11.6 million in 1936 (Table 4.4). As the company's sales soared and its fame spread, it became widely known in China as the King of the Drugstores *(yaofang zhi wang)*.[12]

Five Continents' success at nationwide marketing was made possible because of Xiang Songmao's decision to invest in an infrastructure that reached beyond Shanghai, but his investments alone by no means guaranteed success. Once he committed himself to building branch stores, he

Table 4.5. Distribution of Five Continents' Sales of Man-Made Blood by Macroregion, 1931–1937 and 1938

Macroregion	Percentage of sales volume, 1931–1937	Percentage of sales volume, 1938
Lower Yangzi	23	30
Middle Yangzi	10	5
Upper Yangzi	—	—
Northeast	0.5	0
North	12	20
Northwest	2	1
Southeast and South	15	15
Southwest (including Upper Yangzi)	8	15
Overseas	28	10
Other	1.5	4

Note: In the 1930s Man-Made Blood accounted for one-ninth of Five Continents' total sales revenue. Sales for the Upper Yangzi region are included in the figures for the Southwest. A dash indicates that relevant data are not available.

Source: Shanghai shehui kexue yuan jingji yanjiu suo, *Shanghai jindai xiyao hangye shi* (Shanghai: Shanghai shehui kexue yuan, 1988), 99, 148, 266, 391–392.

had to figure out how to make them attractive to consumers in distant and unfamiliar places.

Controlling Branch Stores and Appealing to Local Consumers

As Xiang Songmao reached out from Shanghai to market goods in other cities of China, he faced a dilemma. How could he retain control at his Shanghai headquarters over his increasingly far-flung branch stores and at the same time make these stores sensitive and responsive to the needs of consumers in their local cities? Xiang's attempt to achieve both central control and local sensitivity is well exemplified by his selection of managers for his branch stores on the one hand and his choice of sites for their stores on the other. He chose managers to give himself unequivocal central control, and he chose sites to give local consumers convenient access.

MANAGING BRANCHES THROUGH A CHINESE SOCIAL NETWORK

To market Five Continents' goods in its branch stores throughout China, Xiang Songmao recruited managers from his Chinese native place. As I noted in Chapter 1, Chinese who were engaged in long-distance trade generally preferred to confine their dealings to associates from their native places because they spoke each other's local dialect and expected eventually to return home. Xiang hailed from Jin county in Ningbo prefecture, one hundred miles south of Shanghai, and in constructing his trading network he followed in the footsteps of others from Ningbo. Since the tenth century Ningbo had built up a reputation for producing merchants who were fiercely loyal to their native place. In the nineteenth century, after Shanghai eclipsed Ningbo as a port, Ningbo merchants created an extensive network of native-place associations that dominated finance in Shanghai and led the way in managing trade between the Lower Yangzi and other regions of China.[13] In the late nineteenth and early twentieth centuries Xiang and other Ningbo merchants adapted these networks—initially to handle industrial products that were imported from abroad and eventually to distribute consumer goods that were mass-produced in their own industrial enterprises.[14]

As the head of Five Continents, Xiang made annual trips from Shanghai to Ningbo to consult his family and friends about prospective recruits for positions in his business. He preferred junior or senior high school graduates who were good-looking and well-spoken. He selected candidates to go to the Shanghai Zhonghua Vocational School, which he commissioned to give written and oral examinations and to provide a six-month training course for those who passed. Once the successful trainees joined the company, he assigned the most intelligent and articulate to marketing; the remainder were employed as shop attendants, administrative clerks, and warehouse employees. This select group in marketing learned about the pharmaceutical business from Five Continents' managers, department heads, and technical experts, and they studied foreign languages with native speakers of English, French, and Japanese. As Ningbo natives beholden to Xiang for their jobs, they were expected to be unswervingly loyal to Five Continents, and their pledge of allegiance included an oath in which they swore not to join any political party or group.[15]

After training new recruits, Xiang appointed them to positions in marketing and continued to test and evaluate them as he subsequently moved them from one of Five Continents' branch stores to another. Generally, he gave them initial assignments at branch stores outside Shanghai. In some cases he kept them in a particular branch store for a long time, as much as eleven or twelve years. For the most promising he reserved coveted positions at the company's Shanghai headquarters in the Department for Administering Branches, which was responsible for building and managing branch stores.[16]

Through this network of native-place associates, Xiang Songmao exercised tight control. He used the Department for Administering Branches to establish and supervise almost all Five Continents' branch stores within and outside Shanghai. The only exception was the Shanghai-based Taihe Drugstore, which he founded in 1915 using his own personal funds, not those of Five Continents' stockholders. Initially he managed it himself without going through Five Continents' Department for Administering Branches, but he eventually brought it into Five Continents and operated it on the same basis as the other branch stores.[17]

PROVIDING CONVENIENT ACCESS

While keeping managerial authority for his branch stores out of local hands, Xiang chose locations for these stores that showed extraordinary sensitivity to local consumers' needs for convenient access. In the context of Chinese history, his placement of these stores is striking because historians have generally asserted that Chinese merchants and businesses have not located their shops in urban neighborhoods that were convenient for consumers.

G. William Skinner has argued that the government of the Qing dynasty prevented merchants from building shops at the geographic center of walled cities because this prime real estate was reserved for official compounds. After the revolution of 1911 overthrew the Manchu-led Qing dynasty and ended imperial rule, some cities lifted these restrictions on commercial investments. One city, Guangzhou, went so far as to create a new business district precisely in the middle of the walled city, where the old Qing official compound had stood, and another, Hangzhou, converted its Manchu garrison into a new business district.[18]

In other Chinese cities, according to specialists in urban history, businesses selling Western-style goods tended to locate their shops in the commercial centers of foreign concession areas, which had been established by foreign governments in treaty ports on land that was leased in perpetuity under treaties between China and foreign governments following China's defeats in nineteenth-century wars. Marie-Claire Bergère and Hanchao Lu have described the biggest treaty port, Shanghai, as having its Western-style shops concentrated exclusively in its foreign concession area, especially along its major shopping street, Nanjing Road.[19] As a result, according to Lu, the majority of the city's consumers had virtually no access to Western-style goods because they lived "away from Nanjing Road."[20]

If, as a rule, Chinese businesses did not give consumers convenient access, then Five Continents was a conspicuous exception to the rule. Xiang Songmao placed almost all his stores near the exact centers of urban populations, with little regard for their proximity to the center of walled cities or the boundaries of foreign concession areas. By the 1920s and 1930s these urban populations had sprawled far beyond the walls of Chinese cities, so Xiang located Five Continents' branch stores near city gates, making them accessible to consumers from both inside and outside walled cities. As a result, Five Continents' stores often ended up near old merchant districts that dated from the late imperial period, but its new stores were on recently widened and paved boulevards, whereas traditional merchants' shops (including Tongren Tang, as we saw in Chapter 2) remained in narrow alleys.

Similarly, Xiang located his branch stores at the demographic center of China's cities rather than concentrating them in the foreign concession areas of treaty ports. Only in China's biggest treaty ports (Shanghai, Tianjin, and Hankou) did he place stores in foreign concession areas. Most of his stores were in other parts of cities under Chinese jurisdiction. In five treaty ports (Jiujiang, Xiamen, Hangzhou, Chongqing, and Guangzhou) he located stores outside foreign concession areas. Moreover, he chose to add branches in seven other cities (Jinan, Beijing, Bengbu, Zhengzhou, Yangzhou, Nanchang, and Chengdu) that never were treaty ports and had no foreign concession areas (Table 4.1 and Map 4.1).

In Shanghai Xiang Songmao made Five Continents' stores even more accessible to consumers than elsewhere. In June 1911, the year that he became head of Five Continents, he opened its new headquarters in the heart of Shanghai's commercial area, the International Settlement's Central District (zhongqu), but Xiang almost immediately began to extend Five Continents' reach to other parts of the city. In 1913 he built a branch store outside the British-controlled International Settlement in the French Concession, locating it near the West Gate of the Old Chinese City, which had existed long before the International Settlement and French Concession were established. By the 1930s, after Shanghai's population had shot up to about three million, Xiang added one more store in the City's Central District and six more in the Northern District, Western District, and French Concession, bringing the total to nine (Table 4.1 and Map 4.2). So, in case workers from industrial suburbs and other consumers living outside Shanghai's Central District were unwilling or unable to shop there, Five Continents went to them, placing stores throughout the city in their own neighborhoods.

Xiang's wide distribution of branch stores in Shanghai and his placement of branch stores in the population centers of other cities show that he chose sites to give consumers convenient access. And then, after selecting locations where Five Continents' branch stores would be seen by a large number of consumers, he made additional bids for attention by constructing strikingly "Western" buildings.

Constructing and Localizing Western Architecture

Xiang Songmao made his stores all "Western" by including features that caused them to stand out in contrast to traditional Chinese shops. In general, Chinese shops were one or two stories high, with wooden fronts, overhanging eaves, lacquered wooden shop signs *(zhaopai)*, and cloth shop symbols *(huangzi)*.[21] These shops rarely had large windows and were dimly lit both inside and out (Figure 4.4). By comparison, Five Continents' stores were taller, made of brick or concrete, and decorated with Western-style balconies, balustrades, and clocks. Perhaps the most striking decoration of all was the company's trademark, a large carving of the world (emblematic of Five Continents) that was plastered high on each of Five Continents' storefronts. The stores' interiors were equally eye-catching, with wide entrances, big plate-glass windows, and brightly lit display cases. At

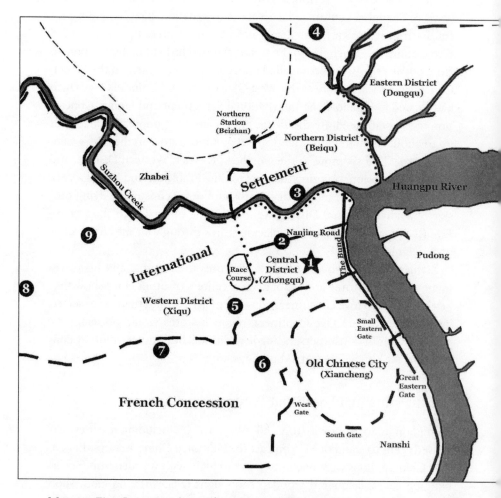

Map 4.2. Five Continents' nine drugstores in Shanghai, 1936.
Map by Eric Singer.

the same time, Five Continents did not make its stores identical to each other or to drugstores in the West. It localized them in the most obvious way by covering their shop signs and facades with Chinese characters that either dwarfed or excluded altogether any roman letters on the stores. It also localized them in more subtle ways.

ADOPTING THE TWO-PART VERTICAL FORM

Five Continents localized designs from Western architecture by adopting Western forms that had been used in the West for commercial buildings other than drugstores. Almost all its drugstores took a form that had become common on the main streets of cities and towns of the United States. The American architectural historian Richard Longstreth has characterized this form as the "two-part vertical block [in which] the façade is divided horizontally into two major zones. . . . The lower zone rises one or two stories and serves as a visual base for the dominant 'shaft,' or upper zone." As Longstreth has noted, a commercial building in this form was commonly "treated as a sculptural tower, rising above its neighbors to punctuate the skyline from all sides." According to Longstreth, this two-part, vertically oriented architectural form spread widely throughout the United States in the early twentieth century and was used for office buildings, department stores, hotels, and, occasionally, public and institutional buildings, but not drugstores.[22]

In all parts of China, Five Continents adopted this two-part design for its drugstores and used a crowning element to give each building the sense of a soaring mass. In the North China cities of Beijing, Tianjin, and Jinan, it used vertical pillars to provide an upward thrust, and it crowned each store with a tower; its Beijing store's tower had a clock that told time in roman numerals. Five Continents added decorations from classical Western history—stately columns, formal balustrades, rusticated masonry—that made its stores stand out as "Western" to Chinese consumers (Figure 4.5). As these stores show, Five Continents localized some of its buildings not by deviating from Western designs but by selecting Western designs that were not used in the West for drugstores.

ADAPTING TO LOCAL TASTES AND CONDITIONS

In some parts of China Xiang Songmao localized Western architecture by modifying Western motifs and designs. In the Lower, Middle, and Upper Yangzi regions, he added Chinese ornamentation. Like the stores in North

China, these were built in the two-part vertical style and were decorated with classical Western ornaments (balustrades, gables, window pediments), but the builders also left spaces on their facades for a Chinese touch. On Five Continents' branch at Jiujiang, craftsmen added Chinese-style floral motifs above the shop sign, and in the Hankou store they constructed vaguely Western columns with capitals that were perhaps of their own creation; they bore no resemblance to Ionic, Corinthian, or any other classical Western capitals (Figure 4.6).[23]

Xiang Songmao further localized Western designs by adjusting them to accommodate local conditions. South of the Yangzi River, his stores were built of reinforced concrete (rather than brick, which he used in North China), and they were taller than their North China counterparts, reaching up four or five stories. While projecting a Western image, these additional floors also served the practical purpose of providing aboveground storage space where Five Continents' goods were prevented from molding in conditions far more humid than those in the dry climate of North China.[24]

In subtropical Southeast China Xiang also adopted a design that accommodated local conditions. Like the stores along the Yangzi River, the Five Continents' branch store in Xiamen was tall (four stories), designed in two parts, made of concrete, and decorated with a trademark and other inscriptions. But unlike the Five Continents stores to the north, its ground floor was set back from the street, so that a covered walkway or arcade (*qilou*) could be erected in front. This feature provided consumers with shelter from the hot summer sun and the torrential downpours of the rainy season, and it gave them the impression that Five Continents was local: the arcade was characteristic of shops throughout Xiamen's commercial district (Figures 4.7, 4.8).[25]

In all these cases Xiang unquestionably used Western-style architecture to make his branch stores stand out in contrast with traditional Chinese shops. In a Chinese expression that was aptly used by a Chinese historian to describe Five Continents' strategy of architectural self-promotion, the company "hoisted the flag on its own separate tree" *(du shu yi zhi)*.[26] But as these examples also show, Xiang added Chinese characteristics to these "Western" stores during a seven-year building spree between 1925 and his death in 1932. Not until after he died did Five Continents build a store whose facade bore no signs of localization.

RELYING ON WESTERN ARCHITECTS

In 1932, at age fifty-two, Xiang Songmao was executed by the Japanese after leading a band of Five Continents' Chinese employees in an act of resistance during the Shanghai Incident (see Chapter 6). At the time Chiang Kai-shek, head of the Nationalist government, wrote a tribute to Xiang, proclaiming that "his spirit will never die" *(jingshen busi),* and ever since—even as recently as the 1990s—other Chinese have celebrated his heroism and martyrdom.[27] In 1936, four years after Xiang's death, his son and successor, Xiang Shengwu, carried out Five Continents' biggest construction project of all, a new Shanghai main store and headquarters, which on the face of it showed no sign of localization.

Xiang Shengwu made Five Continents' new main store explicitly Western in both location and overall design. He sited it on the corner of Fuzhou Road and Henan Road (two blocks south of Nanjing Road and three blocks west of the Bund), at the geographic center of Shanghai's Central District in the British-controlled International Settlement. He gave the commission to architects at Atkinson and Dallas, a British-owned firm that had been founded at Shanghai in 1898 and had established a reputation in China for designing large buildings in accordance with contemporary Western architectural fashions.[28]

In this case Atkinson and Dallas architects designed an Art Deco building, following a style that had become popular in the West in the late 1920s. To construct it they used an up-to-date American building material, "aerocrete," a light and porous form of concrete, and they erected a towering structure ten stories high in its central section and six stories high in each of its two wings. They adopted a two-part design, installing a wall of windows on the ground floor in the lower zone and erecting vertical pillars to accentuate the building's height in the upper zone; the soaring effect was the same as that in Five Continents' branch stores, but on a grander scale. In an elegant touch, they chamfered the building (rounding it at the corners) so that it joined the other buildings around the intersection of Fuzhou and Henan Roads in forming a circle rather than a square (Figure 4.9).[29]

Atkinson and Dallas installed glass windows and lighting fixtures to make the exterior of the building literally glitter. Their entrance centered on a glass revolving door and was flanked by eight huge plate-glass display windows—each twelve feet wide and twenty-four feet high—along

Fuzhou and Henan Roads. In addition to the light radiating from these windows, the entire exterior of the building was outlined with neon lights that created a dazzling silhouette against the night sky (Figure 4.10).[30]

Inside the building the designers also made use of glass and electric lighting to sensational effect. On the main floor they filled the vast shopping area (covering 5,268 square feet) with long rows of glass display cases that were lit both internally and from the ceiling.[31] They added to the rosy glow by erecting huge pink mica stone columns from floor to ceiling and by laying a matching mica stone floor inlaid with copper (Figure 4.11). Outside the shopping area they installed technologically up-to-date amenities that included restrooms, elevators, and heating and air-conditioning systems, and they devoted the upper floors to an auditorium, dining rooms, dormitories, and storage and office space—especially for doctors whose patients were encouraged to fill their prescriptions at Five Continents' pharmacy on their way out of the building.[32]

And yet, for all this building's Western qualities—its Western architectural firm, Art Deco design, "aerocrete," gigantic glass windows, and brilliant electrical lighting—Xiang Shengwu did not leave it completely devoid of Chinese style. On its third floor he paid tribute to his father by building the Xiang Songmao Memorial Hall (Xiang Songmao xiansheng jinian tang). He brought Chinese specialists on Chinese art *(meishu zhuanjia)* from Beijing to design this hall, which served as Five Continents' boardroom, and they created a museum-like space containing exhibits of Chinese interior design and decorative art. Its wooden beams were fitted together by the dovetailing of tenons and mortises, and its walls were covered with scrolls and paintings (Figure 4.12). These and several of its other features have been regarded in the twentieth century as quintessential features of the art and architecture of the Lower Yangzi region dating from at least the Tang dynasty (618–907) and particularly from the Ming (1368–1644) and Qing (1644–1912) dynasties.[33]

Xiang Shengwu gave his father credit for Five Continents' success. He pointed out that Xiang Songmao had conceived the original idea for a tall new main store to replace the three-story one that he had opened twenty-three years earlier, in 1913, at the same location. According to Xiang Shengwu, in the early 1930s his father had gone so far as to submit a proposal to Five Continents' board of directors to construct a nine-story building (one story shorter than the one that was ultimately completed).[34]

On October 10, 1936, at the grand opening, Xiang Shengwu further identified the new store with its Chinese past by hailing its significance in Chinese history. The year of the opening marked the thirtieth anniversary of Five Continents Drugstores (established in 1906), and the day of the opening was the twenty-fifth anniversary of the Republic of China's National Day, "Double Ten," which honored the spark that set off the Revolution of 1911. Xiang personally gave a patriotic speech to the four thousand guests who showed up (of the eight thousand that he had invited), and he delivered an equally nationalistic, buy-Chinese advertising message in all the media, including leaflets dropped from an airplane in a kind of commercial bombing of Shanghai. His advertising was apparently effective, for thirty thousand customers poured into the store on its first day and even more the next.[35]

Whatever gestures Xiang Shengwu made toward his father and Chinese history, he did little else to localize this building for consumers in terms of Chinese taste or style. He discreetly placed the Xiang Songmao Memorial Hall where consumers could not see it while shopping on the ground floor, descending from doctors' offices on the upper floors, or window-shopping outside the building. His building left the impression that Shanghai was fully integrated into the capitalist world because his new headquarters seemed to suggest that, for Shanghai consumers, global taste and local taste amounted to virtually the same thing.

WHO DESIGNED BRANCH STORES?

It is clear that Xiang Shengwu commissioned Western architects to design his Shanghai headquarters and that they constructed a building that was uncompromisingly Western. But it is not clear who designed Five Continents' branch stores and how these stores were architecturally localized. Available documentary evidence gives no precise answer, and available visual evidence (including photographs) suggests that the stores were designed by one of three groups: Western architects who were commissioned by Xiang Songmao in Shanghai, Chinese builders who were dispatched by Xiang from Shanghai, or local builders who were recruited by Five Continents' managers on site. Of these three possibilities, the first is less plausible than the other two. It seems doubtful that Western architects were involved because almost all the stores were built according to the two-part vertical form which was not used for drugstores in the West. It is more likely that Xiang sent Chinese builders from Shanghai to each city: the stores have some features in common—notably the two-part vertical form—and the Chinese with the best reputations as builders in China at the time happened to be from Xiang's native place of Ningbo.[36] It is also conceivable that Xiang's branch managers recruited local builders in each city because, as we have seen, the stores were by no means identical and included features (such as covered walkways) that accommodated local conditions and might well have been modeled after existing local buildings.

The most likely of these three possibilities is that Xiang sent builders from Shanghai to other cities. This conclusion seems warranted because he is known to have taken a personal interest in his stores' architectural design and because he adopted a general policy of retaining his own central authority at Shanghai and preventing local Chinese from gaining managerial control over any aspect of his branch stores.[37]

Localizing the Localizer

As Xiang Songmao extended Five Continents' reach in China, he tried to control its branches and affiliates whether his company owned them or not. In marketing medicine, he was determined to exercise authority at Shanghai over distribution at every level. As it turned out, he was successful at retaining control over Five Continents' wholly owned branch stores but not its locally owned affiliates.

PREVENTING LOCALIZATION OF BRANCH STORES

As noted earlier, Xiang Songmao marketed goods through a Chinese native-place network and retained ownership and managerial authority over Five Continents' branch stores at the company's headquarters in Shanghai. He insisted that Five Continents wholly own all its branch stores, and he dispatched his trusted native-place associates from Shanghai to take charge of each one. With full control over ownership and management, he rigorously prevented local merchants from becoming co-owners or managers of branch stores in their hometowns.

In his early years at Five Continents, Xiang Songmao joined with local co-investors in opening drugstores in medium-sized cities—Hangzhou in 1914, Yangzhou in 1916, and Jiujiang in 1919—but he clearly distinguished these co-owned local stores from wholly owned branch stores, and he made no investments to renovate, enlarge, or replace local stores as long as they were under co-ownership. Only later, after Five Continents bought these stores outright and sent its own managers from Shanghai to take charge, did Xiang build new multistory branch stores and formally open them at these locations: Jiujiang in 1921, Hangzhou in 1928, and Yangzhou in 1931.[38]

Xiang Songmao's central control over ownership and management made Five Continents' branch stores highly resistant to localization. The company's central office required branch managers and franchise holders to submit records of their sales and profits on a regular basis, and in turn, it sent digests and graphs of the sales data to them every month. Along with these financial statements, it also shipped them new advertisements and copies of its promotional magazine, *Chengguang,* on a monthly basis.[39] By all accounts, Five Continents' branch stores followed the policies that emanated from the company's headquarters in Shanghai, but its franchises did not.

SUCCUMBING TO LOCALIZATION BY LOCAL AFFILIATES

If successful at preventing localization at its branch stores in core cities of China's macroregions, Xiang Songmao was not able to do the same at local affiliates in smaller and more peripheral cities and towns. In independent stores he had no direct control over ownership and management. Lacking direct control, he sought indirect control by introducing a new organizational form, the "shop sign affiliate" (*lingpai lianhao,* which literally means "receive a shop sign and affiliate a business"). This was a variation on another organizational form in use at the time, the "affiliate" or the "associated company" *(lianhao),* a business that appeared to be subordinate to the founding patriarch of a "family firm" even as it became largely independent of the founder's control with the passage of time.[40]

In recruiting his shop sign affiliates, Xiang offered to share his company's name and reputation. In late imperial China Chinese merchants had attached great importance to their shop signs, jealously guarding them and actively opposing attempts to imitate or replicate them—as we saw in the case of Tongren Tang. But Five Continents and other drugstores selling Western-style medicine departed from past practice by offering their names to independently owned Chinese shops that became their affiliates. Xiang also recruited affiliates by offering to provide a wide array of advertisements, such as wall paintings, banners, and posters, including posters containing blank spaces where the name of the locality could be filled in (Figure 4.13).[41] As another recruiting device, Xiang negotiated with prospective affiliates over financial arrangements: commissions and profits on the sale of Five Continents' goods, early notifications of Five Continents' promotional price-cutting, and offers of Five Continents' year-end bonuses, which depended on each affiliate's sales volume.

In return, an affiliate was urged to sign an agreement that it would sell only Five Continents' medicines, not the medicines of rivals. Affiliates were also expected to make their shops look and operate like Five Continents' branch stores, thus extending Five Continents' reach. But in practice affiliates deviated from Five Continents' plans and localized or relocalized its advertising in their own ways.

Five Continents' relationship with its affiliate in the medium-sized city of Xuzhou in North China illustrates this kind of localization. In the 1920s, with no branch, affiliate, or other contact in Xuzhou, Five Continents ran newspaper advertisements in search of candidates to serve as its local sales agent. Upon receiving a reply from Lu Shudong, the owner of Xuzhou Puyu Bookstore, Xiang Songmao personally negotiated with Lu. On its side, Five Continents provided Lu with a shop sign and advertisements at no expense. It also supplied goods at wholesale prices, which gave Lu a projected profit margin of 35–45 percent, and it paid a commission to speed up sales, varying the amount from 2 to 5 percent, depending on Lu's rate of turnover.

On Lu's side, he changed the name of his shop to Xuzhou Puyu Bookstore and Great Five Continents Drugstore, put up a signboard with this name on it, and made use of Five Continents' wall paintings, banners, posters, and other advertisements. In 1930, after selling under Five Continents' name for a few years, Lu expanded and added a second building, and even there he mounted a shop sign that bore the words "Branch of Great Five Continents Drugstores" (Wuzhou da yaofang fendian).[42]

While Lu thus lengthened the reach of Five Continents, he did not passively replicate Five Continents' branch drugstores. He stubbornly refused to sign an exclusive dealing agreement with Five Continents, and he carried a variety of its rivals' most popular products, selling not only Five Continents' Man-Made Blood but also Chinese-made Human Elixir and Japanese-made Humane Elixir, and Southeast Asian–made Tiger Balm (described in Chapter 6). Moreover, he did not restrict his offerings to these various brands of Western-style "new medicine." He also sold herbal cures prepared by practitioners of traditional Chinese medicine, and eventually he enlarged his store and diversified his stock to the point where he carried nonmedicinal items, including stationery, photographic equipment, glass, and bicycles. Ultimately Lu dealt with more than one hundred companies in Shanghai. Even as Lu left up his shop sign proclaiming "Xuzhou Puyu Bookstore and Great Five Continents Drugstore," his local customers aptly nicknamed his establishment after China's biggest department store, calling it Xuzhou's "Sincere Department Store of Shanghai."[43]

In these ways the shopkeeper Lu Shudong localized Five Continents' marketing. He used Five Continents' shop sign and advertising to make his affiliate look less like an old-style bookstore and more like one of Five Continents' Western-style branch drugstores, and after adding a branch of his own, he retained his status as an affiliate and made his sales under shop signs for Great Five Continents Drugstores. But along the way he transformed the entire conception of a drugstore, broadening his stock to the point where his business resembled a department store more than it did any of Five Continents' branch drugstores.

Levels of Localization

Five Continents' nationwide marketing was localized in China in ways that the company intended and in ways that it did not intend. At the top Xiang Songmao deliberately attempted to carry out localization under his central control. From Shanghai he invested in the construction of branch stores at core cities in China's regions and sent trusted native-place associates to manage each one. Under his and his branch managers' supervision, Five Continents built stores that all appeared to be Western and made a sharp contrast with traditional drugstores and other Chinese shops. It localized them by selecting sites for them at urban population centers, covering them with Chinese characters, and adding or allowing Chinese builders to add distinctive local architectural features and decorations. It is not clear whether Xiang sent architects and builders from Shanghai to design and construct branch stores in each city, but it seems likely that he had some say in the extent to which each store was localized.

At the macroregional level, Five Continents' branch managers also had some say in the extent to which their stores were localized. As Xiang's appointees, they were expected to follow his orders, and, as Ningbo natives who had been sent from Shanghai, they were more familiar with his spoken dialect, architectural taste, and other cultural values than they were with the dialects, architecture, and local cultures of the cities where they were posted. Nevertheless, they served in any given city for relatively long periods—usually a few years and in some cases eleven or twelve years—so they had opportunities to learn about each city's local customs. Although their actions are not well documented, they probably localized advertising from Shanghai by translating it for local consumers in their branch stores.

At lower levels of the marketing hierarchy, Five Continents' affiliates also localized its advertising and even went so far as to violate company policies. Like Five Continents' branch managers, its affiliates made use of Five Continents' shop signs and advertising, which were supplied from Shanghai. Compared to the branch managers, however, holders of affiliates were not subject to the same central control. They displayed the advertising in ways different from those the company had intended; Lu Shudong's use of Five Continents' advertising to help transform his bookstore not into a drugstore (as his Five Continents' shop sign proclaimed) but into a department store is one example.

At still lower levels of the marketing hierarchy, shopkeepers in small retail stores and itinerant vendors in urban back alleys and rural markets undoubtedly took advantage of Five Continents' advertising too. Although little is known about their business practices, it seems safe to infer that some of Five Continents' massive amounts of advertising reached Chinese retailers and peddlers and created opportunities for them to localize and relocalize Five Continents' "Western" images in their own ways.

Through this vast and intricate network, Five Continents marketed medicine more widely throughout China's macroregions and farther down these macroregions' urban hierarchies than any other business was able to do before the Japanese military invasion of 1937. Moreover, this company continued to operate on a large scale during the Sino-Japanese War of 1937–1945, but by then it ceased to be the most important unit in the drug trade in Shanghai and China.[44] It was surpassed by other Chinese-owned medicine businesses that not only survived but grew spectacularly during the war. While Five Continents, like Great China-France Drugstores and many other prewar medicine companies, continued to operate under the Japanese occupation, its wartime profits fell far short of those of some of its rivals, notably New Asia Pharmaceutical Company.

4.1 Xiang Songmao

4.2 Five Continents' headquarters, 1913

4.3 Man-Made Blood with its Western-style
bottle and Chinese label

4.4 Shops in traditional Chinese architecture

4.5 Five Continents'
Western-style branch
stores in North China

4.6 Five Continents'
branch stores in
the Middle Yangzi
region

4.7 Five Continents' branch store in Xiamen with its arcade, 1930s

4.8 A commercial district in Xiamen, 1920s

新廈外觀

4.9 Five Continents' Shanghai headquarters, 1936

4.10 Five Continents' headquarters at night

4.11 Five Continents' salesroom

4.12 Xiang Songmao Memorial Hall

4.13 A poster advertising Man-Made Blood with a space where each
branch could add the name of its locality

5

Crossing Enemy Lines

> During the period of the [Japanese wartime] occupation, we [Chinese] busi-
> nessmen continued to put profits above all other considerations. To make a
> profit, we fought with each other in a life or death struggle and never
> thought of giving in to rivals. At the time, the most important thing for [Chi-
> nese] leaders of industry and commerce in Shanghai's foreign concessions
> was to become fixers (*lulutong*, a Shanghainese slang expression literally
> meaning "one who takes every road"), so as to maneuver successfully in the
> market, and I was a typical example of a fixer. Those called fixers managed
> to have good relationships with all political parties, including the Japanese
> [military] authorities, Wang Jingwei's puppet government at Nanjing, and
> the Nationalist government's underground agents sent from Chongqing. I
> was pretty successful at establishing friendships with leading figures in all
> these political groups during the war.
>
> Xu Guanqun, "Xinya yaochang sanshinian laide huigu" (1964)

How did Chinese medicine companies market their goods in the wake of
the Japanese military invasion and occupation of China (1937–1945) and
Southeast Asia (1942–1945)? As I mentioned in Chapter 4, Xiang Songmao
was shot dead when he attempted to lead members of Five Continents'
staff against Japanese troops during the Shanghai Incident of 1932. Subsequently other Chinese entrepreneurs found themselves threatened, especially after the Japanese claimed victory in the Battle of Shanghai in 1937.
On the eve of the war Chinese medicine businesses had tended to establish their headquarters in Shanghai and to manage all aspects of their businesses from there. By then Shanghai had surpassed all other cities in
China as a manufacturer of industrial products, a nationwide exporter of
consumer goods, and a publisher of print media (newspapers, magazines,
advertisements). Did the Japanese invasion of 1937 dislodge Shanghai
from its central place in China's industry, commerce, and culture?[1] Some
historians have left the impression that it did. James Reardon-Anderson

notes that only a few Chinese industrialists had teamed up with scientists to conduct research and development in prewar China, and he describes their wartime flight from their bases in Shanghai and other coastal ports to safer inland locations. Similarly, Chang-tai Hung asserts that the leading Chinese journalists, writers, and cartoonists made this same move at the time of the Japanese invasion, precipitating the "decentralization of culture from coastal cities to the interior . . . that shifted China's attention to the countryside."[2]

If Shanghai was devastated by the Japanese invasion and drained of industrial scientists and commercial artists, wouldn't Chinese owners of medicine businesses who had remained there have lacked the expertise needed to manufacture and advertise their goods? Wouldn't they have been marooned in Shanghai and cut off from opportunities for long-distance trade, first in the "solitary island" *(gudao)* of 1937–1941 (when Japanese troops took the Chinese-governed portion of Shanghai, leaving only its foreign concession areas unoccupied), and then under the Japanese military occupation of the entire city, 1942–1945?

The answer would be an unqualified yes if it were not for Chinese fixers. These fixers are difficult to investigate because they were notoriously secretive, but one of them, Xu Guanqun (1899–1972), the self-identified fixer quoted in the epigraph, has provided a window on their world by preserving detailed records of his business, New Asia Pharmaceutical Company (Xinya zhiyao chang), and by writing a revealing and unpublished memoir that describes his dealings with leading wartime figures not only in business but in the wider arenas of politics, medicine, science, and literature.[3] During the war his company's capital and sales rose and its distribution network dramatically expanded throughout China and Southeast Asia (Tables 5.1 and 5.2 and Map 5.1). By the end of the war Xu formed the New Asia Enterprise Group (Xinya qiye jituan), capitalized at more than a billion yuan, which had New Asia Pharmaceutical Company as its cornerstone and included thirty-five enterprises in medicine, printing, papermaking, dyes, textiles, hardware, banking, insurance, and real estate.[4] Xu's successes at building up this remarkable record are traced here through three phases: his operations on the eve of the war, his negotiations with Japanese and Chinese governments at the beginning of the war, and his use of science to achieve commercial expansion and cultural influence during the war.

Table 5.1. New Asia Pharmaceutical Company's Capital and Sales Revenue, 1926–1945

Year	Capital	Sales revenue
1926	1,000	—
1927	10,000	—
1930	50,000	—
1932	50,000	355,000
1933	250,000	614,000
1934	250,000	705,000
1935	250,000	825,000
1936	500,000	1,000,000
1937	500,000	1,303,000
1938	1,000,000	—
1939	1,000,000	3,968,000
1940	3,000,000	—
1941	8,000,000	—
1942	30,000,000	—
1943	120,000,000	52,566,000
1944	120,000,000	248,077,000
1945	120,000,000	121,075,000

Note: No data are available for the years omitted. The currencies used were as follows: before 1935, yinyuan (silver yuan); 1935–1941, fabi (the currency of the Nationalist government); 1942–1945, zhongchuquan (the currency of Wang Jingwei's Japanese-sponsored government.) A dash indicates that relevant data are not available.

Source: Data taken from Chen Lizheng and Yuan Enzhen, eds., *Xinya de licheng—Shanghai xinya zhiyaochang de guoqu xianzai he jianglai* (Shanghai: Shanghai shehui kexue yuan, 1990), 7.

Table 5.2. Wartime Expansion of New Asia Pharmaceutical Company

	1926–1936	1937–1945
Headquarters	Shanghai	Shanghai
Headquarters of branch companies (*fen gongsi*) in China	None	Shanghai (for Jiangsu and Zhejiang)
		Hankou (for Hunan, Hubei, Jiangxi, and Henan)
		Chongqing (for Sichuan, Guizhou, Yunnan, and Tibet)
		Guangzhou (for Guangdong, Guangxi, and Fujian)
		Tianjin (for Hebei, Shanxi, Shandong, and Inner Mongolia)
		Xi'an (for Shaanxi, Gansu, Ningxia, Qinghai, and Xinjiang)
Headquarters of branch companies outside China	None	Hong Kong, Singapore, Bangkok, Manila
Medicine-making plants	Shanghai (1)	Shanghai (4), Chongqing, Beijing, Hong Kong
Sales agencies	27 (all in China)	41 in China and 10 in Southeast Asia

Sources: Shanghai shehui kexue yuan jingji yanjiu suo, *Shanghai jindai xiyao hangye shi* (Shanghai: Shanghai shehui kexue yuan, 1988), 278–280; Xu Guanqun, "Xinya yaochang sanshinian laide huigu" (1964), 66–70; Chen Lizheng and Yuan Enzhen, eds., *Xinya de licheng—Shanghai xinya zhiyaochang de guoqu xianzai he jianglai* (Shanghai: Shanghai shehui kexue yuan, 1990), 6, 224; file Q38–40–11, Xinya huaxue zhiyao gongsi Papers, 104, 107–108.

Prewar Origins and Reforms

Xu Guanqun (Figure 5.1) was able to exploit wartime opportunities because he already had in place sophisticated manufacturing and long-distance marketing systems before the war broke out. In 1926, as a twenty-seven-year-old college graduate, he founded New Asia Pharmaceutical

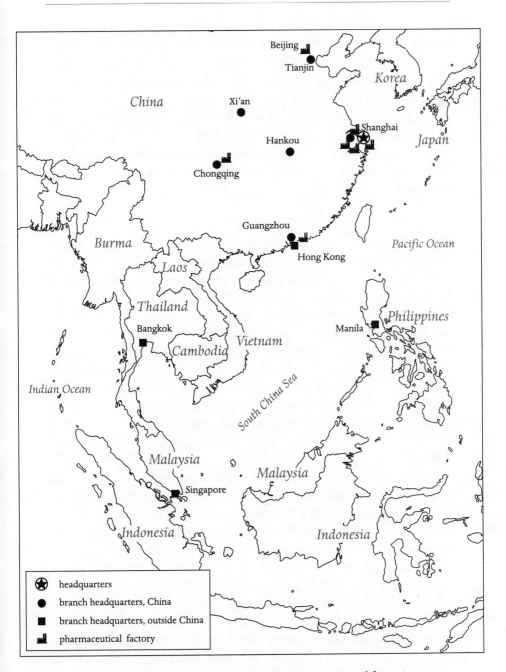

Map 5.1. New Asia's headquarters, branch headquarters, and factories, 1938–1945. Map by Thomas Lyons.

Company and set out to manufacture modern and scientific medicines (as distinct from supposedly pseudoscientific patent medicines), and he opened a Shanghai plant whose first products were distilled water (beginning in 1926) and glass ampoules for holding hypodermic injections (beginning in 1929). During New Asia's first five years, 1926–1931, Xu relied on others outside his business to distribute and promote New Asia's goods beyond Shanghai.[5] Then between 1931 and 1937, with surprising speed, Xu constructed his own sizeable marketing system consisting of a long-distance distribution network and a set of influential promotional publications.

REFORMING A DISTRIBUTION NETWORK

Before 1931, while Xu's marketing system was confined to Shanghai, he distributed through his social network, and only when he extended his marketing system outside Shanghai after 1931 did he begin to modify it. In his early years, like Xiang Songmao and many others, he followed well-established Chinese precedents by basing his distribution network on native-place ties. Xu's native place was Changzhou, a city one hundred miles northwest of Shanghai, and throughout his life he maintained close ties with his fellow Changzhou sojourners. Son of a Changzhou banker, Xu first left Changzhou for Shanghai in 1918 to take a job as an accountant at a textile mill, and he immediately made contacts with Changzhou sojourners by joining the Changzhou student association at the Shanghai College of Commerce, where he enrolled as a part-time student taking night courses.[6]

In 1926, when Xu founded New Asia Pharmaceutical Company, he did so in collaboration with two partners, who were both from Changzhou, and he actively sought out Changzhou natives to fill the ranks of his new business's administrative staff. During the company's first five years he sent recruiters every year by train from Shanghai to Changzhou's schools, where they gave written examinations and signed up successful examinees as company trainees. Xu chose a select few of these Changzhou natives to be his personal disciples *(tudi)* and pupils *(mensheng),* all of whom called him Old Master *(laotouzi),* and he retained many others from Changzhou at all levels of his business.[7] As Xu later recalled, he employed so many people from Changzhou that New Asia Pharmaceutical Company became jokingly referred to in Shanghai as the Changzhou Native-Place Association (Changzhou tongxianghui).[8]

Between 1931 and 1937, when Xu extended New Asia's marketing system outside Shanghai, he retained this Chinese-style native-place network, but he also began to investigate and adopt Western- and Japanese-style approaches to marketing.[9] Since his student days at Shanghai College of Commerce, he had been learning about Western ideas of "scientific management systems" (as he characterized them), and he had become exposed to Japanese business practices through one of New Asia's co-founders, Zhao Rudiao, a Chinese from Changzhou who had earned a degree in pharmacy from Chiba University in Japan during the early 1920s and had subsequently worked for a Japanese trading company selling medicine in China. In 1936 Xu traveled with Zhao to Japan to survey its pharmaceutical industry and, on the basis of what he saw, he resolved to model New Asia after the biggest Japanese pharmaceutical company, Takeda Chemical Industries.[10]

In 1937 Xu carried out a major reform of his distribution network. For the first time he began to appoint to high positions Chinese not from Changzhou, and he began requiring New Asia's recruits to attend his newly opened company school, the Staff Training Institute.[11] To this school he admitted twenty-three high school graduates who had been recommended by their schools on the basis of their academic records and individual accomplishments, not of their native places. Xu selected these young men to become New Asia's business cadres (*gugan*), and he designed for them a three-month curriculum with two aims: to improve technical skills and to instill loyalty. For the teaching of accounting and other technical subjects, Xu enlisted the aid of a vocational program, the China Professional Training Institute (Zhonghua zhiye jiaoyu she), which was operated by the Chinese educational reformer Huang Yanpei. To instill loyalty, he exhorted his recruits to consider themselves soldiers in a military organization so that they would become disciplined members of an aggressive sales force. "The purpose of training was to build up an Army of Sons and Brothers [*zidi bing*]," Xu recalled, "and I promoted several dozens of them to important positions."[12] These "important positions" included appointments as top managers of New Asia's branch offices at core cities in several of China's macroregions: Beijing for North China; Hankou, Nanchang, and Changsha for the Middle Yangzi region; Jian'ou for Southeast China; Wuzhou for South China; and Kunming for Southwest China.[13]

In the same year, 1937, Xu carried out a second major reform of his distribution network by creating a new unit, the General Office for Promotion and Advertising. This unit's mission was to capture the market for medicine by dealing directly with doctors and convincing them to recommend New Asia's products. As Xu later recalled, "We considered medical professionals to be our most important patrons because they had great clout with patients and drugstores. So if we won them over, we would win over the entire consumer society." This unit's "major duties" were, in Xu's words, "to visit local doctors, convince them to order medicines, and introduce them to New Asia's local sales agents." In the doctors' offices, the representatives from New Asia's General Office for Promotion and Advertising set up displays, gave away samples and gifts, invited doctors to banquets, and handed out lists comparing New Asia's goods favorably with higher-priced foreign-made goods. In some cities they even recruited doctors to become New Asia's local sales agents; Drs. Lu Genming of Hangzhou, Xu Boru of Nanjing, and Xu Yuanmo of Changzhou are examples of these recruits.[14]

Xu carried out these reforms—recruiting staff members regardless of whether they were Changzhou natives and training them in his own school—because he needed a disciplined corps of salesmen to staff new offices in New Asia's rapidly expanding distribution network. By 1936, one year before the reforms, this network had grown to include no fewer than twenty-seven offices located in eight of China's nine macroregions—all but the Northeast—and each office employed between three and six staff members.[15] Thus, even though as late as 1931 Xu's distribution network had been limited to a modest group of native-place associates in a single office in Shanghai, by 1937 he presided from his Shanghai headquarters over a large and systematically trained sales force that was deployed in all of China's macroregions except the one already occupied by Japan, the Northeast (Manchuria).

CAPTURING AN AUDIENCE

During the prewar years, while Xu made New Asia's distribution network more extensive, sophisticated, and aggressive, he did the same for the company's promotional publications. Initially, in the late 1920s, Xu despaired of ever successfully promoting New Asia's goods because Chinese consumers showed no faith in any Chinese-owned pharmaceutical company's capacity to match its Western and Japanese rivals' scientific standards in making modern medicine. As Xu later admitted, when he discovered in the 1920s that New Asia's first Chinese-made medical products were unsalable, he resorted to falsifying their national origins by stamping on them "Made in Japan."[16] And yet in his prewar advertising, as in his prewar distribution, he quickly progressed from tentative and limited experiments to aggressive and large-scale operations.

The design of Xu's first promotional device, New Asia's trademark, shows his initial reluctance to reveal his company's Chinese origins and his eagerness to identify it with Japanese and Western medical science. Adopted in 1928, New Asia's trademark consisted of a cross within a five-pointed star. On the surface, these two components simply represented the name "New Asia": the star (pronounced *xing* in Mandarin) was a pun on "New" (pronounced *xin* in Mandarin), and the cross was in the form of the Chinese character for "Asia" (*ya*) (Figure 5.2). But this second component represented more than just part of the company's name. At the time the character for Asia (which was also the written term for Asia in the Japanese language) appeared in the names of Japanese-owned businesses more commonly than in the names of Chinese-owned businesses. So, on seeing this trademark, Chinese consumers might easily have mistaken New Asia's products for Japanese-made goods. Most significant of all in New Asia's trademark, according to Xu, was the innermost portion of the cross, which was printed in red like the symbol of the Red Cross, even though New Asia had no affiliation with this European-based international hospital and ambulance service for victims of wars and other calamities. The red cross, Xu explained, "was to give consumers the impression that our plant and our products were associated with modern medical science."[17]

Not until 1931 and 1932 did Xu begin to advertise New Asia openly as a Chinese-owned company. He was stimulated to do so by a Chinese boycott that was held to protest Japan's seizure of Northeast China in 1931 and Japan's bombing of Shanghai in 1932. During the boycott Xu joined the Association of Allied Manufacturers and Sellers of Chinese National Goods (Zhongguo guohuo chanxiao hezuo xiehui) and introduced nationalistic buy-Chinese advertising (as Huang Chujiu, among others, had done earlier).[18] Once the boycott ended, Xu continued to take the offensive in aggressive advertising campaigns without interruption between 1932 and the end of the war in 1945.

In the 1930s Xu founded medical and health publications so that he could promote his pharmaceutical goods, something his counterparts in the West did not do at the time. In the United States, for example, big American pharmaceutical companies had advertised their goods in conformity with the regulations of the American Medical Association and the federal government since the early years of the twentieth century. On the one hand, these big American businesses had suffered from the regulations insofar as they were forced to trim down the claims in their advertising, and, on the other hand, they had benefited from the devastating effects of the regulations on their smaller rivals who were selling patent medicines. But in any case they did not own or publish American professional journals (such as the *Journal of the American Medical Association*) and American popular magazines (such as *Collier's Weekly* and *Ladies' Home Journal*) that spoke for medical practitioners and led a crusade for the regulation of patent medicines and the prevention of deceptive business practices in the sale of medicine.[19]

In China, by contrast, while Xu was the owner of a big pharmaceutical company, he became the owner and publisher of some of China's most influential publications in the field of medicine. In 1932 he founded the *Journal of New Medicine (Xinyao yi kan),* a Chinese-language professional journal for practitioners of Western-style medicine, and he used it to identify New Asia with the most famous foreign-trained Chinese physicians for the purpose of raising its sales. As he later recalled, "Our special editors all were [Chinese] doctors trained in foreign countries such as Britain, the United States, Germany, and Japan. Their fame and influence boosted the sales of our goods."[20]

As the publisher of the *Journal of New Medicine,* Xu Guanqun set the goal of placing a copy of it in every doctor's office. He kept the price low—ten cents in Chinese currency for each issue, which ran between fifty and seventy pages and included ten to twenty pages of advertisements in color—and he tried to give a free copy to every doctor. With this aim in mind, he assigned his distribution network the task of compiling an address list of all the Chinese practitioners of Western medicine in China, and with the help of this list, he delivered more than twelve thousand free copies of every issue of his medical journal to doctors throughout the country. Not satisfied to stop there, Xu reached still more doctors by publishing an English-language version of the *Journal for New Medicine* and followed a similar procedure for distributing it. Pricing it at fifty cents (in Chinese currency) per copy, he instructed his sales force to track down English-reading doctors (especially in Hong Kong and other British colonies in Southeast Asia) and give each one a free copy of every issue.[21] From then on Xu used the *Journal of New Medicine* as an advertising vehicle for as long as he published it, until 1941.

In 1936 Xu founded a new Chinese-language publication in which he could appeal to consumers directly (rather than indirectly—through doctors—as he did in *The Journal of New Medicine*). He named his magazine *Healthy Home (Jiankang jiating)*, and when he later reflected on his reasons for starting it, he drew a distinction between his "professed aims" and his "real aims" in a revealing passage that is worth quoting at length: "The professed aims of the magazine were to spread knowledge of health, encourage research on family problems, help young people to improve themselves, and promote social services. . . . The real purpose of my publishing *Healthy Home* was, of course, to promote the sale of New Asia's medicines. By publishing the magazine, we were able to penetrate deeply into family life and make our brands into household names. This way of doing business, as the old saying goes, is a matter of 'Never missing a chance to find a way in' [*wukong buru*]."[22]

At the time Xu was by no means the only prewar Chinese entrepreneur who published a popular magazine to advertise his own goods and manipulate progressive ideals for commercial purposes, but compared with the others, he was strikingly successful at capturing a sizeable audience of readers.[23] According to Xu, his first three issues of *Healthy Home,* published in 1936 and early 1937, were snapped up by "several tens of thousands of readers," and by June 1937 he distributed it through twenty-two sales agencies outside Shanghai as well as circulating it within the city. After gearing up to reach a large audience, Xu expected the readership to grow still larger, but he temporarily closed down *Healthy Home* before its fourth issue could be published because of the Japanese invasion in the summer of 1937.[24]

A PREWAR FIXER

This account of Xu Guanqun's prewar marketing shows that he took full advantage of Shanghai's central place in China's commerce and popular culture. Predictably, as Xu's business grew and competed with commercial rivals for China's nationwide market, he became embroiled in political controversies, and in handling these controversies he gained his first experience as a political fixer. In 1933, for example, Xu faced charges from Western pharmaceutical companies that New Asia had been trafficking in an illicit drug, morphine. In response to complaints from the Department of Drug Control in Shanghai's International Settlement, Xu pointed out that New Asia had an official permit from the Nationalist government to import morphine, which it used to manufacture anesthetics. But he did not let the case go to court. Instead, he fixed it by bribing Lu Liankui, head of the International Settlement's Department of Drug Control. Lu was a man well positioned to come to Xu's aid because, according to Frederic Wakeman, he was an influential police detective who had "Green Gang connections and . . . stood as a beat cop who made it good, looking the other way when he had to, and doing what was necessary to get by."[25]

To block future threats, Xu then campaigned successfully for a position on the Public Health Committee of the Chinese Ratepayers Association, which set rules governing the sale of medicine in the International Settlement. In the same year, 1933, Xu founded a lobbying organization, the Shanghai Pharmaceutical Manufacturers Association (Shanghai zhiyaoye tongye gonghui), and installed himself as its president, but his official positions and formal lobbying by no means marked the end of his dealings as a fixer.[26] In 1935, when the German-owned Bayer Pharmaceutical Company sued New Asia for product imitation and trademark infringement, Xu did not settle the issue by turning to lobbying organizations or legal institutions. He preferred once again to fix the case—this time by bribing Li Mianting, the head of the Nationalist government's trademark bureau.[27]

After the war broke out in 1937, Xu's prewar experience as a fixer served him well. Holding together a nationwide business in a politically divided country under a foreign occupation posed problems for a fixer on a grand scale, but he proved to be extraordinarily adept at solving these problems.

Wartime Alliances

When Japan invaded China in the summer of 1937, it did not cut off Xu Guanqun and his Shanghai headquarters from the long-distance marketing network that he had built up in the 1930s. Like the majority of Shanghai's capitalists, he declined to follow Chiang Kai-shek's government as it moved its capital from Nanjing westward, first to Wuhan (1937–1938) and then to Chongqing (1938–1945), but like several other Chinese capitalists, Xu transported a small portion of his equipment from his Shanghai plants first to Wuhan and then to Chongqing. In 1938 he established at Chong-qing a new branch, the New Asia Southwest China Company, and in 1940 he opened there a pharmaceutical plant capitalized at one million yuan.[28] He moved this equipment and opened this new branch, as he later re-called, for commercial rather than patriotic reasons. "Our base for our business was well established in Shanghai, and we had to maintain our pri-mary strength here for the sake of future development," he explained. "But it would have been wrong not to heed the call to move inland. In fact, moving inland was a great opportunity to open vast markets in the provinces of the Southwest. Why should we have let this opportunity slip through our fingers?"[29] During the war Xu continued to reach out from his Shanghai base even after it came under the Japanese occupation, and he was able to exploit markets in other parts of wartime China because of his political alliances across enemy lines.

FORMING POLITICAL ALLIANCES

In the course of the war Xu cultivated Chinese and Japanese leaders of almost all groups in positions of political authority throughout China. Within Shanghai Xu maintained a key contact with the Green Gang, a criminal organization that played an influential role in the city's labor-management relations and business-government relations before and dur-ing the war. In 1936 Xu had recruited onto New Asia's board of directors Gu Kemin, a banker who was a close associate of Du Yuesheng, the head of the Green Gang. Soon after Du fled from Shanghai to Hong Kong in 1938, Xu became Gu's sworn brother. Later, at the end of the war in 1945, when Xu himself fled from Shanghai to Hong Kong, he and his partners showed the extent of their reliance on Gu by leaving New Asia in Gu's hands.[30]

In Shanghai Xu also worked with the Japanese occupying forces and leading Chinese collaborators. He was able to take advantage of preexist-ing contacts because he had already formed ties in prewar Japan through his cofounder and partner at New Asia, Zhao Rudiao. When Xu had trav-eled to Japan in 1936, he had depended on Zhao as his translator and inter-mediary, and, after the Japanese invasion of 1937, Xu had Zhao available to mediate with the Japanese authorities and their Chinese collaborators in Shanghai.[31]

In the early years of the war, 1937–1941, Xu assumed official positions in the government of Shanghai's International Settlement, and in these positions he served with Chinese who gave him access to the Japanese authorities. In 1939 and again in 1941 he was elected to the Shanghai Municipal Council. There he aligned himself with a fellow council member, Yuan Ludeng, and two of Yuan's associates, Wen Lanting and Lin Kanghou, who were known at the time as "The Three Elders of Shanghai" and were later described by Xu as "notorious collaborators" and "leading Chinese traitors" *(da hanjian)*. Through them he made contacts with the Japanese military police and intelligence service.[32]

In December 1941, when Japan occupied Shanghai's foreign concessions, Xu began working directly with the Japanese authorities. He presented himself as a Chinese leader by citing his credentials as president of the Shanghai Pharmaceutical Manufacturers Association, and he merged this association with a related one, the Shanghai New Medicine Trade Association (Shanghai xinyaoye tongye gonghui), for the purpose of dealing with the Japanese authorities.[33]

In 1942 Xu and other Chinese in the pharmaceutical industry lost their direct control over distribution of medicine in China—but only briefly. At first, beginning in April 1942, they had to distribute through a Japanese administrative organization, the Central China Commission for Control of Medicine (Huazhong yiyaopin tongzhi lianhehui), and they were subordinated to its Japanese head, Nakajima Seiichi, a manager in the Japanese-owned Takeda Chemical Industries. Less than a year later, by March 1943, Xu and other Chinese capitalists achieved greater control over distribution with the establishment of the Japanese-sponsored National Commission for the Control of Commerce (Quanguo shangye tongzhi zonghui), which was characterized by the Japanese as a "self-governed merchant group." In August 1943 Xu was recommended for the commission's board of directors by Mei Siping, minister of the interior and one of the most influential figures in Wang Jingwei's Japanese-sponsored government. From then until the end of the war, Xu served as a member of its board and sold medical products (especially alcohol) to Japanese customers, including the Japanese army.[34]

In Japanese-occupied parts of China outside Shanghai, Xu maintained close relations with Japanese-sponsored Chinese governments. In Beijing the head of New Asia's branch company for North China dealt with Wang Kemin, the top Chinese official in the North China Provisional Government, which was set up by the Japanese in 1937. In Nanjing, the capital of the Japanese-sponsored government for central China, Xu worked through Chu Minyi, the foreign minister and vice president of the Executive Yuan of this government, which was led from 1940 to 1945 by Chu's brother-in-law, Wang Jingwei. It was because of Chu's intervention that Xu was able to reopen New Asia's offices in the Japanese-occupied cities of Hangzhou, Hankou, Guangzhou, and Fuzhou during the early 1940s. "We in the new medicine industry knew Chu Minyi most intimately of all the ranking officials in Wang Jingwei's inner circle," Xu later recalled.[35]

Outside Japanese-occupied China, Xu had connections with Chiang Kai-shek's Nationalist government. He arranged for protection of New Asia's goods in areas under the Nationalists' control by winning support from members of the Nationalists' underground in Shanghai. In particular, he financed a unit in Shanghai led by Wu Kaixian and Wu Shaoshu, two prominent figures in the Nationalist party and members of the C. C. Clique, a conservative political faction that took charge of the Nationalist party's intelligence network before the war and became influential with Chiang Kai-shek before, during, and after the war. The C. C. Clique, in return, helped to protect New Asia's branch company in Chongqing and its distribution network in the Upper Yangzi region.[36]

The only major political group with which Xu did not have close relations while he was in Shanghai during the war was that led by the Chinese Communists. Not until he moved to Hong Kong at the end of the war did he begin doing business with the Communists' underground agents.[37] But the Communists were the exception. Xu came to terms with all other major parties during the war.

Xu's success at negotiating this extraordinary range of alliances with leaders of almost every political stripe served more than one of his purposes. It not only protected his distribution network's access to markets both in and outside Shanghai; it also opened financial channels and allowed him to tap sources of capital from outside the city as well as within it.

BROKERING FINANCIAL ARRANGEMENTS

In finance, as in politics, Xu successfully brokered agreements with political rivals outside wartime Shanghai. In financing New Asia, he was particularly adept at raising capital from members of one faction of the Nationalist government, the Political Study Clique (Zhengxue xi), without antagonizing this faction's bitter rival, the C. C. Clique, New Asia's ally.[38] At the same time Xu did not let the C. C. Clique's opposition to the Political Study Clique prevent him from making financial arrangements with members of the Political Study Clique who owned banks based in Chongqing as well as Shanghai.

Before the war Xu had issued New Asia's stocks and bonds through several Shanghai-based banks that were owned by members of the Political Study Clique, but when the war broke out in 1937 some of these banks fled with Chiang Kai-shek's Nationalist government to Chongqing. In 1939 Xu made New Asia's first and second issues of stock in wartime by relying exclusively on banks still remaining in Shanghai. Then in 1940, when Xu announced that he was about to issue more stock in New Asia, he discovered that bankers who had moved their banks to Chongqing had managed to reestablish themselves in Shanghai. The first step was taken by Zhang Jia'ao, head of the Bank of China and an influential member of the Political Study Clique, who sent an emissary to conduct negotiations with bankers in Shanghai. As a result, the bankers from Chongqing and Shanghai jointly formed an investment firm, the Nanyang Enterprise Company (Nanyang qiye gongsi), and in 1940 Xu issued New Asia's stock through this firm.[39]

In the early 1940s Xu started his own financial institutions in Shanghai, and they also had relations with Chongqing. On December 1, 1941, he and other Chinese industrialists opened the China Industrial Bank (Zhongguo gongye yinhang) in Shanghai's foreign concessions with the aim of circumventing the Nationalist government's regulations that limited the amounts of money that depositors could withdraw from their accounts. Before it opened, Xu's plans for the bank encountered resistance from the Nationalist government in Chongqing. One of his banking partners, Zhu Boquan, was offered money by Du Yuesheng's agents to withhold his investment from the proposed bank, and Xu's application to register the bank with the Nationalist government in Chongqing received no reply. Nonetheless, Xu won Zhu's support and opened the bank, which immediately prospered. A little over a year later, Xu added an investment firm, New Asia Reconstruction Company (Xinya jianye gongsi), and he again heard from Chongqing. This time he was contacted by the Shanghai Commercial and Savings Bank and the China Vegetable Oil Company, both of which were owned by members of the Political Study Clique in the Nationalist government in Chongqing. From their owners he received expressions of interest in this venture, and he accommodated them, appointing their representatives along with Shanghai banks' representatives to the board of directors of his new investment firm, which was initially capitalized at 10 million yuan.[40]

In all these cases Xu allowed neither political rivalries nor wartime battle lines to block his financial transactions with investors from outside Shanghai. Far from being financially restricted, Xu seems to have found more room to maneuver during the war. On the one hand, the war did not prevent him from tapping his prewar sources of capital; on the other hand, it did allow him to carry out financial transactions beyond the reach of the Nationalist government's attempts to intervene from Chongqing. As a result, Xu was able to build up New Asia's capital and sales throughout most of the eight-year war. In the late 1930s and early 1940s his company's capital and sales revenue surpassed its prewar levels and did not fall below these levels until hit by runaway inflation between 1943 and 1945 (Table 5.1). As a trained accountant, Xu never let his funds lie idle, and during the war he invested them in New Asia's operations to expand the company and make it more scientific.

Popularizing Science

Xu's political and financial deals opened the way for his wartime commercial ventures but by no means guaranteed their success. It is true that, as consumers suffered under wartime conditions, his product to some extent sold itself; in fact, almost all Shanghai's big Chinese pharmaceutical companies grew rapidly during the war because of a great demand for medical products.[41] But even compared with these other pharmaceutical firms, New Asia grew at an extraordinary rate and emerged as a giant. Why did it become so big so fast? During the war Xu helped to widen the market for New Asia's goods by identifying them with Chinese science.

INSTITUTIONALIZING RESEARCH AND DEVELOPMENT

Xu Guanqun made New Asia more scientific and more Chinese by adding to its staff an illustrious group of Chinese research scientists. Like almost all pharmaceutical manufacturers in the world before the 1930s, he had no scientists on his staff doing serious full-time research and no substantial laboratory in which they could conduct experiments.[42] In 1935 Xu had opened at Shanghai his first modest laboratory, the New Asia Chemical and Pharmaceutical Research Institute, but not until the war was under way did he give New Asia major research facilities by building three large laboratories. In 1937 he opened the New Asia Medical Materials Plant, to which was attached a laboratory for designing and making surgical instruments, adhesive plasters, gauze, bandages, and absorbent cotton. In 1938 he added the New Asia Serum Plant, with a laboratory to produce vaccines to prevent or treat cholera, typhoid, smallpox, diphtheria, rabies, dysentery, tetanus, meningitis, pertussis, and plague. In 1941 he founded his most sophisticated laboratory in the New Asia Biological Research Institute, which specialized in antibiotics, including penicillin.[43]

To staff these laboratories Xu recruited distinguished Chinese scientists trained in Japan and the West as well as in China. In the early 1930s he and his Japanese-trained partner, Zhao Rudiao, had acquired New Asia's first technology and technical expertise by relying on Japanese technical advisers; and in 1935, when he had opened his first laboratory, he had appointed as its director a Chinese holder of a Doctor of Pharmacy degree from Tokyo University, Zeng Guangfang, who employed Japanese technicians and used Japanese-made equipment in the laboratory. But after the war began, Xu recruited for New Asia's top research positions Chinese scientists trained in the West, rather than in Japan. To be the director of the New Asia Serum Plant he selected Cheng Muyi, a Chinese bacteriologist trained at Harvard and formerly the director of the Nationalist government's Central Institute for Medical Testing, and for its associate director he chose Wu Liguo, who had been trained in France. At the New Asia Biological Research Institute he appointed as director Yu He, another Harvard-trained bacteriologist.

To serve under these directors Xu employed additional research scientists who had received training and gained experience in several different institutions and countries. His Chinese scientists trained in China included former members of China's Academia Sinica (Zhongyang yanjiu yuan), former faculty members from China's leading universities, and recent graduates from China's universities, where New Asia recruited every year. His scientists trained abroad included Chinese holders of advanced degrees in medical science from universities in Japan, the United States, Britain, Germany, and France. As Xu proudly recalled, by the end of the war fully 10 percent of New Asia's staff members were experts and trained technicians in one field of medical science or another.[44]

Besides developing highly sophisticated drugs in their research laboratories, New Asia's scientists introduced medical products for popular consumption. Some of these products were designed to treat specific conditions in a limited segment of the population, as in the case of Danggui'er (romanized as Tancnol on the label). An herbal dietary supplement, Danggui'er was designed specifically for young mothers, and it was supposed to nourish their blood and restore their strength after childbirth. (The drug's name literally means "Danggui's' Offspring," a pun that may be construed as a reference either to a root long used in traditional Chinese medicine or to a young woman's "return" to visit her family after being married).[45] By contrast, some of New Asia's other products were aimed at a broad range of consumers and were supposed to relieve widely varied symptoms. One of the company's most popular products, Peishengmeng (literally, "placenta"; the name in roman letters was Placemon), was meant to treat all the following: lower-back pain and weakness down the leg, loss of heart rhythm and sleeplessness, depression, sexual impotence and infertility, low blood count and sperm count, hardening of the arteries, premature senility in adults, and stunted growth in children—a list almost long enough to qualify Peishengmeng as a cure-all comparable to Huang Chujiu's Human Elixir.[46]

New Asia manufactured these and other products almost entirely in new plants built during the war. As Table 5.2 shows, New Asia had only one medicine-making factory in Shanghai before the war, and during the war it added six—three more in Shanghai and one each in Chongqing, Beijing, and Hong Kong—which employed more than a thousand workers.[47] These plants were needed outside Shanghai as well as within it to supply New Asia's growing long-distance distribution network.

TEACHING SCIENCE TO PROMOTE DISTRIBUTION
While recruiting scientifically trained researchers for New Asia's laboratories, Xu also gave scientific training to pharmacists and sales managers who served as its distribution agents. Between 1937 and 1945 he relied less and less on his native-place associates (who, writing in retrospect, have grumbled about their loss of authority and influence at New Asia during the war), and he began recruiting candidates according to their educational credentials rather than their native-place connections.[48] He gave some of these recruits training in science as pharmacists at one of his company's schools, and he gave others training in scientific management as sales managers at another of his company's schools.

In February 1939 Xu opened at Shanghai the Guangcheng Professional

School for Advanced Pharmacy (Guangcheng gaoji yaoxue zhiye xue-xiao), named after his father, Xu Guangcheng. Xu ran the school entirely within New Asia, appointing himself as chairman of its board, his partner Zhao Rudiao as its president, and his longtime chief pharmacist, Liu Buqing, as its dean.[49] Although Xu intended that this school, like New Asia's research laboratories, should raise the standards of pharmaceutical medicine in China, he did not invest in it for purely altruistic reasons. He did not require its graduates to take jobs at New Asia, but he counted on them to promote the company's medicines wherever they were employed. As Xu spelled out this rationale, "We knew that it would cost our company a substantial amount of money to run a private professional school. But we also felt that it was very important for our company to have a basic rank and file. We called the graduates trained by ourselves our 'Army of Sons and Brothers' [*zidi bing*], and we counted on their loyalty." Xu thus inculcated loyalty in his pharmacy students as ardently as in his salesmen, referring to them as members of his "Army of Sons and Brothers," the same militaristic expression that he used to describe his sales organization.[50]

In retrospect Xu expressed satisfaction that the graduates of this school fulfilled his expectations, and it seems likely that they did. After all, upon completing their professional education within his company, they were deeply in his debt, and as they fanned out and took up posts in China's leading pharmacies, they were inclined to promote New Asia's medical products.

While training pharmacists with the expectation that they would informally promote New Asia's products, Xu also trained middle managers with formal responsibility for marketing these goods. Xu had founded New Asia's Staff Training Institute to teach recruits "scientific management" at Shanghai in early 1937, and during the war he appointed Chinese graduates of this institute as managers of New Asia's elaborate, four-tiered marketing system on a national and an international scale. At the top Xu presided from New Asia's Shanghai headquarters over a commercial empire that pushed beyond its prewar borders to encompass all of China proper (excluding the Northeast), Tibet, Ningxia, Qinghai, Xinjiang, and seven Southeast Asian countries. At the second level were ten branch companies (six in China and four in Southeast Asia), each responsible for distribution in a sales region *(yingye qu)* that covered between two and five provinces in China or a country in Southeast Asia (Table 5.2). At the third level each sales region was divided into subregions, with an office *(banshichu)* managing distribution in each subregion. And at the fourth level each subregion was divided into smaller territories, with an agency *(dailichu)* handling local distribution.[51]

From Shanghai Xu sent "posted representatives" *(zhuwai daibiao)* to manage this organization. He assigned them the task of recruiting local merchants to handle New Asia's goods at all levels, but he did not leave supervision to them alone. To monitor them and local merchants, he regularly dispatched from Shanghai teams of inspectors *(fangwen yuan)*, and according to the confidential minutes of the meetings of New Asia's board of directors, he took these on-the-spot inspections very seriously.[52] On February 27, 1943, for example, he made the following statement of policy, with its implied threat: "Every Saturday the General Promotion Office must report on the inspectors' work to the general manager [Xu himself], who may personally review an inspector's work at any time."[53]

During the war New Asia's sales force continued to promote the company's goods as it had before the war—but now with greater intensity. It was able to achieve this greater intensity because it had not only more numerous offices and better trained staff members but also more promotional publications.

USING SCIENCE IN ADVERTISING

During the war, even as Xu recruited specialists in other aspects of his business—scientists to develop his medical products and pharmacists and distribution agents to market them—so too did he recruit editors, literary figures, and artists to promote his goods through popular publications. Even as he built New Asia's laboratories to do scientific research and trained pharmacists in science and sales managers in scientific management, so too did he call upon the magazines' contributors to popularize science and to show the compatibility between modern science and traditional Chinese culture.

In 1938 Xu set out to show this compatibility by founding the *New Voice of Chinese Medicine (Guoyao xinsheng)*, a Chinese-language monthly medical journal for practitioners of traditional Chinese medicine. Xu hired as its editor in chief Ding Fubao, a Chinese author and doctor who had become famous in China for writing books that criticized traditional Chinese medicine in light of Western biological science, even while he continued to practice traditional Chinese medicine in Shanghai. Under Ding's editorship, the magazine was given a hand-sewn binding of the traditional Chinese kind; two to four thousand copies of each issue were printed and sold at .30 yuan per copy.[54]

Through this journal Xu sought to convince traditional Chinese doctors that New Asia's products were based on a kind of science that would serve traditional Chinese medicine as well as modern Western medicine. In this task Xu had to overcome traditional Chinese doctors' anti-Western bias, which had been deepened by their fierce rivalry with Chinese advocates of purely Western-style medical science since the 1920s. Keeping his distance from this dispute, Xu convinced both sides to buy New Asia's goods. As he later recalled, "At the time, [Chinese] Western-style doctors and [Chinese] Chinese-style doctors didn't mix any better than fire and water. . . . As for those of us selling medicine, we didn't really care whether they were Chinese-style or Western-style doctors or which side they were on. We sold to them all."[55]

Besides introducing this new medical journal, Xu also continued to publish his prewar medical journal, his drug catalogues, and his popular magazine, *Healthy Home,* which became his most effective advertising weapon of all.[56] During the war Xu converted *Healthy Home* from a quarterly (which it had been before the war) into a monthly, and he personally dictated editorial policies for promoting sales by popularizing science.

In this magazine Xu's point of departure was the meaning of its title, *Healthy Home,* which he redefined for his own purposes. In the prewar period Chinese intellectuals had originally borrowed the term "health" (*jiankang*) from Japanese and had used the phrase "healthy home" to show the fundamental incompatibility between traditional Chinese values and modern Western values.[57] These intellectuals had argued that the traditional Chinese extended family was "unhealthy" because it was based on outdated and oppressive Confucian notions of filial piety, and they had proposed that it be abolished in favor of the Western-style nuclear family, which, they said, was "healthy."[58]

During the war Xu reacted against this usage and proposed his own definition. "'Healthy' [*jiankang*]," he pointed out on page one of *Healthy Home*'s issue for November 1940, "is made up of two Chinese characters, *jian* and *kang: jian* as in *jianquan,* meaning sound and perfect, and *kang* as in *kangle,* meaning healthy and happy. So a healthy home [*jiankang jiating*] describes a family in which all the members are leading healthy and happy lives because they are sound and perfect in mind and body."[59] By associating health with happiness rather than with liberation from oppressive extended families, Xu thus rejected modern Chinese intellectuals' prewar critique of Confucian filial piety and identified health as a modern scientific idea that was compatible with traditional Chinese values.

Throughout the war Xu sustained his campaign to give new meaning to the term "healthy home." Writing in *Healthy Home* in May 1944, he attacked modernizing Chinese intellectuals for claiming that traditional filial piety and the modern healthy home were not compatible. "Nowadays some self-styled 'modern people' who aspire to distinguish themselves from the rest of us claim that filial piety is an obsolete idea and should be abandoned," Xu observed. But these modernizers were wrong, Xu insisted, because filial piety was "an important Chinese tradition" that should be preserved and adapted to meet the demands of the modern world. He admitted that "old thinking" and "big families" were inherited burdens, but he argued that these problems from the past would solve themselves, disappearing of their own accord as Chinese parents learned to "reproduce eugenically, raise children scientifically, and teach children rationally." Even in a fully modern world of the future, Chinese should continue to value filial piety, he maintained. "Otherwise people will have no moral standard to follow."[60]

Xu did not formulate this new definition of the healthy home as an end in itself. He used it as the basis for campaigns to popularize his magazine and New Asia's goods in wartime China. In editorials he attacked *Healthy Home*'s authors for divorcing science from the traditional Chinese values manifested in everyday life. His magazine *Healthy Home*, he complained in 1940, had too closely resembled "a specialized journal devoted to scholarly discourse," and he proposed that it should become "a magazine for family reading." He wanted no more writing on "solemn" and "heavy" topics. Instead, he called for writing that was "vivid," "lively," and "engaging." Xu urged anyone submitting a piece for publication to address problems within families, with children, and between the sexes, and to "construct the model healthy family," whose solutions could be adopted by readers in their own families.[61]

Xu laid down editorial policies that called on authors to combine science with family life and thereby popularize science with a broad audience. His insistence on this point was evident in the first two editorial policies that he unveiled in 1940:

1. Our magazine will provide our readers with the most up-to-date information on science, education, and health care.

2. Our magazine will be an excellent source of leisure reading that is good for women and children.[62]

These policies showed Xu's determination to make science popular, and during the war these policies were carried out quite fully.

Between 1937 and 1945 numerous contributors to *Healthy Home* wrote pieces that popularized science and showed its compatibility with traditional Chinese family values. In almost every issue of the magazine, authors called on parents (especially mothers) to raise children scientifically, instill traditional filial piety, and achieve these goals successfully and productively by applying the science of home economics (Figure 5.3). In one article, "Science and the Family," New Asia's pharmacologist, Zeng Guangfang, urged *Healthy Home*'s readers to create "the scientific family," which was to be achieved by using science ("the greatest achievement of the West's material civilization") as a means of preserving traditional Chinese family values ("the greatest achievement of China's spiritual civilization").[63]

Among popularizers of these ideas were both nonfiction writers, who gave simple explanations of science with easy-to-follow instructions, and fiction writers, who included members of China's best-known school of popular literature, the Mandarin Duck and Butterfly school. This group has been regarded as resisting change and never innovating—upholding "pre-Western norms and stay[ing] within traditional literary styles," in the words of the literary critic Perry Link—but some Mandarin Duck and Butterfly writers were more adaptable than has been supposed, and the ones who published in *Healthy Home* closely conformed to Xu Guanqun's editorial policies.[64] For example, one of the most famous Mandarin Duck and Butterfly writers, Chen Diexian (Tianxu Wosheng), contributed a piece to *Healthy Home* on the need to conduct scientific "family experiments" for practical purposes such as extracting soda from ashes, refining salt, and salvaging nutrients from burned or spoiled rice.[65]

While these writers used prose to popularize science for the family, commercial artists used visual representations to do the same. During the war New Asia's advertising department employed more than ten painters, including the pioneer cartoonist Ding Song (1891–1972), who in 1927 had founded China's first organization of cartoonists.[66] They reinforced *Healthy Home*'s editorial policies by designing appropriate magazine covers, such as the one by Ding Song showing grandparents (in traditional

Chinese long robes), parents, and children (in Western-style clothing) all living harmoniously under one roof, listening to a radio, reading a newspaper, sitting on overstuffed furniture, and enjoying the pleasures of modern life (Figure 5.4). New Asia's cartoonists also produced full-page and half-page pictorial advertisements and quarter-page cartoons for every issue of *Healthy Home* during the war. Their pictorial advertisements highlighted the scientific nature of New Asia's goods, and their cartoons proclaimed the superiority of scientific medicine and enumerated the deficiencies of "superstitious remedies" and "nonscientific medicine" (Figure 5.5). So, even if looking only at *Healthy Home*'s pictures and ignoring its words, anyone picking up the magazine was able to receive Xu Guanqun's message.

During the war Xu invested heavily in these writers, commercial artists, and other Chinese intellectuals who contributed to New Asia's promotional publications. In 1940, for example, he allocated for advertising 500,000 yuan, which represented 16.6 percent of the company's total capital at the time. He used this money to produce advertising and organize performances in several different media: posters, window displays, neon signs, commercials (on slides) in movie theaters, and mobile libraries; traveling teams of basketball players, martial arts performers, and harmonica players; and radio programs, including "blitzes," in which New Asia monopolized a station as the sole sponsor for twenty-four hours at a time.[67]

In all these media Xu identified New Asia's medical science with Chinese popular culture, and through another vehicle, free clinics (*zhenliaosuo*), he identified New Asia's medical science concretely with wartime conditions. In Shanghai between 1939 and 1945 Xu built ten of these free clinics, all named after New Asia (New Asia Free Clinic No. 1, New Asia Free Clinic No. 2, and so on), and additional ones in Yangzhou, Fuzhou, and other cities and towns. On each clinic's sign New Asia associated itself with the Red Cross and public health by showing a red cross inside the Chinese character for Asia (*ya*), and it printed its own name and trademark in bold characters, leaving no doubt about who deserved all the credit for this scientific contribution to the Chinese struggle for wartime survival.[68]

PRESENTING MEDICINE AS SCIENTIFIC

In all these ways Xu Guanqun achieved success for New Asia in wartime China and Southeast Asia by presenting its goods as scientific. Did Xu's marketing strategy distinguish him from his predecessors in China? A comparison between his marketing of New Asia's goods as scientific and Huang Chujiu's marketing of Ailuo Brain Tonic as Western shows continuities as well as discontinuities. Xu differed from Huang in the extent to which he gave substance to his advertising claims. Contrary to Huang's implicit if not explicit claims, Ailuo Brain Tonic did not come from the West or derive from any Western pharmacology; it was "Western" only in its appearance (style of packaging and advertising). By contrast, Xu's goods were scientific in their contents, which were formulated and tested by professional scientists in New Asia's sophisticated laboratories. The efficacy of both Huang's and Xu's medicines is difficult to evaluate because these entrepreneurs (and the others that are described in this book) kept their formulas secret, but it seems safe to conclude that Xu's investments in research and development produced goods that were scientific by the standards of the time or were at least more scientific than any of Huang's medical products.

It would be a mistake, however, to overdraw the contrast between Xu's and Huang's marketing of medicine. Like Huang, Xu took advantage of print media to promote his goods, and compared to Huang, he exploited these media more fully by founding medical journals, drug catalogues, and a popular health magazine—all publications that pharmaceutical companies were forbidden to own under conflict-of-interest laws in the West at the time. Like Huang, Xu did not allow legal prohibitions or moral scruples to prevent him from making remarkably broad claims for his products; he stopped short of calling them cure-alls (as Huang called his) but went almost that far. Moreover, Xu did not stop short of deliberately misleading consumers when he stamped "Made in Japan" on his Chinese-made goods and imprinted a red cross on his trademark to identify his products with the Western-based Red Cross and medical science from the West. More subtly, again like Huang, Xu did not adopt a Western idea in promoting his goods without first adapting it to make it seem less foreign and more familiar to Chinese consumers. Even as Huang had made "Western" medical ideas seem compatible with the traditional Chinese theory of Yin Orbs and Yang Orbs, so, too, did Xu make "scientific" values seem compatible with the traditional Chinese family value of filial piety. So Xu differed from Huang insofar as he more fully made good on his claims about the contents of his medicines, but Xu closely resembled Huang in his identification of his goods with the West and in his imaginative reinterpretation of Western medical science to make it seem compatible with traditional Chinese thought.[69]

Xu's business strategy served him well during the war, but at its end he was afraid that he would be charged with treason for collaborating with Japan. So in 1945, after remaining at his Shanghai base throughout the war, he fled to Hong Kong. In retrospect he claimed that he could have returned to Shanghai without any risk if he had been able to raise the money needed to bribe the Nationalist intelligence service (*juntong*) when its agents contacted him in Hong Kong in 1945. Be that as it may, even though the Nationalist government did not bring charges against him, he remained in Hong Kong until 1950. Only then, after the founding of the People's Republic, did he return to Shanghai, preside over New Asia's transition to socialism, and write his memoirs. Subsequently, even though he lived in Shanghai as a citizen of the People's Republic of China and witnessed massive campaigns in which capitalists were denounced and punished for profiteering and treason during the Sino-Japanese War, he proudly recorded his wartime achievements as though he still had the unreconstructed mentality of a fixer. Perhaps he was unguarded about his capitalist past because he wrote most of his memoirs during a brief hiatus between two major mass campaigns—the Great Leap Forward, which ended by 1961, and the Socialist Education Campaign, which began in 1963. For whatever reason, he produced a remarkable record of his life as a wartime fixer before he died in 1972 at the age of seventy-three.[70]

Fixers across Enemy Lines

This chapter is based on extraordinary and perhaps unique memoirs, and, in the absence of comparable records, it might well be difficult to document the careers of other Chinese fixers in such detail. Nonetheless, Xu's case is suggestive because it raises questions about the general assertion that Shanghai was stripped of its scientific and cultural resources and cut off from its long-distance trading opportunities during the war.

As noted earlier, James Reardon-Anderson has observed that Chinese industrialists who had joined together with scientists to conduct research and development before the war fled from Shanghai and other coastal ports during the war. In his comprehensive survey of chemistry in Chinese history, Reardon-Anderson discovered only a few Chinese industrialists who "recognized the connections among research, development, and industrial growth" before the war, and he concluded that the "separation in experience and training of China's academic and industrial researchers persisted down to 1949."[71]

If so, then Xu Guanqun distinguished himself as one of the few Chinese who recognized the connections among research, development, and industrial growth, and he overcame the separation between academic and industrial researchers to an impressive extent during the war. He opened laboratories, staffed them with scientists, and took advantage of their research and development in his production of medicines. In addition, he established a pharmacy school to train druggists who were expected to prescribe his medicines in their shops. Xu's recruitment and retention of medical scientists and pharmacists between 1937 and 1945 indicate that he employed more of them during the war than he had done in the prewar period, and his record provides evidence that Shanghai did not lose all its scientific elite to a wartime brain drain.

If Xu's record shows that wartime Shanghai was not devoid of Chinese scientists, it also shows that the city was not devoid of Chinese journalists, writers, and cartoonists. In documenting the work of sojourning Chinese journalists, writers, and cartoonists who left Shanghai during the war, Chang-tai Hung has drawn the inference that their departures deprived Shanghai of its central place as a producer and distributor of Chinese culture. "In the 1930s," Hung has acknowledged, "Shanghai . . . had nearly monopolized the country's learning and publishing to an even greater extent than did Paris in France, . . . [and it] became a pacesetter of modern popular culture." He also has conceded that when the war ended in 1945 "most bookstores and newspapers returned to coastal cities [particularly Shanghai]." But between 1937 and 1945, he has concluded, the war "caused the rapid fading of the urban, elitist character of Chinese culture. . . . The 'ruralization' of Chinese culture had commenced. . . . The War of Resistance . . . created a new political culture that shifted China's attention to the countryside."[72]

Hung's conclusion concerning the fading of Shanghai-centered urban culture, the advent of ruralization, and the shift of China's attention to the countryside is problematic if this account of Xu Guanqun's wartime publications is any indication. Xu published the work of well-known journalists, writers, and cartoonists in his Shanghai-based medical journals, catalogues, and health magazine, and he not only continued but expanded the distribution of these publications from Shanghai throughout China and Southeast Asia during the war.

It would be premature to dismiss Reardon-Anderson's and Hung's well-documented conclusions on the basis of the businesses, scientific research, and publications operating under this single figure, Xu Guanqun. But the possibility that Shanghai continued to be an influential scientific and cultural center during the war seems worthy of further investigation because recent research has shown that it continued to be a dominant commercial center at the time. According to Lloyd Eastman, Shanghai "was the chief supplier of goods traded in the Nationalist area" during the war, and in the Nationalist area, "millions of men engaged in trade, and goods as diverse as tungsten and toothpaste, sheep's wool and vacuum bottles, automobile tires and opium, passed from one side to the other."[73] Eastman's assertion that Shanghai conducted long-distance trade with wartime China has been greatly elaborated, documented, and refined in recently published essays by Brian Martin, Allison Rottmann, and Frederic Wakeman.[74] Their findings and mine suggest that it would be wrong to assume that Shanghai was commercially inert and isolated as a "solitary island" under partial Japanese occupation between 1937 and 1941 and as a wholly occupied city under the Japanese between 1942 and 1945. By the same token, it would also be wrong to assume that Shanghai was scientifically and culturally inert and isolated during these wartime years.

For that matter, Shanghai was not the only city that continued to serve as a dynamic center for marketing goods across enemy lines during the Sino-Japanese War. Some Chinese entrepreneurs established headquarters for long-distance trade in China's other cities, and others set up bases in Southeast Asian cities. Within this latter group, the one that marketed medicine most widely during the war was the maker of Tiger Balm, Aw Boon-haw.

6

Crossing National Borders

> Aw Boon Haw was a collaborator during the Japanese occupation, whose
> activities were freely advertised and who bought his way back into favor with
> the Kuomintang Government in China after the war. At the end of 1948, the
> Hong Kong Police obtained reliable information that he was attempting to
> come to terms with the Communists and at the same time his chain of news-
> papers showed a strong leftist tendency. . . . He is a man of no principles who
> will side with any party he thinks most likely to serve his own interests.
>
> Franklin Gimson, governor of Singapore, to A. Creech Jones, secretary of
> state for Britain's colonies, September 22, 1949

In this top-secret memorandum, Governor Franklin Gimson made his case
to his superiors in London for banning an overseas Chinese entrepreneur,
Aw Boon-haw, from the British colony of Singapore. To the press Gimson
announced that he banned Aw strictly because of pro-Communist pro-
nouncements in Aw's newspapers, but in this secret memorandum he
revealed his "real reasons," as he put it. In 1949 he barred Aw's reentry into
Singapore (where Aw had maintained a home and business since the
1920s) because he could not stand to let Aw go unpunished for his long-
standing record as "a man of no principles" during the Sino-Japanese War
of 1937–1945, the Chinese Civil War of 1946–1949, and the early years of
the cold war.[1]

Whether Aw was guilty of treason is open to debate (as is implied by
Gimson's decision not to make his accusations public), and Gimson's
claim that Aw "bought" his way into political favor, even if valid, begs the
question of how Aw acquired the wealth and influence needed to buy
what he wanted from heads of state such as Generalissimo Chiang Kai-
shek in China and Prime Minister Tojo Hideki in Japan in the 1930s and
1940s. A quarter century earlier, in 1908, on the death of his father, Aw

and his brother had inherited nothing more than one small traditional Chinese medicine shop in Rangoon, Burma—a family-owned, family-operated business, the Hall of Everlasting Peace (Yong'an Tang), with its distribution confined to the local market. Aw's father had migrated from Yongding county, Fujian Province, in Southeast China, to Rangoon but had never entered international markets or distinguished his business from thousands of other small traditional Chinese herbal medicine shops operating at the time in Asia.

How did Aw, with these unpromising prospects at age twenty-six in 1908, end up dealing face-to-face with heads of state in the 1930s and 1940s? To say (as Gimson does) that Aw "bought" his way into power is an oversimplification. Perhaps by tracing the rise of Aw's commercial empire it will be possible to explain more fully how he became able to win over Chiang Kai-shek, Tojo Hideki, and other East Asian political and military leaders.

Riding the Tiger

In 1909, less than a year after inheriting his father's business at Rangoon, Aw (Figure 6.1) took a trip to Hong Kong, China, Japan, and Thailand and made discoveries about media and marketing that proved to be vitally important to his eventual success in business and politics. He financed the trip by using his mother's inheritance of two thousand yuan. He set out to renew contacts with his father's suppliers of herbal medicines, but along the way he noticed Western and Western-style drugstores, and he saw how Western businesses overcame cultural barriers by appealing to Asian customers through eye-catching packaging, posters, and other visual media. He was particularly fascinated by a German-owned drugstore in Japan, and he visited it again and again to observe Japanese consumers and figure out why they were willing to pay more for Western pharmaceuticals than for traditional Chinese medicines. On his return home Aw instructed his younger brother (who, unlike himself, had attended British schools and learned English in Rangoon) to translate the labels on the packages that he had bought abroad.[2] From this point of departure, he conducted experiments in visual advertising, beginning with a trademark that was destined to become famous as the logo for Tiger Balm.

DESIGNING THE TIGER BALM TRADEMARK

It is not clear whether the recipe for Tiger Balm was invented by Aw Boon-haw (as he claimed) or by his father (as other members of the family have claimed), but it is clear that Aw Boon-haw invented the tiger trademark *(hu shangbiao)*.[3] Tiger Balm (as it is called in English) has the name Ten Thousand Golden Oils (Wanjin you) in Chinese, but beginning in 1909 Aw stamped the tiger trademark on it. Since then he and his business successors have done the same on all their ointments, pills, powders, and tonics.[4]

Throughout his career Aw maintained that he selected the tiger as a symbol because it appeared in his own name. (Aw Boon-haw's full name is pronounced Hu Wenhu in Mandarin, and his given name—Boon-haw or Wenhu—means "Cultured Tiger"). His parents, as immigrants to Burma from China, named all three of their sons after animals with symbolic significance in Chinese folklore. Their eldest son, Aw Boon-leng (Hu Wenlong), who died at age eighteen, was named "Cultured Dragon," and their youngest, Aw Boon-par (Hu Wenbao, 1885–1944), was named "Cultured Leopard." Aw's parents did not simply choose Aw Boon-haw's name according to the Chinese zodiac, for the year of his birth, 1882, was not a tiger year. It is probably more than coincidental that Aw's father, Aw Chukin (Hu Ziqin), owned a traditional Chinese medicine shop and had sons named for animals whose real or mythical body parts were supposedly used for ingredients in traditional Chinese medicines.

Whatever lay behind Aw's choice of the tiger for his trademark, it was probably not based on anything he had learned in school, let alone from systematic market research, for Aw had received a very rudimentary formal education, none in English and only a little in Chinese. As a family member recalled, Aw freely admitted that he was "a naughty boy and did not like to study in school," either in Burma or in his native place of Yongding county, in Fujian Province in Southeast China, where he was sent for a few years of schooling before he returned to Rangoon as a teenager to work in his father's medicine shop.[5]

And yet Aw's lack of formal education did not deprive him of a sharp eye and an impressive capacity for visual expression. According to his daughter, he designed Tiger Balm's first posters himself, and his posters all bore the trademark showing his springing tiger. Even from a distance this profile of an animal leaping through the air with its mouth open, paws reaching out, ears back, and tail extended was clearly recognizable as a tiger (Figure 6.2).[6] Moreover, Aw's springing tiger had the potential for transcultural appeal because it was purely visual (with language inscribed only on the trademark, not the tiger's body), and Aw exploited this potential by recruiting some of Asia's leading commercial artists to paint tigers for distribution across national borders in his advertising campaigns.

RECRUITING ARTISTS

Perhaps the most transnational and transcultural artist Aw recruited was a commercial painter named Guan Huinong (Kwan Wai Nung, 1880–1956), who was based in Hong Kong (Figure 6.3). Even Guan's ancestors were transnational and transcultural artists. The most famous of them was his great-grandfather, Guan Zuolin, who modeled his work after a Macao-based British artist, George Chinnery, and, using the name "Lamqua," exhibited his Western-style paintings in London, New York, and Boston during the mid-nineteenth century. Guan's father and grandfather were also well-known artists, and they trained Guan as a Western-style painter.[7]

In 1912, at the age of thirty-two, Guan Huinong moved from Hong Kong to Shanghai to become a member of the Lingnan School of painting. The founders of this school, two brothers named Gao Qifeng and Gao Jianfu, were Cantonese (like Guan), and they had studied painting in Japan. They were already famous for their paintings of tigers, notably Gao Qifeng's *Roaring Tiger* (1908) (Figure 6.4). Soon after Guan Huinong joined them, the three became cofounders of the Lingnan School's most significant publishing venture, a Shanghai-based Chinese-language magazine titled *True Face Pictorial (Zhen xiang huabao)*, with an English subtitle, *The True Record*. To promote it they prominently featured illustrations of tigers on its cover and in its pages (Figure 6.5).[8]

Guan learned about tiger painting from the Gao brothers, but he utilized their techniques to produce tigers for very different purposes. The Gao brothers were political revolutionaries who joined fellow Japan-educated Chinese students in helping to overthrow the Qing dynasty and establish the Republic of China in 1911, and they painted ferocious, snarling tigers as emblems of Chinese nationalism. In the words of Ralph Croizier, the Gao brothers' tiger paintings conveyed an "emotional appeal or even allegorical message about China's need for boldness and bravery."[9] In 1913 Guan decided to part company with the Gao brothers. By then he had worked with them for one year, which ended with the collapse of their magazine.[10] Returning to Hong Kong, he painted tigers for Aw Boon-haw.

Guan adopted the Gao brothers' techniques in designing posters for Tiger Balm (Figure 6.6). Like the Gao brothers, he used shading and cast shadows to give his paintings depth. Like them, he gave his subjects a modern look—in this case by seating a beautiful young Chinese woman at a Western-style easel, giving her a job as a commercial artist with a Western-style brush in her hand, and turning her and draping her arm over her chair in a Western-style pose so that she looks directly and provocatively at the viewer. In all these features Guan followed the Gao brothers' example by identifying his subject with a Western-style modernity.

And yet, compared with the Gao brothers, Guan set a very different tone. He dressed the young woman in a silk gown with a delicate lace collar, and he placed on her wrist a watch (at the exact center of the poster), making her fashionable and identifying her with the most up-to-date commodities of her time. On her painting (within his painting) Guan unmistakably replicated Aw Boon-haw's springing tiger—a commercial logo rather than a political symbol—and, insofar as he linked this tiger with any ideals, they were acquisitiveness and beauty, not boldness and bravery. Instead of exhorting his viewers to campaign for Chinese nationalism, Guan implied his allegiance to Pan-Asian transnationalism and transculturalism in the banner across the top, which gave the name of the Tiger Balm company in more than one language—English and Thai as well as Chinese characters and romanized Chinese.

After returning to Hong Kong in 1913, Guan began distributing his commercial art across national boundaries. He opened his own firm, the Asiatic Litho Printing Press (Yazhou shiyin ju), and before long he reached out from this base in Hong Kong to add branches in the British colony of Singapore and the Chinese cities of Guangzhou and Shanghai. He also expanded his staff, and at his peak in the 1930s he was capable of producing a new calendar-poster advertising painting (*yuefenpai guanggao hua*) every four or five days. As a result, he became known in Hong Kong as the King of the Calendar Poster (*yuefenpai wang*).[11]

Besides commissioning commercial artists like Guan, Aw conducted campaigns to find out what consumers imagined a tiger looked like. In the mid-1920s, for example, he publicly announced an open contest in which all comers—amateurs as well as professionals—were invited to submit paintings of tigers. To the winning contestant he offered a prize of one thousand dollars in Singapore currency and a promise that the design would appear on his Tiger brand medicines' annual calendar poster, which was lithographed and widely distributed as a gift to businesses and customers. Once the results were in, he chose as the winning entry a painting of a glamorous woman snuggling up to a regal tiger, and he featured it on Tiger Balm's annual calendar poster, as he had promised.[12]

TRANSCULTURAL TIGERS IN INTERNATIONAL MARKETS

With images of the tiger in hand, Aw Boon-haw personally carried his goods and advertising outside Burma into international markets. In his first forays as a traveling salesman, he became aware that posters and billboards had a social stigma attached to them—they were seen as vulgar eyesores that defaced the landscape—but he never let this stigma stand in his way. To avoid confrontations with his critics, he sneaked out to put up posters at night, when he would not be seen.[13] As his business grew, he and his staff covered more and more ground, and they broke into markets in the colonies and countries of Southeast and East Asia by using advertising to overcome cultural barriers.

Wherever he sold his goods, he had the tiger trademark stamped on them in Chinese. In China he confined the language on his advertisements to Chinese, but outside China he by no means restricted his appeal to consumers who were literate in Chinese. On the contrary, he emblazoned the name of his product on posters and billboards not only in Chinese but also in whatever language was used in the local market (such as Thai in Thailand). In colonies he went so far as to include the local colonial language as well as the vernacular. For example, he printed his advertisements for the British colony of Burma in Burmese and English, for the British colony of Malaya in Malay and English, and for the Dutch colony of the East Indies in Indonesian and Dutch.[14] Thus did Aw attempt to overcome language barriers through multilingual advertising.

Aw's use of multiple languages is striking, but even more striking is his minimal use of any language. What language appeared on his outdoor advertising generally gave little more than the names of his products, and the words were dwarfed by the images, especially of the tiger. Aw's emphasis on visual images over written words was evident in a wide range of outdoor media. Besides putting up posters and billboards, he erected towers, pavilions, and entrance arches (modeled after Chinese memorial arches), and he covered office buildings with paintings or gargoyles of the tiger and topped them off with statues or banners of the tiger—all in bold colors.[15]

In his advertising Aw used audible appeals along with visual ones. He formed marching bands that played Western-style musical instruments and carried Tiger Balm banners. He organized parades of marchers wearing tiger suits who chanted and set off firecrackers to attract crowds. He had tiger cars custom made in Germany with black and orange stripes, hood ornaments in the form of tiger heads, and horns that roared like tigers. Thus equipped, these cars led promotional caravans around cities and into outlying towns and villages. With their horns roaring, they attracted crowds, and in their wake three-ton tiger trucks dispensed free samples of Tiger Balm and other Tiger brand medicines.[16]

Perhaps Aw's most enduring advertising medium was Tiger Balm Gardens, known in Chinese as Tiger Villa (Hu bieshu) or Tiger and Leopard Villa (Hu Bao bieshu) (Figure 6.7). From the beginning he conceived of the gardens as promotional devices to increase sales of his medicines, and he carefully selected the sites for them in Hong Kong and Singapore.[17] In 1931 he recruited as his designer Kwek Hoon Sua, a Chinese rock carver from Shantou, in Southeast China, and Aw himself personally supervised construction of the gardens in both Hong Kong and Singapore.[18] As early as the 1930s—twenty years before Walt Disney founded Disneyland in the United States—Aw began to attract tourists to his amusement parks. By the time of his death in 1954, Aw had constructed a total of twenty-six castles in Asia.[19]

Within Tiger Balm Gardens Aw built his own homes, and he identified the tiger with his personal life, making himself and members of his family into walking advertisements. He wore a jacket with a tiger embroidered on the pocket, carried a pocket watch with a tiger on its face, and nicknamed all his sons "Tiger": Tiger Number One, Tiger Number Two, Tiger Number Three, Tiger Number Four (Dahu, Erhu, Sanhu, Sihu).[20]

Aw Boon-haw's concern for visual media suggests that he sought to overcome cultural as well as national market barriers. His initial attraction to visual media is perhaps traceable to his limited education and his preference for visual rather than literary expression. But after his trip throughout Southeast and East Asia in 1909, he seems to have embraced visual media not merely as a personal preference but also as a strategy for overcoming language barriers, and subsequently he made use of this strategy by introducing his trademark, recruiting commercial artists, and producing and distributing outdoor advertising across national borders in a wide variety of media. Whereas Aw's image-oriented strategy was designed to overcome language barriers, his use of multiple languages in outdoor advertising served the same purpose. All these techniques were meant to attract non-Chinese as well as Chinese consumers, no matter what languages they did or did not read.

TIGER BALM'S MULTICULTURAL CONSUMERS

Without more detailed data on Tiger Balm's consumers, it is not possible to quantify their market shares by nationality or ethnic group, but anecdotal evidence suggests that consumers from more than one ethnic background not only consumed Aw's goods but also embraced and reinterpreted his advertising.

Overseas Chinese identified Tiger Balm as a Chinese medicine and evaluated it in the context of Chinese popular culture, according to Lynn Pan, a specialist on the history of overseas Chinese. In Pan's words, Tiger Balm consisted of "little more than a mixture of menthol, camphor, clove oil, peppermint oil, cassia oil, and cajuput oil, bound together by wax and petroleum"; it was at best "an effective rub," but "it was popularly believed that the ointment, seen by many to be a cure-all embodying some of the tiger's legendary qualities, contained one or more parts of the animal's anatomy, ground up and mixed in with the rest of the ingredients."[21] If Pan is right, then overseas Chinese consumers made their own addition to the appeal of Tiger Balm beyond the claims in Aw's advertising, for he did not assert (or deny) that Tiger Balm contained "parts of the animal's anatomy."

By contrast with overseas Chinese, Thai consumers considered Tiger Balm to be Southeast Asian and gave it a nickname in Thai: "Ya Maung" (Maung's medicine). In the Thai vernacular, Maung is a humorous and somewhat derisive name for any Burmese man—a mild ethnic slur—so this designation identified Tiger Balm not with China but with Burma (where it in fact originated in the Aw family's shop at Rangoon).[22] Other Southeast Asians who were not of Chinese descent were also attracted to Tiger Balm because of their own beliefs associating the tiger with healing powers, according to the Southeast Asian specialist Robert Wessing. After surveying a rich body of ethnographic literature on the use of the tiger's body parts in amulets, medicines, and aphrodisiacs by Southeast Asians from various ethnic backgrounds, Wessing has suggested that "the tiger as a symbol for curative power may account for the popularity of Tiger Balm in this part of the world."[23]

In general, Aw probably sold more Tiger Balm to overseas Chinese—the largest minority population in most Southeast Asian cities and towns by the 1920s and 1930s—than to other consumers in Southeast Asia.[24] But members of other ethnic groups also bought his product, responded to his advertising, and endowed it with their own meanings. In other words, Aw left his advertising open to multiple interpretations, making the tiger a floating signifier that readily crossed language barriers and took on different meanings in different local cultures.

Introducing Tiger Balm in Rangoon in the midst of multilingual and multicultural Southeast Asia during the 1910s, Aw had every reason to advertise through visual media and appeal to consumers of varied linguistic and cultural backgrounds. But in the 1920s he set his sights on China's market and moved his headquarters from Rangoon to Singapore (whose population was three-quarters Chinese).[25] In expanding and reorienting his business, Aw continued to make a transcultural appeal through visual media, but he also began to invest in a monolingual print medium: Chinese-language newspapers.

Rising Stars

Between 1929 and 1938 Aw Boon-haw founded eleven Chinese-language newspapers in Southeast Asia and China, and he popularized them with extraordinary speed. He used "Star" *(xing)* as the first character in the name of almost all his newspapers, and his Star newspapers shot to the top of their respective newspaper markets. By 1938, for example, his *Xingzhou Daily,* established at Singapore in 1929, had the largest circulation of any Chinese-language newspaper in Southeast Asia; his *Xinghua Daily,* founded in 1931 at Shantou, along the South China coast, had more subscribers than all Shantou's other six newspapers combined; and his *Xingguang Daily,* opened at Xiamen in 1935, delivered copies to several cities in Southeast China and outsold all the other newspapers in Fujian Province. Why did Aw invest heavily in newspapers and how did he make them popular? He made the decision to become a newspaper publisher and to promote his newspapers on a grand scale after fighting an advertising war in newspapers during the early 1920s.

THE WAR BETWEEN THE TIGER AND THE BUDDHA

Before moving to Singapore and starting his first newspaper, Aw Boon-haw discovered the possibilities for newspaper advertising in a battle for the Asian medicine market with an overseas Chinese rival, Wei Shaobo. A Cantonese based in the Vietnamese port of Saigon, Wei had begun manufacturing a medicine named Two Heavens Oil (Ertian you) under a label showing a smiling Buddha in 1905, four years before Aw had taken out a trademark for his similar product, Tiger Balm. Between 1905 and 1920 Wei used more than one language in his advertising and distributed his medicine in more than one colony of Southeast Asia, but his marketing complemented rather than conflicted with Aw's because he concentrated on the French colonies of Vietnam, Cambodia, and Laos, whereas Aw was preoccupied with the British colonies of Burma, Malaya, and Singapore and the Dutch colony of the East Indies. As a result, their businesses were not in serious competition before 1920.[26]

In 1920 Aw and Wei began to compete directly with each other in newspaper advertisements in ports along the South China coast, and their initial skirmishes quickly escalated into the Advertising War between the Tiger and the Buddha *(hu fo guanggao zhang)*, as it was called. Wei made the first move, launching an aggressive campaign for his medicine outside Southeast Asia in the newspapers of the British colony of Hong Kong, the Portuguese colony of Macao, and the Chinese city of Guangzhou. Aw took Wei's campaign as a challenge and began to run competing advertisements in the same newspapers. Further escalating the war, Wei proceeded to take out advertisements in more and more newspapers, eventually reaching well beyond Southeast Asia and South China throughout China—all the way to Shenyang in Northeast China (also known as Manchuria). Wherever Wei ran newspaper advertisements, Aw did the same, always making his advertisements bigger than Wei's.[27]

In 1925, with the two businesses running attack ads against each other, the battle reached fever pitch and caused political leaders to intervene. Wu Tiecheng, formerly chief aide to Sun Yat-sen and a leading figure in the Nationalist government, then based at Guangzhou, urged Aw and Wei to suspend their war during the mourning period following Sun's death in March 1925. It was unseemly, he complained, for Aw's and Wei's spectacular newspaper advertisements to overshadow the coverage of the tributes paid to Sun. Wu criticized not only Aw and Wei but also the newspaper publishers for greedily seeking advertising revenues and "keeping an eye out for money," rather than showing proper respect for Sun, the Father of the Republic of China.[28]

Aw and Wei agreed to no more than a brief cease-fire in their advertising war, and they later resumed the fighting, which continued in China into the late 1920s and early 1930s.[29] But by 1925 Aw, like the political leader Wu, became outspokenly critical of newspapers for their high advertising rates. In particular he was outraged by bills for more than one million yuan in Shanghai alone for the year 1925, and he vowed on the spot to cut his advertising costs by opening his own newspaper. Since he was in the process of moving his headquarters to Singapore at the time, he applied for a license to start a newspaper there.[30]

POPULARITY AT THE EXPENSE OF PROFITS IN SINGAPORE

Aw Boon-haw's first newspaper set the pattern for all his others. He started publishing it at Singapore in 1929, and he named it *Xingzhou Daily* (*Xingzhou ribao* in Mandarin and *Sin Chew Jit Poh* in the romanization used by the newspaper itself). It made a spectacular entrance into Singapore's market because Aw spared no expense in promoting it. From the outset he faced formidable competition from numerous other Chinese-language newspapers (with the oldest, *Le Bao,* dating from 1881). His rival above all others was the city's only other major Chinese-language commercial newspaper, *Nanyang Commercial News* (*Nanyang shangbao* in Mandarin and *Nanyang Siang Pau* in the newspaper's own romanization). The *Nanyang Commercial News* probably served as a model for Aw's newspaper. It had been founded in 1923 by one of the colony's leading Chinese entrepreneurs, the rubber magnate Tan Kah-kee (Chen Jiageng). Even as Tan had used his *Nanyang Commercial News* to advertise his Bell brand rubber shoes and tires, so did Aw proceed to use his *Xingzhou Daily* to advertise his Tiger brand medicines.[31]

In the very first issue of *Xingzhou Daily* Aw unveiled a powerful weapon in his commercial arsenal: underpricing. Whereas his competitors all sold their newspapers at a price of ten cents per copy (in Singapore currency), Aw put *Xingzhou Daily* on the newsstands at the price of eight cents. Charging this lower price plunged *Xingzhou Daily* into the red financially but made it popular within its first year. By the end of 1929 Aw absorbed losses totaling thirty thousand Singapore dollars and captured more than one-third of the market. Its circulation was seven thousand; all Singapore's other Chinese-language newspapers combined had a total circulation of thirteen thousand.[32]

Despite *Xingzhou Daily*'s financial losses in its first year, Aw subsequently continued to spend freely on it for the sake of increasing its popularity. In 1930, its second year, he enlarged it from sixteen to twenty pages and cut its subscription price by 50 percent for schools and other civic organizations and by 80 percent for individuals who had taken it for six months or more. In the same year he brought out *The First Annual Xingzhou Daily Yearbook (Xingzhou ribao yizhounian jinian kan)*, the first Chinese-language yearbook ever published in Singapore, and he distributed it to *Xingzhou Daily*'s regular subscribers free of charge. Apparently imitating the format of the *London Daily Mail*'s popular English-language yearbooks, he devoted its contents to Southeast Asian subjects and included seven hundred pages of articles, photographs, and pictures.[33]

In 1932, *Xingzhou Daily*'s fourth year, Aw gave consumers still more incentives to become subscribers by introducing a Sunday supplement and a morning edition, neither of which had ever previously appeared in Singapore. His Sunday supplement was four pages long and contained sections on business, sports, women, and the arts, in addition to special reports on international news and local issues.[34] He sent it to *Xingzhou Daily*'s subscribers at no additional charge, and, by delivering the new morning edition before noon, he scooped all the other Singapore newspapers, which had only evening editions delivered after six o'clock. He briefly published the morning edition in place of the evening edition, but he soon made *Xingzhou Daily* even more appealing by restoring its evening edition and providing its subscribers with both editions for the price of one.[35]

Using these techniques, Aw Boon-haw steadily boosted *Xingzhou Daily*'s popularity. By 1933 he pushed its circulation up to 10,000 and by 1937 to 60,000–80,000, which made it the best-selling Chinese-language newspaper in Southeast Asia.[36]

POPULARIZING NEWSPAPERS OUTSIDE SINGAPORE

As Aw Boon-haw extended his newspaper empire outside Singapore, he continued to give priority to popularity over profits, and he recruited and trained a staff to start and run newspapers similar to Singapore's *Xingzhou Daily* in other Southeast Asian and Chinese cities. To establish his newspapers, he did not hire people with experience in journalism. Instead, he relied on managers who were members of his social network—Chinese bound to him by family ties, native-place connections, and Hakka minority-group status.

In showing these preferences, Aw resembled other Chinese merchants and industrialists, including manufacturers of medicine. Like them, he groomed members of his family to be his successors, and like them, he had more than the one reason for trusting associates from his native place: they spoke the same local dialect; they knew members of each other's families or lineages; and, even if they lived outside their Chinese native place or outside China (as Aw did), they planned to retire to their native soil (as Aw did).[37] Accordingly, they expected each other to be trustworthy for the sake of protecting the family's reputation in their native place.

In Aw's case his native-place orientation was reinforced by the fact that virtually everyone from his native place was a Hakka (which literally means "guest families"), a Chinese ethnic minority group that had retained its own language and customs as it had migrated over a period of several centuries and had come into conflict with Han Chinese in various parts of China and Southeast Asia, particularly during the nineteenth and early twentieth centuries.[38] Perhaps because of this double bond—a combination of native-place ties and Hakka status—Aw pursued the policy of drawing upon his social network for personnel at all levels of his business. His practices along these lines have been noted by more than one Chinese commentator and have been described firsthand by a Chinese newspaper reporter who worked for Aw's newspapers in Singapore and Penang during the 1930s:

> In his employment policies, Aw Boon-haw preferred to recruit people from his native place of Yongding [in Fujian Province] or people who spoke Hakka dialect. The headquarters and branch stores of the Hall of Everlasting Trust [which produced Tiger Balm] and the "Star" newspapers hired quite a number of Hakkas. . . . Almost all the managers of the Hall of Everlasting Trust's branches and "Star" newspapers were Hakkas from Fujian Province. In 1938, when I was in Singapore, [all the managers and staff members] of the *Xingzhou Daily* were natives of Yongding county. Most of the employees in the medicine plant and newspaper were Hakkas, so Hakka was used as the spoken language in both businesses. In 1939, when I moved to Penang, I found that staff members in the Hall of Everlasting Trust branch office from the top manager down to the lowest clerk were all

Hakkas from Yongding. . . . On the [Penang] newspaper, about half of the staff members and workers were Hakkas from Fujian or Guangdong Province. So when people in Penang talked about Aw Boon-haw's Hall of Everlasting Trust and *Xingbing Daily,* they would say, "It's a Hakka world" [*kejiaren de shijie*].[39]

In retrospect, Aw's dependence on "a Hakka world" and the priority he gave to family and native-place ties over education and experience might seem likely to have limited the scale of his operations, but at the time it did not prevent him from lengthening the chain of his newspapers outside Singapore.

In founding newspapers outside Singapore, Aw relied heavily on his immediate family members, especially his sons, but he entrusted the most responsibility of all to a more distant relative, Aw Chu-chew (Hu Zizhou). Aw Boon-haw's relationship with Aw Chu-chew illustrates how the managers of "Star" newspapers were bound together. Like almost all Aw Boon-haw's top managers, Aw Chu-chew shared with Aw Boon-haw the surname of Aw, hailed from Aw's home village (Zhongchuancun, Yongding county, Fujian Province, in Southeast China), and was a Hakka.[40] Aw Chu-chew lived in Yongding county until 1928, when, at the age of twenty-three, he fled from a local conflict, the West Fujian Insurrection, in which he had participated on the Communist-led losing side, and ended up in Rangoon seeking Aw Boon-haw's help. Although the two men had not previously met, Aw Boon-haw gave Aw Chu-chew refuge in his home, and they became extremely close.[41]

Placing full trust in Aw Chu-chew, Aw Boon-haw trained him as a manager at *Xingzhou Daily* in Singapore and then dispatched him to China to open additional branches and newspapers that were modeled after the ones in Singapore.[42] In 1931 Aw Chu-chew launched Aw Boon-haw's first China-based newspaper at the port city of Shantou (Swatow), on China's southeastern coast. Aw Chu-chew became its head, named it *Xinghua Daily* (*Xinghua ribao* in Mandarin and *Sin Hwa Jit Pao* in its own romanization), and appointed as editor-in-chief Luo Tiexian, another Hakka from Yongding county who had been his high school classmate. They in turn recruited to the newspaper's staff still more Hakkas from Yongding. Once this staff had been put in place, Aw Chu-chew invested heavily in up-to-date printing presses and began boosting circulation in Shantou as Aw Boon-haw had done in Singapore. By 1937 *Xinghua Daily* had twelve thousand subscribers—more than were taking all Shantou's other six newspapers combined.[43]

In 1935 Aw Boon-haw transferred Aw Chu-chew and Luo Tiexian from Shantou to Xiamen (Amoy), in Fujian Province, where they once again assembled a staff consisting of Hakkas from Yongding, founded a newspaper, and spent freely to make it popular. They named this newspaper *Xingguang Daily* (*Xingguang ribao* in Mandarin and *Sin Kwong Jit Pao* in its own romanization), and they housed it in Xiamen's tallest building, a five-story mansion, which Aw Chu-chew bought for one hundred thousand yuan. He then installed new German-made printing presses that were valued at two hundred thousand yuan and were capable of producing newspapers at the rate of four thousand sheets per hour. On September 1, 1935, he began publishing *Xingguang Daily* at twelve pages per issue in a morning edition every weekday. Following the precedent set by Aw Boon-haw's Singapore newspaper, he provided a Sunday supplement (in this case two pages long) at no expense to regular subscribers, and he added an evening edition under the name *Xingxing Evening News* and delivered both editions to regular subscribers for the price of one.

In Xiamen, as in Singapore, Shantou, and other cities, Aw Boon-haw's newspaper immediately attracted a following and became the local favorite. Using its own trucks, Aw's publishing firm distributed its newspapers in not only Xiamen but also Fuzhou, Quanzhou, and other nearby cities and towns, and it boosted its circulation to ten thousand, the largest of any newspaper in Fujian Province in the 1930s.[44]

Aw Boon-haw captured all these newspaper markets in China and Southeast Asia by operating at a loss. In 1938 he remarked, without regret, "The many newspapers that I have founded have cost me no small amount of money every year," and the evidence bears him out.[45] By then he had started eleven newspapers in seven Southeast Asian and Chinese cities, and his losses on them the following year were $250,000 in Singapore currency. To make up these deficits, he routinely drew upon profits from sales of Tiger Balm and other Tiger brand medicines.[46]

Aw Boon-haw did not simply allow these losses to occur by default. On the contrary, he actively pursued a marketing strategy in which losses on his newspapers were a key component. He once explained this strategy to Yu Dafu, a leading Chinese literary figure whom he was recruiting as a staff writer. In 1938, at a welcoming dinner honoring Yu in Singapore, Aw confessed that his goals as a newspaper publisher were neither purely patriotic nor wholly separate from his goals as a seller of medicine. "The first goal of my newspapers is, of course, to serve the interests of our country. But frankly speaking, I also intend to use them to advertise my Tiger brand medicines. We Hakkas have a saying: If a tailor wants to make a pair of trousers for his wife, he doesn't buy the cloth himself—he uses leftover cloth that his customers have brought him to make their clothes. So in making my own advertisements, I don't want to buy space myself—I want to use leftover space in my newspapers."[47] This Hakka saying is apt to the extent that Aw sold advertising space in his newspapers to other businesses—even other medicine companies, as long as their products did not compete directly with his own—and he used the remaining space for advertising his own products. But his image of "leftovers" should not obscure the fact that he set aside for his own products the lion's share of advertising space in his newspapers. He advertised his Tiger brand products to the exclusion of all other commodities on pages where news stories appeared, and he filled more than half of his newspaper's total advertising space with advertisements for his own goods.[48] Packing his newspapers with these advertisements, Aw used them as weapons for capturing medicine markets in the Chinese diaspora as well as China.

TRANSNATIONAL NEWSPAPERS AND NETWORKS

Since Aw's newspapers were published exclusively in Chinese, he was not able to use them to promote Tiger Balm and other medicines on a transcultural basis in Southeast Asia as broadly as he did through image-oriented and multilingual outdoor advertising. But if he did not make his newspapers transcultural, he certainly made them transnational. He envisioned a plan for establishing newspaper offices and Tiger Balm's business offices side by side in all the major cities of Southeast Asia and China, and he carried out this plan to a remarkable extent before the outbreak of the Sino-Japanese War of 1937.[49]

In the Chinese diaspora of Southeast Asia, Aw established branch offices for Tiger Balm in several cities and deployed newspapers that were strategically positioned to support them. In 1925 he moved his headquarters to Singapore and in 1929 started three newspapers there. In the islands of Southeast Asia, as he proceeded to add branch offices for his medicine business in Java and Sumatra in the 1930s, he advertised by exporting his newspapers from Singapore. Similarly, in mainland Southeast Asia he exported his newspapers from Singapore to the British colonies of Burma

and Malaya, and in 1939 he founded another Chinese-language newpaper
at Penang in northern Malaya. In short, his newspapers reached all the
major markets of island and mainland Southeast Asia except French
Indochina, where his rival, Wei Shaobo, was based (Table 6.1).

In China and Hong Kong Aw also opened newspapers in conjunction
with branch offices of his medicine business. In 1929 he established a
branch office at Hong Kong for South China, and within the next decade
he introduced two newspapers in the region: *Xingyue Daily* in nearby
Guangzhou in 1934 and *Xingdao Daily* in Hong Kong in 1938. In 1931 he
started *Xinghua Daily* at Shantou before setting up a branch office of his
business there three years later. In 1935 he opened *Xingguang Daily* at Xiamen, and in the same year he added a business office at the nearby city of

Table 6.1. Aw Boon-haw's Business and Newspaper Offices in Southeast Asia
through 1937

Location	Sales territory	Year established	Approximate annual revenue from sales of medicine
Singapore	Headquarters	1925	
Xingzhou Daily		1929	
(60,000–80,000 circulation)			
Xingzhong Daily		1935	
Batavia (Jakarta)	Java and South Sumatra	1933	Over one million guilders
Penang	North Malaya	1934	Several million Singapore dollars
Xingbing Daily		1939	
Medan	North and West Sumatra	1935	Several hundred thousand guilders
Surabaya	East Java	1937	Several hundred thousand guilders

Sources: Li Fengrui and Wang Dong, *Hu Wenhu pingzhuan* (Shanghai: Huadong
shifan daxue, 1992), 34–36; Chen Danxin and Li Fengrui, "Hu Wenhu fengyun lu,"
Hu Wenhu yanjiu 1 (1985): 17; Hu Zhifei and Chen Danxin, "Hu Wenhu dashiji," *Hu
Wenhu yanjiu* 2 (1987): 14; Li Fengrui, "Hu Wenhu zai kangri zhanzheng shiqi," *Hu
Wenhu yanjiu* 3 (1988): 3; Laopai jizhe, *Hu Wenhu fada qushi* (Macao: Yuzhou, 1960)
48, 53.

Fuzhou. Also in 1935 he established a branch office in Chongqing in the Upper Yangzi region, and within two years he began publishing *Xingyu Daily* in that city. He refrained from opening newspapers to go along with branches for his medicine business only in China's biggest metropolises (Shanghai, Tianjin, Hankou), which were already served by numerous newspapers (Table 6.2).

Table 6.2. Aw Boon-haw's Principal Business and Newspaper Offices in China through 1937

Location	Sales territory	Year established	Approximate annual revenue from sales of medicine
Shanghai	Lower Yangzi	1929	5 million yuan
Hong Kong *Xingyue Daily* (Guangzhou)	South China	1929 1934	1 million Hong Kong dollars
Shantou *Xinghua Daily* (12,000 subscribers)	South and Southeast China	1934 1931	20 million yuan
Hankou	Middle Yangzi	1934	1 million yuan
Tianjin	North, Northeast, and Northwest China	1934	1 million yuan
Fuzhou *Xingguang Daily* (Xiamen) (10,000 subscribers)	Southeast China	1935 1935	Several hundred thousand yuan
Chongqing *Xingyu Daily*	Upper Yangzi	1935 1937	Several hundred thousand yuan

Sources: Li Fengrui and Wang Dong, *Hu Wenhu pingzhuan* (Shanghai: Huadong shifan daxue, 1992), 34–36; Chen Danxin and Li Fengrui, "Hu Wenhu fengyun lu," *Hu Wenhu yanjiu* 1 (1985): 17; Hu Zhifei and Chen Danxin, "Hu Wenhu dashiji," *Hu Wenhu yanjiu* 2 (1987): 14; Li Fengrui, "Hu Wenhu zai kangri zhanzheng shiqi," *Hu Wenhu yanjiu* 3 (1988): 3; Laopai jizhe, *Hu Wenhu fada qushi* (Macao: Yuzhou, 1960) 48, 53.

ASIA-WIDE REACH

As the data in these two tables indicate, by 1937 Aw's business operated internationally on a large scale. Based in Southeast Asia at Singapore, he registered his highest sales of medicine in the colonies of Southeast Asia and South and Southeast China, but he also achieved considerable success in other, more distant regions of China, notably the Lower, Middle, and Upper Yangzi and North China.

After the Sino-Japanese War broke out in 1937, Aw's business continued to grow. He extended his distribution network westward from Southeast Asia to India, and in China his goods were so popular that they were used as substitutes for currency in all parts of the country—in territory occupied by the Japanese, territory under the control of Chiang Kai-shek's Chinese troops, and even across enemy lines between Japanese-occupied and Chinese-occupied territories (Map 6.1). According to Aw's cousin who was manager of Aw's branch in Chiang Kai-shek's capital of Chongqing during the war, Aw generated more than two billion yuan in total annual sales revenue from his medicines during the wartime years of 1937–1945. This era was, in the words of Aw's cousin, Tiger Balm's "golden age."[50]

Aw also published newspapers during the war. Although some of his newspapers were shut down by successive Japanese invasions and occupations (in Shantou and Xiamen, 1937–1945, and in Hong Kong, Singapore, and Penang, 1941–1945), he continued to operate *Xingyu Daily* in Chongqing, and in Hong Kong he opened a new newspaper, *Xiangdao Daily* (*Xiangdao ribao* in Mandarin and *Heung Tao Jit Pao* in his own romanization). Both were published throughout the Pacific War, 1942–1945.[51]

Thus did Aw Boon-haw create a business empire that was transnational (extending throughout China and Southeast Asia) and transcultural (reaching other consumers in Asia besides Chinese). His empire was based on cultural media and commercial networks rather than government institutions or military forces, but it was substantial, and it gave him a solid basis for dealing face-to-face with leaders of the Chinese government and the Japanese empire.

Making Politics Pay

In the 1930s and 1940s Aw Boon-haw met with political and military leaders who were at odds or even at war with each other. And yet, in nearly every case, he negotiated successfully with them. He gained what he

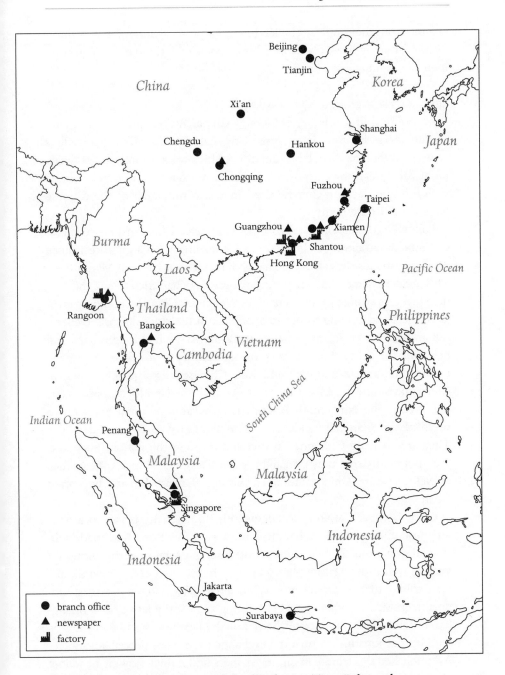

Map 6.1. Aw Boon-haw's network for distributing Tiger Balm and newspapers, 1930s. Map by Thomas Lyons.

wanted from them not by challenging their political and military authority but rather by shrewdly turning his contacts with them to his own commercial advantage.

CELEBRATING GENERAL CAI TINGKAI

With political and military leaders in China, Aw adopted a two-phase strategy. First, he ingratiated himself by making a donation to a leader's cause, and then he turned his donation to his own advantage by publicizing it for advertising purposes.[52] In an early example, he experimented with this approach on General Cai Tingkai, commander of the Chinese Nineteenth Route Army.

Following the Japanese takeover of Northeast China in 1931, General Cai quickly attained celebrity status by leading the Chinese resistance against a Japanese attack in the Shanghai Incident of January–March 1932. This incident had begun when the Japanese navy had tried to end the Chinese protests against Japan's seizure of Northeast China by bombing civilian targets and landing troops in Shanghai. In the city's defense, General Cai and his troops in the Nineteenth Route Army had fought back and held out for thirty-three days, showing bravery that was widely celebrated and publicized in Aw's and other Chinese-language newspapers in China and Southeast Asia at the time. As the historian Lloyd Eastman has observed, "The Nineteenth Route Army became national heroes as a result of the Shanghai Incident. . . . The names [of its commanders, Cai Tingkai and Jiang Guangnai] resounded through the nation. Such was their popularity that they overnight became legends."[53] In Southeast Asia as well as China, Chinese heralded this act of resistance and boycotted Japan.

Once General Cai and the Nineteenth Route Army began to attract attention during the Shanghai Incident of 1932, Aw Boon-haw made substantial donations to their cause, contributing a total of thirty thousand yuan as well as medical supplies.[54] In reply, he received from General Cai a brief tribute that read in its entirety as follows: "We had the strongest support from Mr. Aw when we were fighting against the Japanese in Shanghai. He shares with us a bitter hatred of the Japanese, and he inspires us with his patriotism." To turn the exchange to his commercial advantage, Aw published this tribute in his newspapers under the following headline: "National Hero, General Cai Tingkai, Revered by People throughout the Country, Gives His Support to Tiger brand Medicines."[55]

In thus exploiting General Cai's celebrity status, Aw Boon-haw capitalized on the most newsworthy Chinese leader of the moment. At the time
other entrepreneurs also made use of General Cai's popularity—featuring
his name in brands of cigarettes and advertisements for other goods—but
no one else put words in General Cai's mouth as audaciously as Aw did.[56]

Characteristically, Aw Boon-haw followed up and sustained his publicity beyond the fleeting events of the Shanghai Incident. In 1933, after
Chiang Kai-shek transferred General Cai and the Nineteenth Route Army
to Fujian Province, Aw published *Xingzhou Daily*'s annual yearbook under
the title *New Fujian* and devoted it to a celebration of the Nineteenth
Route Army's valiant efforts to establish a government and carry out
reforms in the province—from which many overseas Chinese families
(including Aw's own) had migrated to Southeast Asia.[57]

AIDING GENERALISSIMO CHIANG KAI-SHEK

In his relations with Chiang Kai-shek and the Nationalist government of
China, Aw followed this same pattern of first making donations to a political leader and then turning them to his advantage. In 1930, three years
after Chiang nominally unified China and set up the Nationalist government's new capital at Nanjing, Aw paid Chiang a formal visit at the
Chinese leader's official residence there, and when Chiang asked for a contribution toward the construction of Central Hospital in Nanjing, Aw
promised on the spot to cover the entire cost of 375,000 yuan.

Poised at the scene, Aw's newspaper reporters covered the meeting and
celebrated his generosity in their stories. Subsequently Aw received still
more favorable publicity because he erected a bronze statue of himself at
a cost of twenty-five thousand yuan in front of Central Hospital, and he
received a jade citation in honor of his philanthropy from the Nationalist
government. Perhaps most valuable of all for Aw's purposes was a photograph that he had taken of himself with Chiang in Chiang's home during
the meeting. Aw had large copies of the photo hung on the walls of his
own home and in the central shop of every Chinese city where his medicines were sold. When asked why he did so, he replied that he used it not
only to promote his goods but also to scare off government officials, local
thugs, and others who threatened his business or placed official obstacles
in his path.[58]

Throughout the 1930s Aw Boon-haw repeatedly invoked his friend-
ship with Chiang Kai-shek and prohibited his newspapers from criticizing

Chiang by name. After Japan seized Northeast China in the Mukden Incident of 1931, Chiang was widely denounced by the Chinese media for his policy of nonresistance.[59] Nonetheless, Aw instructed his newspapers that they should not attack Chiang in their stories and editorials. Aw's censorship in this case was striking because it was an exception to his general policy of editorial nonintervention. Although he set up the Star Newspapers Management Headquarters in Singapore in the early 1930s, he subsequently left decisions on editorial policies to each newspaper, and his newspapers became known for adopting widely varied political stances—including some that were actively pro-Communist.[60] Under Aw's decentralized organization, his newspaper editors and reporters were free to criticize anyone else, but not Chiang Kai-shek.[61]

In 1935 Aw Boon-haw once again offered philanthropic support to Chiang's government. At China's Sixth National Games, held at Shanghai in anticipation of the 1936 Olympics, Aw spoke as a sponsor of this athletic event. To the press he announced that he had pledged 3.5 million yuan over a ten-year period to finance the construction of one thousand elementary schools throughout China.

As he had with his earlier pledges, he used this one to derive favorable publicity. In this case he specified that each of the one thousand schools would be named "Aw Boon-haw Elementary School" (Hu Wenhu xiao-xue). In addition, each would have its library, laboratory, auditorium, and gymnasium named after himself and his brother (for example, Tiger and Leopard Library [Hu Bao tushuguan]), the names inscribed on prominently placed placards. Later, in negotiations with provincial officials, he promised one hundred of these schools to his home province of Fujian, fifty to each of the other southern provinces, and ten to each of the northern provinces. Between 1935 and 1937 Aw began to fulfill his promise by building two hundred of these schools at a cost of 1.5 million yuan.

When this project was interrupted by the Japanese invasion of 1937, he called a news conference to announce that he would finish the rest of the schools after the war. In the meantime, he contributed the remaining two million yuan from the school fund to the Chinese struggle against Japan by buying war bonds from Chiang Kai-shek's Nationalist government.[62] In Southeast Asia, as in China, he also built schools, hospitals, orphanages, nurseries, temples, and other charitable institutions, always specifying that his name (with the "Tiger" in it) should appear on each one.[63] For his philanthropy in British colonies he received the Order of the British Empire from King George VI in 1938.[64]

In February 1941, three and one-half years after Japan's invasion and occupation of China, Aw reaffirmed his commitment to Chiang Kai-shek with great fanfare. He flew to Chiang's wartime capital at Chongqing, in western China, where Chiang had retreated in the wake of the Japanese invasion, and he accepted an appointment as a member of the Nationalist government's National Political Assembly. Upon his arrival in Chongqing, Aw announced that he would buy five hundred thousand yuan worth of war bonds from Chiang's government and would contribute two million yuan to the government's relief fund for wounded soldiers and war refugees.

As he had in his previous meetings with Chiang, Aw again exploited the opportunity to generate favorable publicity. On his way to Chongqing he stopped in Rangoon and told newspaper reporters that Chiang had personally invited him to Chongqing and had asked him to serve as the representative of all overseas Chinese in the National Political Assembly. On his first day in Chongqing he met with Chiang and had a photograph taken of the two of them shaking hands and beaming at each other (Figure 6.8). He then left Chongqing after attending only the first day of the National Political Assembly's ten-day session. The next day he featured a photograph of himself with Chiang Kai-shek on the front page of his newspapers. Following up in characteristic fashion, Aw also published and distributed a pamphlet that publicized his trip and prominently featured the same photograph of himself with Chiang.[65]

DICKERING WITH PRIME MINISTER TOJO HIDEKI

Although Aw used his newspapers to project an image of himself as a Chinese nationalist supporting Chiang and resisting Japanese aggression, he also used his newspapers to publicize his successful negotiations with Chiang's foreign enemy, Prime Minister Tojo Hideki, the head of imperial Japan's wartime government. In March 1943, at the height of the Pacific War, Aw granted an interview to a reporter from his new Hong Kong newspaper, *Xiangdao Daily*, and announced his plans to see Tojo in Tokyo. Fifteen months earlier, in December 1941, when Japan's military forces had bombed Pearl Harbor and launched their invasion of almost all the countries of East and Southeast Asia, Aw Boon-haw had been in Hong

Kong and had been placed briefly under house arrest by the Japanese military. But within a few months he had regained control of his business, reopened his medicine factory in Singapore, and built a new factory in Hong Kong. By 1943 he was doing a booming business under the Japanese occupation.[66]

In anticipation of his trip to see Tojo in 1943, Aw reminisced nostalgically about his visit to Japan as a young man more than thirty years earlier, and he credited Japan with success at winning the respect of "white men" throughout the early twentieth century. Lamenting China's failure to do the same, he drew this comparison:

> In my travels around the world and my long residence in Southeast Asia [Nanyang], I have often noticed how our own people are scorned and insulted by white men, who never treat Japanese the same way. On the contrary, they always give Japanese special privileges. Why is there such a marked difference in white men's attitudes toward Japanese and Chinese, who are all East Asians? Searching for an answer, I came to realize that it is because the Japanese have a strong state and we do not. Admiration filled my heart for the Japanese, a people I have always enjoyed befriending for thirty years. . . . The Chinese and the Japanese are brothers because they share the same culture and the same race [*tongwen tongzhong*].[67]

Later, in claiming to have been a lifelong Chinese nationalist, Aw had difficulty explaining his endorsement of Japan's "strong state" and his expression of "admiration" for the Japanese people in nationalistic terms, but at the time his statement prepared the way for his visit to Tokyo.

In June 1943 Aw Boon-haw flew on a Japanese military aircraft from Hong Kong via Shanghai to Tokyo with an official invitation in hand. He was probably invited at this time because, after Pearl Harbor, Tojo had introduced new guidelines for seeking aid from non-Japanese Asian businesses to obtain raw materials for wartime purposes. As the historian Akira Iriye has summarized these guidelines, "Japan must secure resources that were essential for the prosecution of the war, prevent natural resources from reaching the enemy, ensure self-sufficiency for its armed forces throughout Asia, and try to get existing business enterprises to cooperate with the war effort."[68] Aw's invitation was delivered by an influential (and unnamed) Japanese intermediary who visited him in Hong Kong twice during the spring of 1943. On the first visit the Japanese was favorably impressed with Aw's proposal for teaming up with the Japanese in transporting surplus rice from Burma, Thailand, and Vietnam to South China, which suffered from a rice shortage. On the second visit the Japanese intermediary officially invited Aw to meet with Tojo for a discussion of Aw's proposal.[69]

On his arrival in Tokyo, Aw was given accommodations in the Japanese prime minister's official guesthouse and was ushered into an audience with Tojo. According to the official Japanese transcript of their conversation, Tojo initially responded to Aw's proposal by making a proposal of his own. He urged Aw to use Tiger Balm's business network to extract from unoccupied China materials such as tungsten, cotton, and tung oil, which Japan would find useful for military purposes. Aw replied that it was "impossible to secure those materials from inland China and transport them here [to Japan] while there were no relations between your government and the government [of Chiang Kai-shek] at Chongqing."[70]

Despite his rejection of Tojo's proposal, Aw won the prime minister's endorsement of his own plan for transporting rice from Southeast Asia to South China under Aw's management and on steamships supplied by the Japanese government. In support of this plan, Aw said, "I'll exert what little influence I have to help bring people relief. I can't bear to see Chinese people suffer without doing something." For his part, Tojo promised that he would supply the steamships and that he would, in Tojo's words, "instruct everyone concerned to provide for your convenience."[71] Before they parted, Aw expressed admiration for a tiger skin hanging on the wall of Tojo's residence and mentioned his own affinity for tigers, as the manufacturer of Tiger Balm and other Tiger brand medicines. Seeing Aw's keen interest, Tojo promptly took down the tiger skin and presented it to Aw as a gift.

In June 1943, on Aw's return from Tokyo to Hong Kong, he published an article in his *Xiangdao Daily* under the title "Why I Visited Tokyo." Aw maintained that he had been an advocate for the Chinese people and had urged Tojo to alleviate rice shortages, restore Chinese organizations, lift a ban on overseas Chinese remittances to China, and improve Hong Kong's government under the Japanese occupation. Though Aw's newspaper presented his views in a favorable light, other newspapers attacked him, accusing him of collaboration with the Japanese and calling upon Chiang's Nationalist government to arrest him for treason.[72]

Aw was not arrested, and he intended to carry out his plan for transporting rice from Southeast Asia to South China, but it proved to be unfeasible because of the threat of American bombing in the South China Sea. Despite this limitation, Aw took advantage of Japanese support for his management of the rice trade between Hong Kong and the Pearl River delta in South China. In particular, he worked closely with a Japanese liaison officer named Chiba, who remained on favorable terms with Aw throughout the war and during the postwar period.[73]

At the end of the war, Aw Boon-haw once again used his newspapers to recast himself in the image of a Chinese nationalist who had unwaveringly resisted Japan and supported Chiang Kai-shek. In December 1945, four months after Japan had surrendered, Aw told reporters from his Hong Kong newspaper *Xingdao Daily* (which had recently reopened for the first time since 1941) that he had never been convinced that Japan's leaders could implement the Greater East Asia Co-prosperity Sphere because "Chinese believed that China could never perish, and the Thais and Burmese (and Indians) were not willing to cooperate with the Japanese." He had "risked his life" traveling to Tokyo and seeing Tojo during the war because he had been "enraged by the arrogant and domineering behavior of Japanese, who treated Chinese like slaves," and he had told Tojo to "take immediate action against such outrageous behavior." Aw said that he had urged Tojo to go in person to Chiang's wartime capital of Chongqing and to negotiate a peace in which "Japan had to make an immediate withdrawal of all troops from China without leaving a single soldier behind." When Tojo had declined to do so, Aw had returned to Hong Kong with renewed determination to relieve the suffering of wartime Chinese. With this aim, he had established the Zhongqiao Trading Company to transport rice from Guangdong Province in China and from Southeast Asia to starving people in China, and he claimed to have operated it at a loss of 40 million Hong Kong dollars during the war.[74]

In postwar interviews Aw maintained that he had been consistently loyal to Chiang Kai-shek during the war. Despite threats from Japanese interrogators, he had steadfastly insisted that "Mr. Chiang Kai-shek is the only legitimate leader of our country." As further evidence of his loyalty, he told this anecdote:

> I have always covered the walls of Haw Par Villa [Aw's mansion in his Tiger Balm Gardens in Hong Kong], the office of *Xingdao Daily*, and the headquarters of the Hall of Everlasting Peace [which manufactured Tiger Balm and other medicines] with photographs of me taken with officials of the

central government [of Chiang Kai-shek]. When a group of Japanese offi-
cers paid visits [during the war], they asked me why I had left these pictures
hanging. I replied, "Maybe you don't like them, but they are my old
friends, and I have a right to hang pictures of my old friends." I suppose
that my home and newspaper office were the only places in Hong Kong
where huge pictures of Chairman Chiang Kai-shek remained on display
[during the war].

After telling the press of his tenacious loyalty to Chiang and his defiant
attitude toward the Japanese authorities during the war, he said it was
ironic and outrageous that anyone would consider charging him with
treason. The British government, he pointed out, rescued and repatriated
its citizens who had survived the Japanese occupation, but "those of us
[Chinese] who survived the occupation are labeled 'dupes' [*shunmin*] or
'collaborators' [*weimin*]. What a tremendous difference!"[75] At the end of
the war, Aw Boon-haw's name did not appear on the Nationalist government's list of wartime traitors, although the name of one of Aw's sons,
Aw Swan (Hu Shan), did appear on the list until another of his sons, Aw
Kow (Hu Hao), intervened and had it removed.[76]

APPEALING IN VAIN TO THE PEOPLE'S REPUBLIC

In the 1930s and 1940s, while attentive to Chiang and Tojo, Aw did not
overlook the Chinese Communists. During the Sino-Japanese War of
1937–1945 he made financial contributions to the Communists' war effort
against Japan, met with Communist leaders such as Zhou Enlai and Ye
Jianying, and made use of the favorable publicity that the Communists
had given him in news releases from their New China (Xin Hua) News
Agency. Subsequently, during the Chinese Civil War of 1946–1949, Aw
continued to remain open to both the Nationalists and the Communists,
leaving some of his newspapers aligned with one side and some aligned
with the other.[77] But after Mao and the Communists triumphed over
Chiang and the Nationalists in 1949, Aw was not able to continue business
as usual in the People's Republic of China.

In 1950 and 1951 Aw made every effort to win over the new government of China. In the spring of 1950 he tried to exploit his old contacts by
appealing directly to Ye Jianying, his fellow Hakka and a Cantonese, who
by then had become vice chairman of the Military and Administrative
Commission of Central and South China and chairman of its Committee

on Finance and the Economy. In three successive letters Aw repeatedly contrasted the success of the Communist government's economic policies with the failure of the Nationalist government's past economic policies, especially at fighting inflation. "Previously the Nationalist government's past economic policies caused uncontrollable inflation, which was tantamount to depriving people of their property," Aw wrote from Hong Kong to Ye in Beijing, apparently making his bid to be classified positively as a member of the "national bourgeoisie" rather than negatively as an "enemy of the people," in the Communist leaders' terminology of the early 1950s. "I have always considered it my obligation to help our people . . . so I sincerely endorse the new government's new policies, which will relieve the people from the hardships of inflation." At the same time, Aw instructed managers of his branches in Guangzhou, Shantou, and Xiamen to obey the government's new regulations, pay new taxes, and buy new government bonds. In 1951 he made his single grandest gesture, sending one of the Aws from Hong Kong to Guangzhou to buy government bonds worth 300 million yuan.[78]

Despite these efforts, Aw did not prevent his business from being shut down in China. In 1950 he was officially branded a "reactionary capitalist" (*fandong zibenjia*) for having supported Chiang Kai-shek and the Nationalist government and for having collaborated with Japan's wartime government. All his newspapers and all the branch offices of his medicine company in China were confiscated by the governments of the provinces in which they were located, and his personal property in his native place was taken over by the government of Fujian, his native province. A year later, in July 1951, even his hopes for exporting to China were dashed when the central government in Beijing banned Tiger Balm and all Tiger brand products from the country.[79]

Angry and incredulous, Aw never forgave the Chinese Communists for dismantling his business and cutting him off from China's market. In 1951 he made a series of speeches, saying that he could not understand why the leaders of the People's Republic were hostile to him.[80] Shortly thereafter he abandoned his lifelong policy of giving his newspapers managerial autonomy and editorial latitude. In the early 1950s all the newspapers in his "Star" chain became vehemently anti-Communist—"the most anti-Communist newspapers in Southeast Asia," according to a report at the time from United Press International.[81]

Outside China Aw found governments more accommodating. As we saw at the beginning of this chapter, he was banned from Singapore by the British governor in 1949, but he succeeded in having the ban lifted within three months, and in the early 1950s he invested heavily in Southeast Asia, expanding his existing network of Tiger Balm branches and newspapers in Singapore and Penang and adding new ones in Jakarta, Rangoon, Bangkok, and Sarawak.[82] In 1953 Aw visited Chiang Kai-shek in exile at the Nationalist government's new capital in Taipei and found that his old ally was receptive. Aw pledged to support Chiang, and on the same trip he promoted Tiger Balm in Taiwan.

In the 1950s Aw's Tiger brand medicines and newspapers survived the loss of the China market, and they continue to operate on a large scale today, but in his final days Aw remained obsessed with the People's Republic's unwillingness to come to terms with him.[83] While in a Boston hospital for a stomach operation, he told a reporter from the *Boston Globe*, "There is no room for compromise with the Communists. There are only two alternatives: we conquer them or they conquer us."[84] A few weeks later, in September 1954, Aw died at the age of seventy-two.

AW'S EFFECTIVENESS AGAINST STRONG GOVERNMENTS

In all these cases Aw dealt with governments that were strong, according to several political historians' evaluations. By 1910 (just as Aw was making his start) Western colonial governments in Southeast Asia were so powerful that, in the words of Carl Trocki, they had already integrated "the overseas Chinese into the global capitalist system."[85] As early as 1927 Chiang Kai-shek's Nationalist government began forcibly extracting wealth from Chinese capitalists, and in the 1930s and 1940s it greatly extended its control over Chinese-owned businesses, imposing comprehensive state capitalism, in the view of several historians.[86] During the Sino-Japanese War of 1937–1945, Japan's military imposed its authority on businesses in China and elsewhere in the empire.[87] And in the early 1950s the People's Republic cracked down on Chinese capitalists most decisively of all, especially in carrying out the Five Antis campaign of 1952, the year after Aw's goods were banned from China.[88]

If powerful Western, Chinese, and Japanese governments in Asia supposedly intervened in Chinese businesses and imposed their authority on Chinese capitalists, what is the explanation for Aw's success at evading official intervention and even benefiting from his relations with governments? Aw's case suggests that political historians might have underestimated Chinese entrepreneurs' capacities for dealing with governments. Aw's record does not provide a basis for reversing their verdict and concluding that businesses unilaterally dictated political and military decisions to governments, but it does suggest that government-business interaction was a two-way process. Aw's effectiveness in official negotiations and his success at turning philanthropic donations, influential media, and social networks to his own commercial advantage show that even as governments acted on him, so too did he act on them.

In trying to understand this process of government-business interaction, it might be helpful to adopt the distinction that the political scientist Joseph Nye has drawn between the "hard power" of political authority and military forces and the "soft power" of commercial enterprises and cultural media. Aw lacked hard power, but he built up an arsenal of soft power, and he used it, as possessors of soft power generally do, for the purpose (in Nye's words) of "getting others to want what you want."[89]

Exploiting Asian Advantages

This interpretation of Aw Boon-haw's commercial rise and political influence complicates the interpretation of Aw as "a man of no principles" who "bought" his way into political favor—the charge made by the governor of the British colony of Singapore. Aw did in fact make cash payments to Chinese leaders (the military hero General Cai Tingkai, the Nationalist leader Generalissimo Chiang Kai-shek, the provincial authorities of the newly founded People's Republic), and he did cut deals with political leaders outside China, including Prime Minister Tojo Hideki in Japan and Western colonial authorities in Southeast Asia. But Aw's effectiveness in negotiating with political leaders was not simply the result of buying them off. He also exercised leverage over them because he had the capacity to protect them from criticism on the editorial pages of his widely circulated newspapers (as he did for Chiang), and he had the potential to serve their economic purposes through his far-flung distribution networks (as he declined to do for Tojo).

In evaluating Aw's use of media, it is worth noting Aw's concern for timeliness. His heavy investments in daily newspapers show his awareness of the value of transmitting up-to-date advertising to consumers as rapidly as possible. He recruited commercial artists like Guan Huinong to keep his advertising fashionable, and he relied on branch managers like Aw Chu-chew to adjust quickly to changing conditions in local markets. Perhaps the timeliness of Tiger Balm's marketing helps to explain why consumers of more than one ethnic background, Chinese and Southeast Asians alike, speedily localized its product.

All these historical figures—Aw Boon-haw, Guan Huinong, Aw Chu-chew, and Chinese and Southeast Asian consumers—deserve to be characterized as agents of consumer culture, even though they differ from agents of consumer culture as conventionally characterized in studies of Western corporations and their interactions with consumers. As a Chinese entrepreneur, Aw Boon-haw resembled Western entrepreneurs because he built up his business through marketing, just as Walt Disney did in the entertainment industry and as Ray Kroc did with McDonald's fast-food restaurants. Compared with them, however, Aw did not rely as heavily on corporate hierarchies for managing marketing; he preferred to operate through social networks based on family, native place, and Hakka minority status. As a Chinese commercial artist, Guan Huinong supplied Aw's business with advertising images in the same way that Western advertising agencies supplied Western businesses, but Guan's background and training as a Chinese artist qualified him to mediate between elite and popular taste as no Western artist was capable of doing in Asia at the time. Similarly, as a Chinese branch manager, Aw Chu-chew took responsibility for promoting sales at the local level, just as Westerners did for John D. Rockefeller's Standard Oil Company and James B. Duke's British American Company in China and Southeast Asia at the time, but his command of the Chinese language and his personal contacts enabled him to manage media (including Chinese-language newspapers) and accommodate local differences (including political rivalries) as no Westerner did at the time.

By the same token, Asian consumers of Asian-made Tiger Balm localized it in much the same way that other non-Western consumers have localized Western-made products, but they did so much faster. Whereas consumers in non-Western cultures have not generally begun to believe that Western-made goods originated in their non-Western home localities until at least one generation has passed, Asian consumers needed no such interval before claiming Tiger Balm as their own in China and Southeast Asia.[90]

These Asian figures deserve their place in the history of consumer culture for more than one reason. If they were to be included merely for the sake of historical comprehensiveness, it would be difficult to justify bothering with them. Recently a historian of Chinese art, Craig Clunas, has criticized historical studies of consumer culture for being Western-centered, and he has pointed out the dangers of this trend for specialists in non-Western as well as Western studies. In his words, "Nothing is more tedious and unproductive than for the historian of China (or India, or Mexico, or Sweden, or Morocco, or Turkey, all equally outside the ambit of 'Culture and Consumption' here) to engage in a bout of 'me-too,' or worse, 'me-first.'"[91] By comparison with Western agents of consumer culture, Asian agents of consumer culture as described here may be viewed as mere counterparts ("me-too") and as mere antecedents ("me-first"), but they also have a larger significance because they provide a basis for reconsidering why consumer culture has spread throughout the world.

5.1 Xu Guanqun

5.2 New Asia Pharmaceutical
Company's trademark with
a red cross at the center

庭家康健
HEALTHY HOME

29

Vol. 3, No. 5
August 30th 1941

Published by The Publishing Association of The Healthy Home, Shanghai, China.

第三 卷　第五期（總第二十九期）上海健康家庭出版社發行

內政部登記證警字第七〇一四五號
上海公共租界警務處登記證C字第四三三號
上海法租界政事處　特許發售
中華郵政登記認為第一類新聞紙類

南洋　傳價依當地當制幣計算
香港　傳價港幣貳毫郵費加酌
內地　傳價每冊七角港幣
上海　傳價每冊七角法幣

民國三十年八月出版

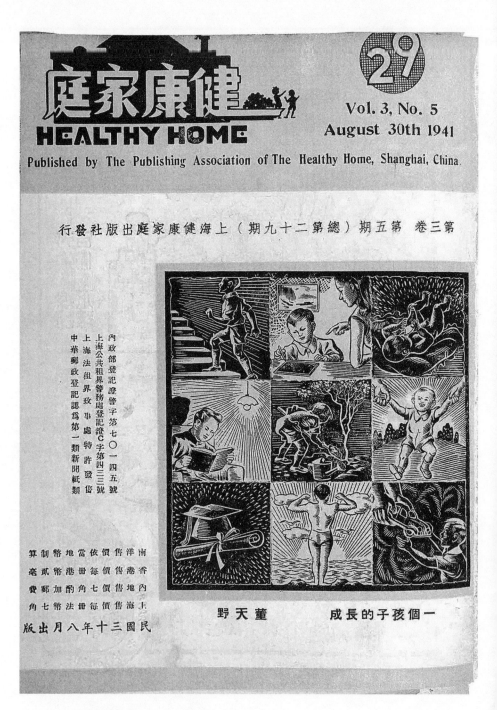

野天童　一個孩子的長成

5.3 A Child's Growth to Manhood

庭家康健

期二十一第　　卷三第

━━━━━版出社庭家康健海上━━━━━

VOL. 3 NO. 11 & 12　HEALTHY HOME　DECEMBER　1942

PUBLISHED BY THE PUBLISHING ASSOCIATION OF THE HEALTHY HOME, SHANGHAI, CHINA.

5.4 The compatibility of the traditional and the modern in a Chinese family

5.5 *Nonscientific Doctors of the Masses*

6.1 Aw Boon-haw

6.2 The springing tiger on an early twentieth-century tin of Tiger Balm

6.3 Guan Huinong, a commercial artist

6.4 *Roaring Tiger* (1908), by Gao Qifeng,
a political revolutionary

真相畫報

第十式期

THE TRUE RECORD

(ILLUSTRATED MAGAZINE)

THREE TIMES MONTHLY. VOL. 1, NO. 12

Office 45 Wu Fon Lau, Foochow Road, Shanghai.

6.5 A tiger on a magazine founded by Guan and Gao

6.6 A poster for Tiger Balm, with print in Chinese, Thai, and English by Guan Huinong

6.7 Tiger Balm Garden in Hong Kong

6.8 Aw Boon-haw with Chiang Kai-shek

7

Agents of Consumer Culture

> When within less than a decade [between the mid-1980s and mid-1990s in China] millions of people gained access to new modes of communication, new vocabularies of social discourse, and novel forms of leisure through newly commercialized outlets, it does not seem an exaggeration to claim that there was a revolution of consumption.
>
> Deborah S. Davis, *The Consumer Revolution in Urban China* (2000)

What or who have been the agents of consumer culture? As I noted in Chapter 1, this question has generated a contentious debate and has yielded two different answers. On one side of the debate are those who identify big, Western-based transnational corporations as the primary or even sole agents of consumer culture. According to proponents of this interpretation, Western corporations like McDonald's fast-food restaurants and Walt Disney entertainment industries have used mass marketing to spread consumer culture throughout the world and reshape the consciousness of individual consumers. On the other side of the debate are those who maintain that individual consumers in local cultures have been the primary agents of consumer culture. In this view, wherever big Western corporations have introduced consumer culture through mass marketing, individual consumers have transformed it through a process of localization. Ultimately these two approaches point to starkly contrasting visions—one of the world becoming ever more culturally uniform and the other of the world becoming ever more culturally diverse.

With stakes so high, it is worth reflecting on what this book might contribute to the debate over agents of consumer culture. Its most important contribution, I think, is that it has uncovered previously overlooked agents of consumer culture by turning the spotlight on Chinese history. The aim of this final chapter is to evaluate the significance of these Chinese agents by comparing them with agents in other times and places: institutions acting from the top down, consumers participating from the bottom up, and brokers mediating in between. Within this comparative perspective, it becomes possible to consider whether Chinese agents brought about "a revolution of consumption" in presocialist China comparable to the one in socialist China that is described by Deborah Davis in the epigraph.[1]

Institutions from the Top Down

Advocates of the top-down approach have concentrated almost exclusively on Western-based transnational corporations as their examples of institutions capable of spreading consumer culture. Generally, proponents of this interpretation have focused on structural features of corporations and have traced the spread of consumer culture by using a modified version of the influential model of the world capitalist system.[2] They claim that, just as capitalism originated in the West and has been diffused from the core of the system in the West outward and downward through a commercial and administrative hierarchy to non-Western peripheries of the world, so too has consumer culture been diffused. Those on the diffusion side of the debate have suggested that Western-based transnational corporations have unilaterally imposed consumer culture on consumers throughout the world.

Chapters 1 through 6 call into question the assumption that transnational corporations operating from bases in the West have been the only institutions to impose consumer culture from the top down. G. William Skinner, William Rowe, and Takeshi Hamashita have described Chinese institutions—native-place associations, guilds, informal organizations in a tributary trade system—that engaged in long-distance trade in the nineteenth century, and the findings in this book show that Chinese businesses surpassed their predecessors in pushing out the frontiers of long-distance trade and introducing consumer culture in the early twentieth century. Whereas Skinner has concluded that Chinese trade was somewhat confined within China's semiclosed macroregions during the nineteenth century, I have shown here that Chinese-owned businesses readily crossed macroregional boundaries in the early twentieth century. Rowe has described Chinese guilds that traded throughout China's land-based national market in the nineteenth century, but it is evident here that Chinese-owned businesses covered this ground and reached beyond it to capture international markets overseas in the early twentieth century. Although Hamashita has attributed the dynamism and control of China's coastal and overseas trade to a tributary trade system that ended in 1911, the businesses described here expanded and managed the coastal and overseas trade in medicine throughout the first half of the twentieth century.

On these marketing frontiers, Chinese medicine businesses introduced new cultural forms as well as new commodities. As Kaoru Sugihara has shown, as early as the nineteenth century other Asian merchants had already exploited cultural advantages in their competition with Western rivals. In his words, they had created an exclusively Asian "commodity chain" and had made a "close study of tastes and customs of local people and the identification of suitable price ranges."[3] In the early twentieth century Chinese medicine businesses exploited these same cultural advantages, and then they went further by making use of Western organizational and cultural forms: chain stores, affiliates, architectural designs, posters, billboards, newspapers, magazines, and other print media. By adapting these forms for their own purposes, Chinese-owned medicine companies surpassed Western-based transnational corporations in spreading consumer culture throughout China and Southeast Asia.

Even in wartime Chinese medicine businesses (particularly the ones described in Chapters 5 and 6) continued to operate across macroregional and national borders and steadily extended their reach. They did not oust political leaders or behave as though national governments had withered away (as advocates of the top-down approach have often asserted that Western-based transnational corporations have been able to do). Although they did not possess political authority or military might themselves, they dealt directly with Chinese, Japanese, and Western political leaders, and they used cash payments, philanthropic contributions, publicity campaigns, and commercial networks to gain approval from political leaders for the marketing of medicine across enemy lines and national boundaries before, during, and after World War II.

If we are to take into account the reach and resilience of these Chinese-owned businesses as agents of consumer culture, we must revise both the spatial and the chronological schemes that underlie the conventional Western-centered top-down approach. Spatially, a global top-down approach needs to acknowledge that institutions have produced consumer culture in more than one regional "core" of the world and have distributed it downward through hierarchies from more than one "top"—not only from New York or London in the West but also from Singapore, Hong Kong, Tianjin, and especially Shanghai in Asia.

Chronologically, a top-down approach should take into account events in East Asian as well as Western history. The most present-minded, Western-oriented commentators have dated globalization's point of origin as recently as the end of the cold war, which they set at 1989, the year that the Berlin Wall came down. Others have taken a longer view and allowed for the possibility of two eras of globalization, one under way since 1989 and the other beginning in 1870 and ending in 1914, with the outbreak of World War I in Europe. In particular, leading specialists on the history of Western-based transnational corporations have accepted 1914 as a key turning point in these businesses' integration of international markets.

In his authoritative historical survey of American, British, and German businesses between 1880 and 1945, Alfred Chandler has catalogued the sequence of events that have served as chronological guideposts marking ruptures in business history. "In the decades following 1914," he has written, "the drive for long-term profits through growth by expansion into new markets had been held back by the traumatic events of world history. The devastating First World War, followed by continuing crises into the 1920s, the Great Depression of the 1930s, the even more gigantic, global war of 1939 to 1945, and the massive reconstruction that had to follow— all these delayed the increased international and inter-industry competition that such growth made almost inevitable."[4] Chandler's richly documented book has made a strong case that these "traumatic events" held back Western businesses from expanding into new markets and integrating them, but he has perhaps overstated the global significance of such events by identifying them with "world history."

Like their counterparts in the West, Chinese-owned businesses in East Asia were repeatedly—almost incessantly—touched by political and military events (albeit different ones) in the early twentieth century: the Chinese revolution of 1911, the fall of the Qing dynasty and the two-thousand-year-old imperial system in 1912, a series of political campaigns such as the May Fourth Movement of 1919 and the Northern Expedition of 1926–1928, prolonged rivalry between Chiang Kai-shek's Nationalist government and Mao Zedong's Communist movement dating from the late 1920s, and half a century of military conflicts that culminated in the Sino-Japanese War of 1937–1945 and the Chinese Civil War of 1946–1949.

As I mentioned in Chapter 1, several Chinese historians have concluded that Chiang Kai-shek's Nationalist government exploited opportunities during some of these events—especially the Northern Expedition and Sino-Japanese War—to extract revenue from Chinese capitalists and subordinate them under state capitalism. But this conclusion does not seem to be well borne out in the history of Chinese-owned medicine businesses. In prewar and wartime China and Southeast Asia, Chinese selling medicine repeatedly evaded, overcame, or benefited from the Nationalist government's and Japanese occupying forces' interventions in their industries.

This conclusion can be reconciled to some extent with seemingly contradictory conclusions that William Kirby and Parks Coble have reached about government-business relations during the Sino-Japanese War of 1937–1945. Since my interpretation is based on a light industry (by far the largest part of China's industrial sector in the first half of the twentieth century), it does not challenge Kirby's contention that the Nationalist government came to dominate heavy industries during and after the war.[5] Similarly, since my conclusion is based on examples of Chinese entrepreneurs who readily dealt with the Japanese occupying forces, it refers to a group of entrepreneurs who, unlike the group described by Coble, showed no reluctance to negotiate with the Japanese invaders. But my interpretation does differ from theirs insofar as they have maintained or implied that Chinese or foreign governments severely restricted or totally closed down marketing by Chinese businesses during the Sino-Japanese War.

The Chinese-owned businesses that are described here continued to use their networks to manage trade and integrate markets nearly without interruption between the late nineteenth and mid-twentieth centuries. Distant from political and military events in the West and undeterred by political and military events in East and Southeast Asia, they almost all steadily expanded until the 1950s, when the government of the newly founded People's Republic began to restrict and control trade across China's macroregional and international borders, and even then these Chinese-owned firms were not permanently cut off from long-distance trade. Since the late 1970s, as Mark Selden has noted in his study of East Asia's contemporary political economy, "Informal networks . . . particularly those centering on China, involving the Chinese diaspora and cutting across borders in ways indicative of the growth of a cohesive regional economy, suggest resonances with Asia's historic tributary trade system and its associated business networks."[6]

So although Western transnational businesses were apparently held back from enlarging and integrating markets by events in the West during the first half of the twentieth century, Chinese businesses have not been so categorically held back from enlarging and integrating markets for medicine and other consumer goods by any military conflict or political intervention except one: the trading policies of the People's Republic and its cold war enemies, especially the United States, between the mid-1950s and the late 1970s.

Taken as a whole, these observations by no means amount to a refutation of the idea that consumer culture has been imposed by capitalist institutions from the top down. Instead, the point here is to call into question a top-down approach that focuses exclusively on Western-based corporations and ignores or oversimplifies non-Western businesses in regions on the "periphery." Chinese-owned businesses deserve attention because they also imposed capitalist institutions and reached from the top down in ways somewhat different from those employed by Western-owned businesses. Like Western entrepreneurs, Chinese adopted business practices that varied from one entrepreneur to another, as is evident in the various Chinese entrepreneurs' organizational innovations that are described here: Yue Daren's introduction of chain stores, Huang Chujiu's creation of advertising departments, Xiang Songmao's recruitment of locally owned affiliates as distribution agents, Xu Guanqun's construction of laboratories for research and development, Aw Boon-haw's founding of newspapers for advertising purposes. But compared to Western entrepreneurs in China, Chinese entrepreneurs as a group tended to rely more heavily on social networks that were based on family ties, native-place connections, and Hakka minority-group solidarity, especially when their businesses were in their early phases. It would be an oversimplification to say that all Chinese-owned firms reached down exclusively and continuously through social networks (even as it would be an oversimplification to say that all Western-owned firms reached down exclusively and continuously through impersonal corporate hierarchies). As I illustrated in Chapter 5, Chinese businesses selectively appropriated Western-style corporate hierarchies (even as Western businesses delegated authority to Chi-

nese social networks).[7] But it is indisputable that at one point or another
all the Chinese entrepreneurs described here made use of social networks
as a major vehicle for marketing. In fact, it is impossible to analyze the
organizational forms of their businesses without taking the distinctive features of their social networks into account.

Even as Chinese businesses reached from the top down differently from
the ways Western ones did in China and Southeast Asia, so too did businesses in other parts of the world probably reach from the top down in
their own distinctive ways. Although historians have barely begun to document the spread of consumer culture elsewhere in the world, they have
already given early indications that local businesses based in Tokyo and
Osaka, Mexico City and Buenos Aires, Istanbul, and other cities outside
Western Europe and the United States pushed out the frontiers of (their
versions of) consumer culture in their own regions.[8] Not until more is
learned about locally owned businesses in these and other regional centers will it become possible to evaluate their worldwide significance in
comparison with Western-based transnational corporations as agents of
consumer culture. But it already seems clear that anyone taking up this
subject should be mindful of a broad generalization that Peter Katzenstein and Takashi Shiraishi have made about the Asian region and the contemporary world: "regionalization and globalization appear here as
interrelated processes that cannot be analyzed in isolation."[9]

Consumers from the Bottom Up

Proponents of the bottom-up approach have generally concentrated on
geographically limited communities, interviewing local residents in a
single city, town, or village. In this fieldwork, they have found that consumers have not passively accepted or uncritically internalized the ideas,
images, forms, and discourses that Western-based transnational corporations have distributed. Using the "representations" definition of consumer
culture, they have concluded that consumers have actively reinterpreted
and selectively appropriated Western ideas, images, forms, and discourses—accepting some, rejecting others, and creating new inflections
and combinations. As the anthropologist James Watson has pointed out,
the process of localizing a foreign business requires time, usually about
one generation. The first generation of local consumers who grow up
with a Western-made product like a McDonald's hamburger recognizes

its foreign origins, he notes in the epigraph at the beginning of this book, but "by the time the children of these original consumers enter the scene, McDonald's is no longer perceived as a foreign enterprise."[10]

It is impossible when conducting historical research to match the richness of anthropologists' ethnographic data, which makes a historian yearn for the opportunity to interview the dead. Nonetheless, even in the absence of interviews, polls, questionnaires, and similar surveys from the past, the evidence in this book provides a basis for reappraising bottom-up localization and its relationship to homogenization by testing it over a longer chronological span and a wider spatial scheme than its proponents have generally done.

If evaluated over time, the examples given here suggest that Chinese consumers localized Chinese-made goods faster than foreign-made ones. As we saw in Chapter 3, they took more than one generation to localize the products of a foreign-owned business, Humane Elixir (Jintan). They readily started the process of localizing Humane Elixir by taking the mustache from the picture of the Japanese man on its logo and making it a model for Chinese men's facial hair—a fashion immortalized in the expression "Humane Elixir mustache" (Rendan *huzi*), which is still embedded in the Chinese language. But they did not complete the process of localization for at least half a century because Chinese nationalists seized on Humane Elixir as a symbol of Japanese imperialism and made it a target of anti-Japanese boycotts in the 1910s, 1920s, and 1930s; they thus provided repeated reminders of its foreign origins.

By contrast, consumers seem to have localized Chinese-made goods without delay. In perhaps the most apt example, both Chinese and Southeast Asian consumers claimed Tiger Balm as their own. Chinese believed that it came from the Chinese medical tradition and therefore jumped to the conclusion that it contained parts of a tiger's body, even though Tiger Balm's marketing campaigns did not claim (or deny) that this was so. At the same time Thai consumers assumed that it was a Southeast Asian medicine and gave it a Thai nickname (which did not appear in Tiger Balm's advertising), attributing its origin to Burma. These examples suggest that Chinese and Southeast Asian consumers unhesitatingly localized Chinese-made goods, and they show that the process of localization in China and Southeast Asia is not unique to the current era of globalization. It occurred long before globalization supposedly began, with the fall of the Berlin Wall in 1989, long before McDonald's opened its first restaurants in Hong Kong (1975), Taiwan (1984), and China (1990), and, for that matter, long before the People's Republic launched its first official campaigns to remold Chinese consumers' attitudes in the 1950s.[11]

While emphasizing that consumers have a long history of localizing consumer goods, it is also important to recognize that they have a long history of exposure to the process of cultural homogenization. In the first half of the twentieth century, as Chinese businesses aggressively used mass marketing to give the impression that their medicines were either Chinese or Western, did consumers homogenize their medical pluralism into a Chinese-Western medical dualism? Did they come to distinguish clearly between Chinese medicine and Western medicine? On these questions, this book contains little direct evidence, but it provides circumstantial evidence suggesting that the sharpness of consumers' distinctions between Chinese and Western medicines probably varied according to where they lived and worked in the urban hierarchies of China and Southeast Asia.

In Shanghai, the city at the pinnacle of China's urban hierarchy, it seems likely that consumers generally learned to distinguish between Chinese and Western medicines during the first half of the twentieth century. It was no coincidence that the biggest Chinese, Western, and Japanese businesses all tended to locate their headquarters in Shanghai, China's most central metropolis in the sense that it was the site of the largest interurban commercial flows of any city in China. Nor is it surprising that all the businesses described in this book established their headquarters in Shanghai, attempted to do so, or established larger-than-usual branch offices there. These businesses advertised intensively in Shanghai and distributed goods and advertising extensively through wholly owned branch stores at widely spaced locations in the city. Under exposure to intensive and extensive advertising campaigns, consumers probably learned to distinguish between Chinese and Western medicines in the early twentieth century not only in Shanghai's Central District but throughout the city.

At the next level of China's urban hierarchy, in cities at the cores of macroregions, consumers were not subjected to agents of consumer culture as much as in Shanghai, but the difference was only a matter of degree. Chinese entrepreneurs built wholly owned branch stores selling both traditional Chinese medicine and Western-style medicine in all nine of China's macroregions and in mainland and island Southeast Asia. Even as they constructed some of the tallest and most sensational eye-catching structures in Shanghai, they did the same in cities throughout the subcontinent: at Dalian, Tianjin, and Xi'an in China's northern macroregions; Hankou and Chongqing in the Middle and Upper Yangzi; Xiamen, Shantou, Guangzhou, and Kunming in China's southern macroregions; and Singapore, Jakarta, Rangoon, Bangkok, and Penang in Southeast Asia. Even as Shanghai's consumers were exposed to a steady stream of advertising, the same was true for consumers in other core cities. Perhaps the buildings were not quite as tall and the advertising was not quite as massive as in Shanghai, but the buildings were tall enough to break the urban skylines, and the advertising included the full array of visual media—newspapers, posters, billboards, wall paintings, towers, gates, parades, decorated cars and trucks. Moreover, the buildings were centrally located in relation to each city's population density and prominently placed at busy intersections and other transportation nexuses. With this access and exposure to consumer culture, it was probably almost as common for consumers in China's core cities to distinguish between Chinese and Western medicines as it was for consumers in Shanghai to do so during the first half of the twentieth century.

Consumers in China's smaller cities and towns had fewer opportunities to see medicine companies' tall buildings and less exposure to these businesses' advertising campaigns. But it is important to note that consumers in these places were touched by consumer culture too. Chinese-owned businesses became affiliated with locally owned shops that were located outside core cities in numerous smaller cities and towns. These affiliates were concentrated in China's most populous macroregions, and they left control in the hands of local shopkeepers, who may or may not have promoted Shanghai-based companies' goods and advertising in the ways that the companies intended. Nonetheless, especially in the heavily populated macroregions of the Lower and Middle Yangzi and North China, consumers in smaller cities and towns had exposure to packaging and advertising that gave them a clear basis for distinguishing between Chinese and Western medicines during the first half of the twentieth century.

Of all Chinese, the ones living in the villages and market towns in China's countryside had the least access to consumer culture and the fewest opportunities to observe differences between Chinese and Western medicines. Neither Chinese-owned chains of drugstores nor any other large-scale businesses opened branches or started affiliates in China's market towns and villages. And yet, even peasants were not completely cut off from consumer culture. As I mentioned in Chapter 4, in 1992 an art critic and her team of researchers found hundreds of pre-1949 calendar posters hanging on walls in the homes of peasants. For more than four decades these rural consumers had retained posters from the presocialist past, and in all likelihood many other peasants saw similar advertisements in rural markets on a regular basis during the first half of the twentieth century.

These examples suggest that Chinese had opportunities to localize and homogenize their perceptions of consumer goods according to their places at each level of China's urban hierarchy. Exactly what terms and images consumers used to exploit these opportunities is difficult to say, since we lack documentation, but it seems safe to conclude that Chinese consumers made very broad distinctions between "Chinese" and "Western" medicines. Their notions of what was "Chinese" included both old medicine and new "olde" medicine; and their notions of what was "Western" included Chinese-made "new medicine" as well as Western-made products.

Distinguishing along these lines, Chinese consumers probably thought of the differences between Chinese and Western medicines in terms that have been concisely summarized by Perry Link in his book on popular literature in Shanghai during the late nineteenth and early twentieth centuries. In his formulation, "Two horns of a dilemma . . . pervaded modern urban life: whether to be modern, foreign-influenced, stylish, and aggressive or old-style, purely Chinese, plain, and retiring. The general distinction, perhaps best captured by the Chinese terms *t'u* (earth, and hence "local, native") and *yang* (ocean—from across the ocean, foreign), dates in Shanghai from the late nineteenth century."[12] In these terms, if Chinese in Shanghai began distinguishing sharply between *tu* (local, native) and *yang* (foreign-influenced) from the late nineteenth century, then it is no exaggeration to say that Chinese consumers in all parts of the country began to distinguish, with varying degrees of exactitude, between medicines that were *tu* (both old and "olde") and medicines that were *yang* (both Western-made and Chinese-made) during the first half of the twentieth century.

Brokers in Between

In the debate over agents of consumer culture, adversaries in the top-down versus bottom-up debate have all generally taken the same point of departure: the point where a Western-based corporation has crossed national and cultural boundaries and made contact with consumers in a local culture. Preoccupied with Western corporations acting from the top down or local consumers acting from the bottom up, the debaters have paid little attention to brokers acting in between. Nonetheless, whether viewed from the top down or the bottom up, the brokers that are described in this book played key roles in mediating the spread of consumer culture. They "diffused" goods (in the process central to the top-down interpretation), and they reinterpreted the "representations" of goods (in the process highlighted by the bottom-up approach).

Perhaps advocates of the top-down approach have made little mention of brokers as mediators in the spread of consumer culture because they have assumed that only intellectual elites—especially politically engaged intellectual elites—appropriated Western ideas, images, forms, and discourses. As I mentioned in Chapter 1, many intellectual historians of China have implicitly or explicitly made this assumption, but this book calls it into question. To be sure, Chinese entrepreneurs outside the intellectual elite were not pioneers of cultural change in the sense that they appropriated Western ideas, images, forms, and discourses directly from the West. But they were certainly legitimizers of cultural change in the sense that they readily appropriated "Western" ideas, images, forms, and discourses from other Chinese and aggressively popularized them at all levels of China's urban hierarchy.

At the top of each business's managerial hierarchy, Chinese entrepreneurs played pivotal roles between intellectual elites and nonelites. Although generally lacking in formal education, they recruited highly educated elite artists to paint images for use in calendar posters, billboards, wall paintings, magazine covers, and cartoons. Moreover, they commissioned elite architects to design buildings and amusement parks and hired sophisticated scientists to research and develop products in laboratories. In all these cases, Chinese entrepreneurs gained access to "Western" ideas, forms, signs, and discourses as understood by elite Chinese intellectuals, and they carried out localization in the sense that they freely added Chinese ideas, forms, signs, and discourses—even when these seemed to contradict the "Western" ones—thus creating new hybrid representations of what was "Chinese" (like the "olde shoppes" in Chapter 2) and "Western" (like the drugstores and advertisements in Chapters 3–6).

If advocates of the top-down approach take into account this role that non-Western entrepreneurs played as brokers, then interpretations of the institutional dynamics behind the spread of consumer culture will become more complicated. Since Chinese entrepreneurs who had never been employed by Western-based corporations were capable of localizing Western-style consumer culture, it cannot be assumed that Western-based corporations have had unmediated access to everyone who has been touched by consumer culture. In evaluating the dynamics of top-down "diffusion," it is necessary to examine more than one link in the chain reaching down from Western-based corporations to local societies. It is not enough to consider Western corporations' direct impacts on local consumers or even Western corporations' direct dealings with their non-Western local employees. Besides focusing on relations between Westerners and non-Westerners, one needs to look closely at relationships among non-Westerners within local societies. At the very least, the researcher needs to analyze non-Western rivals of Western corporations and their roles as brokers in relation to non-Western intellectual elites, and, if possible, it is preferable to go further down the marketing chain that connects additional levels of non-Westerners.

By contrast with the advocates of the top-down approach, advocates of the bottom-up approach have emphasized the importance of nonelites as participants in the spread of consumer culture, but they have generally confined their investigations of nonelites to individual consumers. As a result, they have ignored nonelite brokers as much as proponents of the top-down approach have done. But to understand what consumers reacted to, it is important to pay attention to these brokers and their localizing effects on consumer culture at every level of the marketing hierarchy.

Below the top managers presiding over the businesses that are described here were another set of agents of consumer culture: the companies' branch managers. These branch managers were charged with the task of mediating between their business's headquarters and its local branches in cities at the cores of China's macroregions. They generally had even less exposure to the West than their bosses did, and, when projecting images of their stores and products as "Western," they took into account macroregional and local differences in dialects, architectural styles, visual cultures, and political attitudes in China and Southeast Asia. They localized their headquarters' representations of their stores as

"Western" in the sense that they revised their headquarters' blueprints for "Western" branch stores and "Western" advertising images for the sake of appealing to local tastes.

While Chinese branch managers localized top managers' representations of "the West" in core cities, Chinese owners of affiliated drugstores localized branch managers' representations of "the West" in smaller cities and towns. Once a Chinese business's advertising was in an affiliate's hands, the affiliate did not necessarily use it as the business intended; instead, affiliates appropriated it for their own purposes, and still other independent shopkeepers and peddlers probably did the same with posters and handbills in smaller-scale operations. Although not under the ownership of Chinese producers of goods and advertising, these affiliates and other independent shops and vendors carried out localization in the sense that they made use of Chinese businesses' representations of "the West" in settings that were different from and beyond the control of the businesses' own stores.

Whether viewed from the top down or the bottom up, these various Chinese brokers formed links in a chain that extended consumer culture deeply into Chinese society. Taken as a whole, they show that nonelite brokers translated terms and idioms between cultures in early twentieth-century China, and they exemplify a category of people—nonelite cultural brokers in local societies—who were highly influential agents of consumer culture and yet have been almost entirely omitted from the debate between advocates of top-down and bottom-up approaches.[13]

Agents of Consumer Revolution

This book has identified numerous historical agents—corporations acting from the top down, consumers participating from the bottom up, brokers mediating in between—all promoting the spread of consumer culture, and their reach and dynamism raise the question of whether they carried out a consumer revolution. The concept of consumer revolution has recently been applied to China by the sociologist Deborah Davis. Davis used this concept in her editor's introduction to a recent book, *The Consumer Revolution in Urban China*, in which she and several other social scientists reported on fieldwork that they did in China between the mid-1980s and the mid-1990s. In it they have explored a wide variety of contemporary developments, but they have made no attempt to place

China's consumer revolution since the 1980s in the context of Chinese history. As a result, they have left the impression that agents of consumer revolution in China should be understood strictly as a contemporary phenomenon, and their preoccupation with the recent past challenges historians to take a longer view, identify earlier phases of consumer revolution, and consider the possible relevance of these earlier phases to the present and future.

By Davis's criteria for assessing consumer revolution, it is reasonable to conclude that a consumer revolution occurred in China during the first half of the twentieth century. Within the decade between the mid-1920s and the mid-1930s (to select a temporal unit comparable in length to her period of study), it can be claimed that in China "millions of people gained access to advanced modes of communication, new vocabularies of social discourse, and novel forms of leisure through newly commercialized outlets." In this book I have documented the creation of some of the advanced modes of communication (especially print media), new vocabularies of social discourse (particularly through advertising images), and newly commercialized outlets (such as nationwide chain stores and their locally owned affiliates). In addition, in recent studies others have uncovered evidence that points toward the conclusion that China underwent a consumer revolution in the early twentieth century.[14] Although precise figures on the number of consumers participating in this revolution are not available, it is estimated that between 500 and 550 million people lived in China between the mid-1920s and mid-1930s. So it is readily conceivable that tens of millions of people in China gained access to its consumer culture as window-shoppers, occasional customers, or regular patrons at that time.[15]

These similarities between China's pre-Maoist and post-Maoist consumer revolutions suggest that the history of China's current consumer revolution has pre-1949 origins and deserves a place in the worldwide history of consumer culture that occurred before World War II. In other words, the beginnings of Chinese consumer culture need to be pushed back in time to the pre-1949 period, and the boundaries of worldwide consumer culture need to be pushed outward in space to encompass Chinese history.[16]

What, if any, is the connection between pre- and post-1949 agents of Chinese consumer revolution? Hanlong Lu, the only contributor to *The Consumer Revolution in Urban China* who has discussed pre-1979 China, has identified central planners in government as the key agents molding consumers' attitudes during the Maoist era (1949–1976). In Lu's words, "Central planning suppressed the normal processes of personal consumption by rejecting normal market mechanisms." As a result, Chinese consumer culture was "massified" *(dazhonghua)* to the extent that "the vast majority of the people" conformed to a single pattern of consumption, eating the same food, wearing the same clothes, using the same transportation, celebrating the same holidays in the same way.[17]

Lu's interpretation raises a crucial issue for understanding relations between the past and present. On the one hand, his characterization of central planners as new agents of "massification" under Mao implies that China had no mass consumer culture before 1949. On the other hand, his use of the word "normal" to describe the consumption process and market mechanisms that were suppressed by Maoist central planners suggests that, in its consumer culture, pre-Maoist China bears a closer resemblance to contemporary China than Maoist China does. These two potentially contradictory points, in turn, pose a question: If pre-1949 China had consumption processes and market mechanisms that were "normal" by the standards of mass culture in today's China, then wasn't there something "massified" about it too?

This question brings us back to the thorny issue of how to define mass culture. In Chapter 1 I faulted Leo Lee and Andrew Nathan for applying to early twentieth-century China a definition of mass culture that was historically unrealistic and for concluding flatly that before 1949 China had no "truly mass audience." Perhaps nuance can be added to Lee and Nathan's assertions about Chinese cultural history by taking advantage of a tripartite set of chronological categories that has been proposed by Michael Kammen in his recent synthesis of American cultural history.

Besides making the conventional distinction between popular and mass cultures (as Lee and Nathan have done), Kammen has added a third category: proto–mass culture. This category seems apt as a characterization of China's culture in the early twentieth century for at least two reasons. First, it describes a culture in which there was an "overlap" between popular culture and mass culture. As Kammen has emphasized, "The word 'overlap' (rather than 'transition') is deliberately chosen because there was, undeniably, a great deal of simultaneity."[18] As I have shown, a similar overlap was pervasive in the consumer culture of early twentieth-century

China and is illustrated by the coexistence of (reinvented) traditional Chinese "olde shoppes" and "Western" drugstores (under Chinese ownership and management).

Second, proto–mass culture seems an apt concept because it describes a culture that has an organic relationship with mass culture. Kammen has noted numerous examples of departures from American popular culture that did not result in direct transitions to American mass culture, and he has shown how proto–mass culture did grow directly into American mass culture. In his summary, "Mass culture sank roots earlier in the twentieth century, but only blossomed into full flower directly following World War II [in the United States]."[19]

In China Chinese agents of consumer culture that were comparable to contemporaneous ones in the United States similarly sank roots for mass culture in the early twentieth century, and in retrospect it seems likely that they would have helped to bring it into full flower following World War II if the Maoist revolution had not intervened. Throughout the first half of the twentieth century, Chinese entrepreneurs and businesses kept pace with American, European, and Japanese cultural trends in everything from women's fashions to Art Deco architecture, and in the late 1940s they seemed poised to promote a consumer revolution at a higher level; this was illustrated by their appropriation of science and their plans for extending the reach of newspaper empires and amusement parks. By then these top-down agents of consumer culture had already acted in concert with consumers from the bottom up and brokers in between to carry out a consumer revolution and had given rise to the first sprouts of mass culture. Surely they would have continued to follow this trajectory if Mao had not come to power in 1949 and if his central planners had not eliminated them as agents of consumer culture by shifting the distribution of goods from commercial to noncommercial channels.

If recognizing that Chinese agents of consumer revolution sank roots in mass culture and helped to produce a proto–mass culture in China during the first half of the twentieth century, then it is easier to explain why the Chinese-owned medicine businesses that are described in this book have reappeared as agents of consumer revolution in China since the 1980s. After a hiatus during the Maoist era, they are all currently once again marketing medicine by commercial means under the same names that they adopted during the early twentieth century. A new generation of

Chinese entrepreneurs has taken charge, and these new managers have shown awareness of the past by commissioning and publishing histories of all these businesses.[20]

Since the 1980s Chinese entrepreneurs operating medicine companies have aspired to some of the same goals that were set by their predecessors during the first half of the twentieth century. In advertising, as the sociologist Gail Henderson discovered in recent interviews with Chinese managers of contemporary medicine companies, "the techniques that Huang [Chujiu] used [as I described them in Chapter 3] are just being duplicated today."[21] Similarly, she found that they, like earlier Chinese entrepreneurs, are striving to capture a national market. When she questioned one of the current Chinese managers at New Asia, he told her that he hopes to extend his company's distribution to "the whole country, but there are just different ways to enter it."[22]

While contemporary Chinese entrepreneurs seem to share many of their historical predecessors' goals for using advertising media and reaching a national market, they have begun to formulate somewhat different strategies for achieving these goals. According to Henderson, the ones selling Western-style medicine have not cast their advertising in traditional medical terms, as Huang Chujiu and other pre-1949 Chinese advertisers once did. Perhaps they assume that under the influence of cultural homogenization Chinese consumers have universally come to recognize a clear-cut duality between traditional and modern medicine. In seeking to capture a national market, today's Chinese entrepreneurs have not reached as widely as their pre-1949 predecessors were able to do. If they are to overcome new forms of local protectionism in today's China, Henderson has observed, they will need to "re-invent" pre-1949 systems of marketing medicine through the kinds of chain stores, affiliates, and other retailers that I have described.[23]

These indications that contemporary Chinese entrepreneurs have begun to duplicate some pre-1949 Chinese business practices and will eventually reinvent others are not a basis for concluding that they simply picked up in 1979 where their predecessors left off in 1949, as though China's decades under Mao had never happened. It is undeniable that to some extent the government of the People's Republic "massified" Chinese consumer culture between 1949 and 1979 (as Hanlong Lu has shown). Perhaps it is even conceivable that the Chinese state has "managed"

China's consumer culture since 1979 in a "new type of cultural globalization," as the anthropologist Yunxiang Yan has recently suggested.[24]

And yet, even if consumer culture might appear to be new in today's
China, its principal direct agents bear a striking resemblance to those of
the pre-1949 era. Once again transnational corporations, Chinese intellectuals, and the Chinese government are among its leading agents in China,
and once again Chinese-owned businesses are promoting it too.[25] Will
Chinese entrepreneurs deal as effectively with these other agents of consumer culture as their predecessors did in the medicine business before
1949? Will they surpass transnational rivals as distributors, recruit Chinese
intellectuals as designers of advertising, and turn alliances with the Chinese government to their commercial advantage? Derived from the pre-
1949 past, these questions set an agenda that Chinese entrepreneurs might
well follow in the twenty-first century.

ABBREVIATIONS USED IN NOTES

BJTRTS Zhongguo Tongren Tang jituan gongsi Beijing Tongren Tangshi
bianweihui (Editorial Committee for the History of Tongren
Tang from the Tongren Tang Group of Companies of China), ed.
Beijing Tongren Tangshi (The history of Tongren Tang in Beijing).
Beijing: Renmin ribao, 1993.

Longteng Shanghai shehui kexue yuan jingji yanjiu suo (Shanghai Academy
of Social Sciences, Institute of Economics). *Longteng huyao bashi
nian: Shanghai Zhonghua zhiyaochang chang shi* (Eighty years of the
dragon soaring and the tiger leaping: A factory history of the
Zhonghua medicine factory of Shanghai). Shanghai: Shanghai
renmin chubanshe, 1991.

Xiyao Shanghai shehui kexue yuan jingji yanjiu suo (Shanghai Academy
of Social Sciences, Institute of Economics). *Shanghai jindai xiyao
hangye shi* (A history of the modern medicine trade in Shanghai).
Shanghai: Shanghai shehui kexue yuan, 1988.

Zhongxi Shanghai shehui kexue yuan jingji yanjiu suo (Shanghai Academy
of Social Sciences, Institute of Economics). *Zhongxi yaochang
bainian shi* (A history of one hundred years at the China and the
West Medicine Factory). Shanghai: Shanghai shehui kexue yuan,
1990.

1. CONSUMER CULTURE IN CHINESE HISTORY

1. Friedman, *The Lexus and the Olive Tree*, 291–297; Watson, "Introduction," 35–38. Among critics of big Western-based corporations, see Schiller, *Communication;* Hamelink, *Cultural Autonomy;* Barnet and Cavanagh, *Global Dreams*. For more examples, see Tomlinson, *Cultural Imperialism*. Several proponents of this top-down approach have drawn inspiration from the influential Frankfurt School of the 1930s and 1940s. For a classic work on "the culture industry" by two leaders of the Frankfurt School, see Adorno and Horkheimer, *Dialectic*. Among anthropologists defending the bottom-up approach, see Comaroff and Comaroff, introduction to *Modernity and Its Malcontents;* Appadurai, *Modernity at Large;* Hannerz, *Transnational Connections*.
2. See Watson, "China's Big Mac Attack," 121–122.
3. On these definitions of consumer culture, see Tiersten, "Redefining Consumer Culture," especially 137–138.
4. Cochran, *Big Business in China*, chap. 2; Cochran, *Encountering Chinese Networks*, chaps. 2 and 3.
5. On patent medicine businesses as early advertisers and promoters of consumer culture in American history, see Young, *Toadstool Millionaires;* in English history, see Corley, "Interactions," 115–116; in Canadian history, see Loeb, "George Fulford"; in Japanese history, see Yamamoto, *Kokoku no shakai shi*, 60–61, and *Jintan kara JINTAN e*, 26–45.
6. *Xiyao*, 23–27, 322–338; Scientific Terminology Association, comp., *Dictionary;* Saenz, "Squibb," 452; Wilkins, *Emergence*, 208–209; Corley, "Interactions," 126; Wang Duyuan, "Baowei yaohuang shimo," 251–269, Loeb, "George Fulford," 135. Of these Western-based corporations, Bayer seems to have had the most extensive operations in China during

the early twentieth century, but it concentrated on exporting dyestuffs more than pharmaceutical products. See Haber, *Chemical Industry,* 331–333, and Beer, *Emergence,* 94–96. Some of these Western companies currently maintain historical archives that contain primary sources. By far the richest or at least the most accessible collection of historical documents on the marketing of Western medicine in China is at the Bayer Archives in Leverkusen, Germany. I have also consulted materials at the Wellcome Foundation in London, the Merck Archives in Whitehouse Station, New Jersey, and the Squibb Archives in Princeton, New Jersey.

7. The influence of indirect agents on Chinese consumer culture is a topic worthy of a separate study, especially in light of numerous recent publications in history and anthropology on ideas about the body and hygiene. An excellent example of new work in this field is Ruth Rogaski's *Hygienic Modernity* (2004), which contains an up-to-date review of the literature on the subject.

8. Skinner, "Regional Urbanization."

9. Skinner, "Mobility Strategies," 361.

10. Rowe, *Hankow,* 60–62.

11. Hamashita, "Intra-Regional System," 120, 128, 135.

12. Hamashita, "Tribute and Treaties," 20.

13. Cartier, "Origins," 123, 127.

14. Ibid., 117–118.

15. In his recent work Skinner has begun to give more attention to human agency and its consequences. For example, in a sweeping synthesis of China's urban history, 1895–1995, he has shown continuity in China's "system of cities" (in keeping with his earlier work), but he has also distinguished "cities themselves" from these systems and has argued that within cities human actions have resulted in "dramatic transformations." See his "Chinese Cities."

16. Eastman, *Abortive Revolution,* 226–239; Coble, *Shanghai Capitalists;* Bergère, *Golden Age,* quotation from 274.

17. Kirby, "Continuity and Change," 128.

18. Kirby, "Chinese War Economy," 204.

19. Coble, *Chinese Capitalists,* 188–189.

20. Trocki, *Opium and Empire,* 30, 34.

21. On Han relations with non-Han peoples, see Rawski, "Presidential Address"; Ho, "In Defense of Sinicization."

22. For examples of intellectual biographies, see Meisner, *Li Ta-chao;* Grieder, *Hu Shih;* Alitto, *Last Confucian.* For collective portraits, see Spence, *Gate;* Schwarcz, *Chinese Enlightenment;* Chang, *Chinese Intellectuals;* Dirlik, *Origins.* For cultural studies, see Barlow, "Theorizing Woman."
23. Barlow, "Theorizing Woman," 262.
24. Cohen, *Between Tradition and Modernity,* 242.
25. Lee and Nathan, "Beginnings of Mass Culture," 360, 375.
26. Sivin, *Traditional Medicine,* 195.

2. INVENTING IMPERIAL TRADITIONS AND BUILDING OLDE SHOPPES

1. Cameron moved from his home country of Scotland to China in 1921 and lived there until 1940, eventually becoming the chief pharmacist at Peking Union Medical College. See Bowen to Pearce, January 10, 1940, 121/178 Peking Union Medical College Papers, Rockefeller Archives.
2. Cameron, "Some Sidelights," 665–666.
3. Cameron and Chen, "Old and the New in Pharmacy," 636.
4. While Tongren Tang was the largest of China's traditional drugstores, other big ones included Leiyunshang of Suzhou, Huqingyu of Hangzhou, Yekaitai of Wuhan, and Chenliji of Guangzhou. For sketches of these and other big traditional Chinese medicine stores, see Chen Xinqian and Zhang Tianlu, *Zhongguo jindai yaoxue shi,* and Xie Mu and Wu Yongliang, *Zhongguo.*
5. BJTRTS, 1–5.
6. According to one source, the Yues chose the name Tongren Tang for an inn before they used it in their medicine shop. Zhang Bingxin, "Tongren Tang," 4.
7. Zhongguo minzhu jianguo hui, "Tongren Tang," 29–39; BJTRTS, 1–5; Chang Te-chang, "Economic Role," 251–259; Naquin, *Peking,* 331–337.
8. Xie Mu and Wu Yongliang, *Zhongguo,* 1:52; Wang Yingkui, "Chutan Tianjin shangbiao," 133.
9. BJTRTS, 1–2, 5; Li Chunsheng, "Qingdai gongting dang'an," 40.
10. Liu Yongcheng and He Zhiqing, "Wanquan Tang," 2. On Dashalan, see Naquin, *Peking,* 623–632. On merchants' rationales for locating shops in Beijing during the Qing dynasty, see Skinner, "Introduction: Urban Social Structure," 533.
11. BJTRTS, 5–6.

12. Xie Mu and Wu Yongliang, *Zhongguo*, 1:51–57.
13. BJTRTS, 3, 149; Zhang Bingxin, "Tongren Tang," 4. On Shaoxing natives' domination of Qing bureaucracy, see Cole, *Shaohsing*, chap. 6.
14. BJTRTS, 14–16; Zheng Tianting, "Zheng Tianting jiaoshou xu," 10. The Imperial Hospital had served China's emperors since the Six Dynasties period (222–589) and came under the Imperial Household Agency after it was established by the Qing in 1661. The hospital had a hierarchy of medical staff members during the Qing as follows: a director of the fifth-class official rank, thirteen doctors with imperial honors, twenty-six officials of the eighth- or ninth-class ranking, twenty doctors of the ninth-class ranking, and thirty other doctors as well as several pharmacists. See Ha Yi, "Qingdai tai yiyuan," 40.
15. BJTRTS, 19–23.
16. Ibid. The unit of currency used in this book unless otherwise specified is the Chinese yuan, a silver dollar. During the late nineteenth and early twentieth centuries, the yuan varied in value between twenty and fifty cents (U.S. currency), until it fell sharply in the 1940s, during wartime inflation. Another unit, the liang, is translated here as an ounce of silver. It weighed, more precisely, thirty-seven grams.
17. Hamilton and Lai, "Consumerism without Capitalism," 259.
18. Zhang Bingxin, "Tongren Tang," 4.
19. BJTRTS, 12–13, 24, 28–30, 19–23.
20. Ibid., 32–33; Yuan Shude, "Beijing Tongren Tang," 59–63. On the purchasing of degrees in Qing China, see Chung-li Chang, *Chinese Gentry*, 5–6, 11–13, 19–20, 103–111, 139–140, and Ho, *Ladder of Success*, 30–34, 46–50, 104.
21. Alford, *To Steal a Book*, 16–17.
22. BJTRTS, 8–10. Here I have used Susan Naquin's terminology. As she has pointed out, the civil officials who administered each of Beijing's five boroughs at the time "were called censors but are better thought of as superintendents of police" (Naquin, *Peking*, 360). In this case, the name of the police force was Qinming xunshi zhongcheng chuan (Office of Police for the Central Borough).
23. BJTRTS, 8–10.
24. In theory these examinations for the top-tier metropolitan degree were given once every three years, but in practice they were held three of every four years during the Qing, sometimes at both levels in a single year. See Naquin, *Peking*, 415–416.

25. On this elite, see Kia-ngau Chang, *Inflationary Spiral;* Ho, *Ladder of Success;* Meskill, "Conferral of the Degree"; and Elman, *Cultural History.*

26. BJTRTS, 3–4; Xie Mu and Wu Yongliang, *Zhongguo,* 1:52.

27. BJTRTS, 33–34; Imahori, *Peipin shimin,* 88–94; Naquin, *Peking,* 660–662. On fire brigades in Hankou and Tianjin at the time, see Rowe, *Hankow,* 317–321, and Kwan, *Salt Merchants,* 94–95.

28. BJTRTS, 30–35.

29. Ibid., 36–40.

30. Ibid., 19–23, 150.

31. Ibid., 40–41; Yue, "Beijing Tongren Tang," 141. In the early 1930s, when China went off the silver standard, the Yue family's joint management began to pay each branch in cash at fourteen thousand yuan per year rather than in silver. Otherwise, the family's regulations of 1907 remained basically unchanged until 1956.

32. BJTRTS, 40–41; Yue, "Beijing Tongren Tang," 132; Wang Ziran, "Yueren Tang," 118–119.

33. Bai, "Tongren Tang," 106.

34. BJTRTS, 156.

35. An, "Tongren Tang chuanren Yue Songsheng," 154.

36. Roger Yeu, son of Yue Duzhou, interview by author, Montvale, N.J., June 28, 1999.

37. Wang Ziran, "Yueren Tang," 120–121.

38. Outside Beijing during the early twentieth century, Chinese entrepreneurs who were not related to the Yue family operated medicine shops under the name Tongren Tang in at least four places: in the Middle Yangzi region at Zhangshu, Jiangxi Province (established 1910); in North China at Juxian, Shandong Province (established 1924); in the Lower Yangzi region at Bangbu, Anhui Province (established 1944); and at Chengdu as described above. See Zhang Zhiyu, "Tongren Tang," 202; Chuan Anying, "Huiyi Tongren Tang," 72–73; Wang Jinyuan, "'Tongren' Yao fang shimo," 201–207.

39. Chi Zehui, Lou Xuexi, and Chen Wenxian, *Beipingshi,* 387–392; Shen Hongxian, "Qiantan Tongren Tang," 128.

40. BJTRTS, 40–41; Yue, "Beijing Tongren Tang," 132; Wang Ziran, "Yueren Tang," 118–119.

41. Yue, "Beijing Tongren Tang," 143–144; An, "Fazhan zhong de Beijing Tongren Tang," 563–582.

42. Zhang Weihan, "Tianjin Daren Tang," 143–144.

43. Ibid.; He, "Tianjin Daren Tang," 261–262.

44. BJTRTS, 51; Yue, "Beijing Tongren Tang," 143; Wang Ziran, "Yueren Tang," 120; Ju, "Yueren Tang," 111; Yeu, interview.

45. BJTRTS, 51; Yue, "Beijing Tongren Tang," 143–145; Wu Hong and Wu Tingkai, "Daren Tang," 67. On the spread of chain stores in Europe, see Chandler, *Scale and Scope*, 255–257, 420.

46. Yue, "Beijing Tongren Tang," 144–145; Liu Zhaoqi, "Daren Tang," 239–241.

47. Ji Shihua, interview by author, Tianjin, China, January 14, 1999; Shen Wenxiu, interview by author, Tianjin, China, January 16, 1999. Both have had longstanding affiliations with Daren Tang.

48. Wu Hong and Wu Tingkai, "Daren Tang," 67; Zhang Weihan, "Tianjin Daren Tang," 143–144; Bai, "Tongren Tang," 106; An, "Fazhan zhong de Beijing Tongren Tang," 563–582.

49. Zhou, *Jinghua ganjiu lu*, 7.

50. Cameron, "Some Sidelights," 668.

51. Wu Hong and Wu Tingkai, "Daren Tang," 67.

52. Ibid.

53. Cameron, "Some Sidelights," 665.

54. Wu Hong and Wu Tingkai, "Daren Tang," 67.

55. Yue, "Beijing Tongren Tang," 144–145; Zhang Weihan, "Tianjin Daren Tang," 143–147. Yue Daren presided over the entire business and divided management at his headquarters in Tianjin into departments—general management office *(zong chuanli chu)*, business office *(gongshifang)*, production department *(yaofang)*, department for main and branch stores *(zong fen dian)*, and deer park department *(luyou,* for raising animals that were used in making medicines)—and he assigned members of his family to manage each one. Even after the business grew and began to distribute goods throughout China, he continued to make all its medicines in Tianjin.

56. Wu Hong and Wu Tingkai, "Daren Tang," 68–69; Zhang Weihan, "Tianjin Daren Tang," 144, 147. Near the end of his life Yue Daren made plans for a new training center, the Academy for New Studies (xinxue shuyuan), for preparing employees to staff stores in the British colony of Hong Kong and other cities in Southeast Asia. He went so far as to select candidates for the school from his staff members and to devise a curriculum that included the study of English. But he died in 1934, and his scheme for training employees and expanding Daren Tang's business into Southeast Asia was not carried out because of the Japanese military invasion of 1937. See Yue, "Beijing Tongren Tang," 144–145.

57. Zhang Weihan, "Tianjin Daren Tang," 144, 146–147.

58. Wu Hong and Wu Tingkai, "Daren Tang," 68–69.

59. Chen, "Chinese Drug Stores," 104; Cameron, "Some Sidelights," 667–668; Cameron and Chen, "Old and the New in Pharmacy," 633–634.

60. For examples of newspaper advertisements run by Tongren Tang and Daren Tang in Tianjin newspapers, see *Beiyang huabao (North China Pictorial News)* (February 26 and 28, 1931); and *Dagong bao* (December 5, 1933). For examples of newspaper advertisements by Great China-France Drugstore, New Asia Pharmaceutical Company, and Tiger Balm (all Western-style drugstores) using pictorial advertisements and modern calligraphy in one of the same newspapers, see *Dagong bao* (November 20, 1932; January 4, 1933; April 26 and July 25, 1934; January 9, February 15, March 25, and November 23, 1936; January 22, 1937).

61. John Yueh, son of Yue Daren, telephone interview by author, August 9, 2000; Roger Yeu, letter to author, September 24, 2000; Cameron, "Some Sidelights," 665.

62. Jones, "Trade," 126, 130. In North China the biggest medicine fairs were held twice a year in three-month cycles (from the third through the fifth and the ninth through the eleventh lunar months) at Qizhou, in Anguo county, about 125 miles southwest of Beijing. In South China the biggest medicine fairs were held at Zhangshu, in Jiangxi Province. Both sites have long histories in this local specialization, and both are currently continuing to pursue it; see Chen Xinqian and Zhang Tianlu, *Zhongguo jindai yaoxue shi*, chap. 6; Liu Haopu and Xu Zisu, "Qizhou miaohui"; Yu Yue and Wu Liyue, eds., *Jiangxi*, chap. 5; Qiu, ed., *Zhangshu yaosu*, chaps. 2–3.

63. Zhang Weihan, "Tianjin Daren Tang," 143.

64. Ibid., 147–148; Ji Shihua, "Tianjin Daren Tang," 100–101.

65. Zhang Weihan, "Tianjin Daren Tang," 148. On Sun Simiao, see Sivin, *Chinese Alchemy*, 81–144. Sun Simiao's birthday was a widely celebrated annual event in Tianjin. Every neighborhood had its own Temple to the Medicine God and held a fair for the occasion. See Rogaski, *Hygienic Modernity*, 67–69.

66. BJTRTS, 51; Yue, "Beijing Tongren Tang," 143; Wang Ziran, "Yueren Tang," 120; Ju, "Yueren Tang," 111; Yeu, interview.

67. BJTRTS, 51–52; An, "Dui zi gaizao zhong de daibiao renwu Yue Songsheng," 23.

68. Han Wenwei and Li Xiu, "Tongren Tang," 249; Shi Chuan, "Tongren Tang," 94–96; Ke Mu, "Xianggang," 97.

69. Bayer proposed that it and Daren Tang cooperate on the construction of a major new medicine-making plant in China. The two companies held discussions, but negotiations soon broke down over the name and location of the joint venture. Yue Daren preferred to build it under Daren Tang's name near his headquarters in Tianjin, whereas Bayer wanted to keep it under Bayer's name and locate it 250 miles southeast of Tianjin in the coastal city of Qingdao, which had been the center of German influence in China since the nineteenth century (Yue, "Beijing Tongren Tang," 144–145; An, "Tongren Tang chuanren Yue Songsheng," 133).

70. Lao She, "Lao zi hao," 326.

3. ADVERTISING DREAMS

1. Lu Xun, "Lu Xun," 2–3. Among Chinese intellectuals, Lu Xun was perhaps the leading critic of Chinese commercial artists, but he was by no means the only one. For other examples, see Laing, *Selling Happiness*, 37–39.

2. Marchand, *Advertising*, xvii.

3. *Xiyao*, 236.

4. Gong, "Huang Chujiu zhuan," pt. 2, 75–77; Kong et al., eds., *Zhongguo*, 2:427–428.

5. On "private" schools, see Evelyn Rawski, *Education and Popular Literacy*, 162–167.

6. Gong, "Huang Chujiu zhuan," pt. 1, 53–56, and pt. 2, 72–74; Guan, "Huang Chujiu," 138; *Xiyao*, 231–232; *Longteng*, 2. Many who migrated from Huang's home county of Yuyao to Shanghai in the late nineteenth century became financiers. According to some estimates, their native banks were very powerful in early twentieth-century Shanghai. See Cole, *Shaohsing*, 79–80.

7. *Longteng*, 2.

8. Guan, "Huang Chujiu," 138; Kong et al., eds., *Zhongguo*, 2:427–428; Gong "Huang Chujiu zhuan," pt. 2, 74–75.

9. Gong, "Huang Chujiu zhuan," pt. 2, 72–73.

10. Porkert, *Theoretical Foundation*, 107, 161.

11. Gong, "Huang Chujiu zhuan," pt. 2, 75.

12. Ibid.; Guan, "Huang Chujiu," 139; Kong et al., eds., *Zhongguo*, 2:428.

13. Gong, "Huang Chujiu zhuan," pt. 2, 75; Guan, "Huang Chujiu," 138–139.

14. Guan, "Huang Chujiu," 139.

15. The other "one and a half" were Shi Dezhi, a man of mixed Sino-Western descent who sold fake antiques, and Wu Jiangang, a fortune-teller. Ping, "Mantan Huang Chujiu," 146–147.
16. *Xiyao*, 36–37, 41, 233–235; Gong, "Huang Chujiu zhuan," pt. 2, 73–75; Shanghai Municipal Police Files, "File on the affairs of the late Huang Cho Chiu," D-1949 (1931).
17. *Xiyao*, 93; Gong, "Huang Chujiu zhuan," pt. 3, 94.
18. Croizier, *Traditional Medicine*; Zhao Hongjun, *Jindai Zhongxiyi*; Xiaoqun Xu, *Chinese Professionals*, chap. 7.
19. Sammons, *Proprietary Medicine*, 4.
20. "Jintan."
21. *Tsuien*; Ito Yoichiro, "Morishita Hiroshi," 387.
22. *Jintan kara JINTAN e*, 34.
23. *Tsuien*; *Longteng*, 1–2, 5; *Xiyao*, 56–57.
24. Sammons, *Proprietary Medicine*, 4.
25. Hirschmeier and Yui, *Development of Japanese Business*, 181.
26. Sanger, *Advertising Methods*, 67.
27. *Tsuien*.
28. Lin Yutang, *Moment in Peking*, 576; Wu Tsu-hsiang, "Fan Village," 404.
29. *Xiyao*, 121, 234; Guan, "Huang Chujiu," 139; Gong, "Huang Chujiu zhuan," pt. 3, 93.
30. *Shenbao*, July 26, 1911.
31. *Longteng*, 3.
32. Gerth, *China Made*, chap. 3; Remer, *Study*, 47; Kikuchi, *Chugoku*, 164–165; Joseph T. Chen, *May Fourth Movement*, 93.
33. *Shenbao*, May 18 and 23, August 30, 1915.
34. *Guohuo diaochalu*.
35. For a graphic visual representation of this image, see the thirteenth-century painting *Dragon and Tiger Embracing (Long hu tuzhu)*, formerly attributed to Chen Rong, at the Museum of Fine Arts, Boston.
36. Zhang Yanfeng, *Lao yuefenpai*, 2:47; *Shenbao*, August 30, 1915.
37. Guan, "Huang Chujiu," 139; Gong, "Huang Chujiu zhuan," pt. 3, 94; *Xiyao*, 234.
38. Gong, "Huang Chujiu zhuan," pt. 3, 93–94; *Xiyao*, 235; *Longteng*, 4, 6–7.
39. Guan, "Huang Chujiu," 139; *Xiyao*, 234–235; *Longteng*, 6.
40. *Longteng*, 7–8, 11; *Xiyao*, 131, 235, 315; Gong, "Huang Chujiu zhuan," pt. 3, 93.
41. Remer, *Study*, 245.
42. Hou Chi-ming, *Foreign Investment*, 151–55.

43. On the persistence of the national goods movement, see Gerth, *China Made,* chap. 4. For an example of a sales agent promoting Humane Elixir as "Eastern goods" in China in 1936, see Cochran, Hsieh, and Cochran, *One Day in China,* 244–245.

44. Zhang Yanfeng, *Lao yuefenpai,* 1:29.

45. Ibid., 88.

46. Ibid. In her portrait of Zheng, Ellen Laing has given this lucid description of his technique: "The rub-and-paint technique used by Zheng involves applying carbon for what would be shaded parts of the figure and gently rubbing the carbon into the paper and then carefully applying water-soluble pigments. The shadows created by the carbon impart a quality of volume and mass to flesh and fabric, giving a heightened sense of realism." Laing, *Selling Happiness,* 116.

47. Laing, *Selling Happiness,* chap. 6.

48. Kao, "China's Response," 77, 110–111.

49. Link, *Mandarin Ducks,* 66. A rare exception was a female nude appearing in an advertisement for a Japanese medicine in the Shanghai newspaper *Shenbao* in May 1911. Cited by Laing, *Selling Happiness,* 118.

50. Buji, "Jiefangqian de 'yuefenpai' nianhua shiliao," 51; Laing, "Chinese Palace-Style Poetry," 291; Zhang Muhan, "Cong meiren," 24.

51. Huang's advertising manager was Zhou Minggang, and his best writer was Xu Zhuodai, a popular humorist known for his "comic stories" *(huaji xiaoshuo).* On Xu, see Link, *Mandarin Ducks,* 158.

52. *Xiyao,* 113–114; Gong, "Huang Chujiu zhuan," pt. 3, 96; Buji, "Jiefangqian de 'yuefenpai' nianhua shiliao," 52–53.

53. Ding Hao, "Ji lao Shanghai," 13–17.

54. Zhang Yanfeng, *Lao yuefenpai,* 2:29, 33, 89, 90; Buji, "Jiefangqian de 'yuefenpai' nianhua shiliao," 53; Wu Hao et al., *Duhui modeng,* 5, 161–164.

55. Zhang Yanfeng, *Lao yuefenpai,* 1:28, 33, 60, 84; 2:18, 121.

56. Ibid., 1:77–78; Buji, "Jiefangqian de 'yuefenpai' nianhua shiliao," 55.

57. Zhang Yanfeng, *Lao yuefenpai,* 1:33; 2:22–24.

58. Ibid., 1:21, 29, 60; 2:14, 86, 121. On the popularity of the "one bare breast" motif in Chinese calendar posters during the late 1920s and 1930s, see Laing, *Selling Happiness,* 216–217.

59. Zhang Yanfeng, *Lao yuefenpai,* 1:10, 11, 88, 95, 96, 106, 117–121; 2:38, 106; Cochran, "Transnational Origins," 40–45.

60. Zhang Yanfeng, *Lao yuefenpai,* 1:65, 70–71, 77–78, 85–86, 90; Buji, "Jiefangqian de 'yuefenpai' nianhua shiliao," 53, 55. On British-American

Tobacco Company's advertising in China, see Cochran, "Transnational Origins," and Laing, *Selling Happiness,* chap. 8.

61. Elvin, "Tales of *Shen* and *Xin,*" 267–268, 275, 292, 312.
62. Weidner, "Women," 23; Hay, "Body Invisible in Chinese Art?" 43.
63. Cahill, "Three Zhangs," 61, and "'Where Did the Nymph Hang?'" 9–10.
64. On this point Laing has reacted against Buji, "Jiefangqian de 'yuefenpai' nianhua shiliao," 51.
65. Laing, *Selling Happiness,* 118–119.
66. Elvin, "Tales of *Shen* and *Xin,*" 268.
67. Lee and Nathan, "Beginnings of Mass Culture," 368–370; Chen Xinqian and Zhang Tianlu, *Zhongguo jindai yaoxue shi,* 31, 39; *Xiyao,* 66–67, 79.
68. *Zhongxi,* 12–13; *Xiyao,* 114; Gong, "Huang Chujiu zhuan," pt. 3, 97.
69. *Xiyao,* 237; Guan, "Huang Chujiu," 139; Gong, "Huang Chujiu zhuan," pt. 3, 96, and pt. 4, 105, 107.
70. *Xiyao,* 109, 114–115, 235–236; *Zhongxi,* 23.
71. *Xiyao,* 80, 95, 108, 114, 240; Chen Xinqian and Zhang Tianlu, *Zhongguo jindai yaoxue shi,* 37.
72. On the contrast between the advertising policies of "old-style" and "new-style" drugstores, see Huang, "Cong *Shenbao* yiyao guanggao," 150–153.
73. Yang and Tao, *Study,* 68–78.
74. Spence, *Search,* 377–378.
75. Certeau, *Practice of Everyday Life,* xi–xii, chap. 12.

4. CAPTURING A NATIONAL MARKET

1. Bacon, "Pharmacy in Shanghai," 658. Great Five Continents also had an English-language name, The International Dispensary, Ltd., but I have used an English translation of its Chinese name because it published the overwhelming majority of its advertising in Chinese and thus targeted consumers who read its name in Chinese, not English.
2. Gan, ed., *Shanghai bainian,* 138–139; *Xiyao,* 260.
3. On this pattern of migration, see Skinner, "Mobility Strategies."
4. Shen Zuwei, "Xiang Songmao," 1; *Xiyao,* 60; Gan, ed., *Shanghai bainian,* 138–139; Sun, "Xiang Songmao," 172.
5. Shen Zuwei, "Xiang Songmao," 2; *Xiyao,* 262.
6. *Xiyao,* 258, 260–261; Tan, "Wuzhou," 16–17.
7. Kulp, *Country Life,* 265.
8. Zhang Yanfeng, *Lao yuefenpai,* 1:3, 104.
9. *Wuzhou,* 203.

10. Gan, ed., *Shanghai bainian*, 138–139. Of Five Continents' nonmedical products, the best known was Guben soap. See Xiang, "Wuzhou guben feizao"; Xiang, "Wuzhou zaochang."
11. *Xiyao*, 266.
12. Tan, "Wuzhou," 16.
13. Shiba, "Ningpo," 437; Rowe, *Hankow*, 231; Leung, "Regional Rivalry," 29–50; Jones, "Ningpo Pang," 73–96.
14. Zhang Zhongli, ed., *Jindai Shanghai*, 740–741; Cochran, *Encountering Chinese Networks*, chaps. 2 and 7.
15. *Xiyao*, 109–111, 267–268.
16. *Wuzhou*, 113–125; *Xiyao*, 273.
17. *Wuzhou*, 113–115.
18. Tsin, "Canton Remapped," 27–28; Wang Liping, "Tourism," 113.
19. Bergère, *Golden Age*, 114–117.
20. Hanchao Lu, "Away from Nanking Road," 93–123. See also Honig, *Sisters and Strangers*, 184–185.
21. Wilson, "Architecture," 248.
22. Longstreth, *Buildings of Main Street*, 45, 82.
23. *Wuzhou*, 122.
24. Ibid., 121–122, 124.
25. Ibid., 124.
26. *Xiyao*, 102.
27. Sun, "Xiang Songmao," 178; Xiang and Tan, "Aiguo shiyejia," 314–315; Wang Renze, "Kangri xunshen," 190–191; Zhuang, "Rijun qiangkou xia de jushang fuzi," 15; Shen Zuwei, "Xiang Songmao," 1, 13. In May 1995, during the celebration of the fiftieth anniversary of the victory over Japan in the Pacific War, Xiang Songmao's role in defense of Shanghai in 1932 was the subject of a series of television and radio programs that were produced and broadcast in Shanghai under the title *Years of Tears and Bloodshed (Qixue nianliu)*.
28. Wright, *Twentieth Century Impressions*, 628–630; Feldwick, ed., *Present Day Impressions*, 243–245, 261, 349–357.
29. *Wuzhou*, 107; "Engineering and Industrial Notes," 101.
30. *Wuzhou*, 182.
31. Ibid., 108.
32. Newspaper clippings, September 9 and October 9, 1936, Liu Dajun Papers.
33. *Wuzhou*, 201; newspaper clipping, October 9, 1936, Liu Dajun Papers; cf. Zhang Baohao and Fan Nengchuan, *Shanghai*, chap. 16.

34. *Wuzhou,* 103, 105.
35. Ibid., 183–185, 191–194; newspaper clipping, October 18, 1936, Liu Dajun Papers.
36. Feldwick, ed., *Present Day Impressions.*
37. *Wuzhou,* 105.
38. Ibid., 119, 121, 123; see Table 4.1.
39. File Q38–37–29, minutes of the meetings of the board of directors, 1940–1941, Wuzhou da yaofang Papers.
40. Choi, "Competition among Brothers," 96–114.
41. Zhang Yanfeng, *Lao yuefenpai,* 2:205.
42. Hu Jiru and Li Baochen, "Puyu shuju," 90–95.
43. Ibid.
44. File Q38–37–29, minutes of the meetings of the board of directors, August 4 and 8, 1940, October 30, 1940, and February 19, 1941, Wuzhou da yaofang Papers.

5. CROSSING ENEMY LINES

1. Zhang Zhongli, ed., *Jindai Shanghai,* 148–152, 1130–1159; Lee and Nathan, "Beginnings of Mass Culture," 368–375; G. William Skinner, "Regional Urbanization," 17, 24n.
2. Reardon-Anderson, *Study of Change,* 100–101, 151, 170, 294–295; Hung, *War and Popular Culture,* 281–282, 285.
3. Xu Guanqun, "Xinya."
4. Ibid., 131–133.
5. Ibid., 62–66; *Xiyao,* 276, 278; Chen Lizheng and Yuan Enzhen, eds., *Xinya de licheng,* 2.
6. Xu Guanqun, "Xinya," 1–2; *Xiyao,* 274.
7. Qi, "Xu Guanqun," 51, 70.
8. Xu Guanqun, "Xinya," 79.
9. For a comparison of Western, Japanese, and Chinese business practices that were used in China at this time, see Cochran, *Encountering Chinese Networks,* chap. 1.
10. Xu Guanqun, "Xinya," 32, 38–40, 72–76; *Xiyao,* 278; Chen Lizheng and Yuan Enzhen, eds., *Xinya de licheng,* 5. On Takeda, see Fruin, *Japanese Enterprise System,* 103–104.
11. Qi, "Xu Guanqun," 51, 70.
12. Xu Guanqun, "Xinya," 79; *Xiyao,* 285; Chen Lizheng and Yuan Enzhen, eds., *Xinya de licheng,* 19.

13. Xu Guanqun, "Xinya," 65–66; *Xiyao,* 285.
14. Xu Guanqun, "Xinya," 56–60, 62, 64, 126; *Xiyao,* 282; Chen Lizheng and Yuan Enzhen, eds., *Xinya de licheng,* 19–20.
15. *Xiyao,* 278; Xu Guanqun, "Xinya," 62–66; Chen Lizheng and Yuan Enzhen, eds., *Xinya de licheng,* 30–32; Qi, "Xu Guanqun," 50–51; Chen Lizheng and Yuan Enzhen, eds., *Shanghai Xinya,* 136–139.
16. Xu Guanqun, "Xinya," 8; *Xiyao,* 276.
17. Xu Guanqun, "Xinya," 3–4.
18. Ibid., 8, 65; Gan, ed., *Shanghai bainian,* 31.
19. Starr, *Social Transformation,* 127–134. In China during the early twentieth century, practitioners of Western-style medicine made proposals that were modeled after American efforts to regulate advertising of patent medicines, but they did not attempt to regulate big pharmaceutical companies' ownership and control of medical journals and health publications. The first concerted efforts to regulate medical advertising in China date from 1909. See Cochran, "Marketing Medicine," 84–85.
20. Xu Guanqun, "Xinya," 57–58; *Xiyao;* 282; Chen Lizheng and Yuan Enzhen, eds., *Xinya de licheng,* 13. In 1932 Xu recruited as the first members of the editorial board at the *Journal of New Medicine* three distinguished physicians, Drs. Zhao Yuhuang, Xu Naili, and Gu Yuqi. In 1936 he added to New Asia's board of directors two of China's most famous men of medicine, Drs. Wu Liande and Yan Fuqing (Xu Guanqun, "Xinya," 31–32).
21. Qi, "Xu Guanqun," 52–53.
22. Xu Guanqun, "Xinya," 59.
23. For other examples, see Benson, "Consumers Are Also Soldiers," and Glosser, "Business of Family," 80–116.
24. Xu Guanqun, "Women," 1; Chen Lizheng and Yuan Enzhen, eds., *Xinya de licheng,* 256–58.
25. Xu Guanqun, "Xinya," 22–23; Wakeman, *Policing Shanghai,* 288.
26. Xu Guanqun, "Xinya," 22–23, 25; *Xiyao,* 301–303, 319–320; Chen Lizheng and Yuan Enzhen, eds., *Xinya de licheng,* 5.
27. Xu Guanqun, "Xinya," 32, 35–36.
28. Ibid., 42–43; *Xiyao,* 279–280. For a survey of the wartime relocation inland by a minority of Shanghai's capitalists, see Coble, *Chinese Capitalists,* chap. 1.
29. Xu Guanqun, "Xinya," 42.
30. Ibid., 34, 148, 155; *Xiyao,* 279, 288. On Du, see Martin, "Resistance and Cooperation."

31. Xu Guanqun, "Xinya," 38–40; *Xiyao,* 278; Chen Lizheng and Yuan Enzhen, eds., *Xinya de licheng,* 5.

32. Xu Guanqun, "Xinya," 67, 102; *Xiandai Shanghai dashiji,* 740, 796; *Xiyao,* 171–172. Cf. Wang Ke-wen, "Collaborators and Capitalists," 51, and Yuan Yuquan, "Rikou," 83–85.

33. *Xiyao,* 301–303, 319–320; Chen Lizheng and Yuan Enzhen, eds., *Xinya de licheng,* 5; Xu Guanqun, "Xinya," 25. The organization resulting from this merger was known as the Alliance of the New Medicine Trade and the Pharmaceutical Industry (Xinyaoye zhiyaoye lianhehui). It existed barely a year, until April 1943, when it once again was divided into two organizations because of orders from Wang Jingwei's government that all prewar guilds and trade associations be restored (*Xiyao,* 301–302).

34. Wang Ke-wen, "Collaborators and Capitalists," 49–50; Gan, ed., *Shanghai bainian,* 32; *Xiyao,* 170–171, 287, 302; Chen Lizheng and Yuan Enzhen, eds., *Xinya de licheng,* 27.

35. Xu Guanqun, "Xinya," 68, 127; *Xiyao,* 171–172.

36. Xu Guanqun, "Xinya," 68–69. On Wu Kaixian and Wu Shaoshu in wartime Shanghai, see Martin, "Resistance and Cooperation." On the C. C. Clique, see Tien, *Government,* 47–52, and Eastman, *Seeds of Destruction,* 27–28, 100–102, 109–116.

37. Xu Guanqun, "Xinya," 162–163.

38. On the rivalry between the C. C. Clique and the Political Study Clique before, during, and after the war, see Tien, *Government,* 70–71, and Eastman, *Seeds of Destruction,* 111–113, 125–127.

39. Xu Guanqun, "Xinya," 119–121.

40. Ibid., 128–133.

41. See Cochran, "Marketing Medicine," 87–88, and Chapter 6 in this volume.

42. The only exceptions to this generalization were in Germany, where the leading pharmaceutical company, Bayer, was producing synthetic drugs developed in its laboratories as early as 1900. In the United States and Britain the leading pharmaceutical companies did not open their first laboratories for serious research until the decade preceding World War II: Eli Lilly in 1929, Merck and Company in 1933, Squibb in 1938. See Chandler, *Scale and Scope,* 478; Cowen and Helfand, *Pharmacy,* 164, 214; and Young, *Pure Food,* 113–120.

43. Xu Guanqun, "Xinya," 44, 49–50, 125.

44. Ibid., 37–39, 49, 125, 197; *Xiyao,* 276, 278; Chen Lizheng and Yuan Enzhen, eds., *Xinya de licheng,* 13.

45. *Jiankang jiating* 3, nos. 9–10 (1942); 4, nos. 1–2 (1943).

46. Danggui (a.k.a. Angelica sinensis) was first popularized in China in the eleventh century and was commonly used in late imperial China to treat menstrual irregularity. See Bray, *Technology and Gender,* 320–321n.9, 332–333.

47. Chen Lizheng and Yuan Enzhen, eds., *Xinya de licheng,* 66.

48. Qi, "Xu Guanqun," 51, 70.

49. Xu's appointments to the school's board of trustees illustrate his techniques for cultivating political figures in positions of authority. In deference to the Japanese, he appointed to the school's board three of Shanghai's leading Chinese collaborators, Wen Lanting, Yuan Ludeng, and Lin Kanghou. To give representation to Wang Jingwei's Japanese-sponsored government for Central China, Xu appointed as a trustee Chu Minyi, who was Wang's brother-in-law and a high official in Wang's government. Xu's choice as a representative of the Green Gang among the school's trustees was Gu Kemin, Xu's sworn brother and a leader of the gang in wartime Shanghai (Xu Guanqun, "Xinya," 102).

50. Ibid., 102, 79.

51. Ibid., 66–72; *Xiyao,* 279–281; Chen Lizheng and Yuan Enzhen, eds., *Xinya de licheng,* 5–8.

52. Xu Guanqun, "Xinya," 64–66, 69–72; *Xiyao,* 278–280; Chen Lizheng and Yuan Enzhen, *Xinya de licheng,* 17–19; Tan, "Xu Guanqun," 263.

53. File Q38–40–11, Xinya huaxue zhiyao gongsi Papers.

54. Xu Guanqun, "Xinya," 58–59; *Xiyao,* 282; Qi, "Xu Guanqun," 54–55.

55. Xu Guanqun, "Xinya," 58. On the rivalry between advocates of Chinese- and Western-style medicine, see Croizier, *Traditional Medicine;* Zhao Hongjun, *Jindai Zhongxiyi;* and Xiaoqun Xu, *Chinese Professionals,* chap. 7.

56. Xu's other wartime medical publications included *The Catalogue of Superior Medicines from [New Asia's] Star Brand (Xingpai liangyao ji)* (in Chinese), which started in 1929 and went through a total of twenty editions by the end of the war (Chen Lizheng and Yuan Enzhen, eds., *Xinya de licheng,* 256–258); the *Journal of New Medicine (Xin yiyao kan)* (in Chinese), which, as mentioned earlier, had been founded in 1932 and continued to be published until 1941; and *Modern Therapeutics,* an English-language medical manual whose first edition of five thousand copies was shipped in 1939 from Shanghai to Singapore for distribution throughout Southeast Asia (Xu Guanqun, "Xinya," 59–60; *Xiyao,* 282).

57. On the etymology of the Japanese term for health *(kenko)* in the Meiji period, see Tatsukawa, *Meiji iji orai,* 50–58. I am indebted to Ruth

Rogaski for this reference. She has analyzed the etymology of the related Chinese term *weisheng* (health care, hygiene, or sanitation) and its derivation from the Japanese term *eisei;* see Rogaski, *Hygienic Modernity,* chap. 3.

58. Yeh, "Progressive Journalism," 205–214, esp. 213–214.
59. Xu Guanqun, "Women," 1.
60. Xu Guanqun, "Fumujie yougan," 5–6.
61. Xu Guanqun, "Women," 1.
62. Ibid.
63. Zeng, "Kexue."
64. Link, *Mandarin Ducks,* 178.
65. Chen Diexian, "Shiyan jiating." Other writers from the Mandarin Duck and Butterfly school contributing to *Healthy Home* included Zhou Shoujuan, Fan Yanqiao, Gu Mingdao, Qin Shou'ou, Xu Zhuodai, and Zhang Henshui. On them and their early writings, see Link, *Mandarin Ducks,* 117–118, 124, 148, 158, 164, 168–169, 257–258.
66. Qi, "Xu Guanqun," 54–55. On Ding, see Hung, *War and Popular Culture,* 30, and Laing, *Selling Happiness,* 103, 189.
67. Xu Guanqun, "Xinya," 55–61.
68. Ibid., 101.
69. To place Xu's marketing in historical perspective, it is worth noting that he was not the first to use images of the family in advertisements for Chinese-made medicine. Others had done so at least as early as 1926 (see Lee, "Cultural Construction," 49–50). But he differed from earlier advertisers in explicitly identifying his image of the healthy family as a distinct alternative to the image of the healthy family that had been advocated by prewar intellectuals.
70. Xu Guanqun, "Xinya," 142–146. On the campaigns against Chinese capitalists in Shanghai during the 1950s, see Gardner, *"Wu-fan* Campaign."
71. Reardon-Anderson, *Study of Change,* 151, 170.
72. Hung, *War and Popular Culture,* 14, 18, 19, 279, 282, 285.
73. Eastman, "Facets of an Ambivalent Relationship," 276–278.
74. See Martin, "Resistance and Cooperation," Rottmann, "Crossing Enemy Lines," and Wakeman, "Shanghai Smuggling."

6. CROSSING NATIONAL BORDERS

The letter cited in the epigraph is in the collection "Political Development: Aw Boon Haw" (see Archives).

1. Gimson to Jones, September 22, 1949, CO 717/183/52928/26, ibid.
2. Li Fengrui and Wang Dong, *Hu Wenhu pingzhuan*, 29–31.
3. Aw Kow (Datin), transcript of interview A000041/04, 7, 1984, Singapore Archives; Chen Danxin and Li Fengrui, "Hu Wenhu fengyun lu," 12–13.
4. Brandel and Turbeville, *Tiger Balm Gardens*, 22.
5. Aw Kow (Datin), transcript of interview A000041/04, 6, 1984, Singapore Archives; Hu Zhifei and Chen Danxin. "Hu Wenhu dashiji," 13.
6. Brandel and Turbeville, *Tiger Balm Gardens*, 22.
7. Yan Shufen, "Guanshi jiazu shilue," 10–13; Crossman, *China Trade*, 26–29.
8. Wu Hao et al., *Duhui modeng*, 13, 17, 161; Zhuo Botang, "Guan Huinong yu Zhongguo zaoqi de shangpin haibao," 4; Gu, "Guan Huinong shengping jianjie," 14–15; Croizier, *Art and Revolution*, 68–70.
9. Croizier, *Art and Revolution*, 40.
10. Guan was not the only Chinese artist to work with the Gao brothers and then apply what he had learned to painting calendar posters. In 1914, one year after Guan parted company with them, Zheng Mantuo (discussed in Chapter 3) collaborated with them and, as a result, improved his painting. See Laing, *Selling Happiness*, 121–124.
11. Wu Hao et al., *Duhui modeng*, 13, 161; Zhuo Botang, "Guan Huinong yu Zhongguo zaoqi de shangpin haibao," 7; Lu Jin, "Yuefenpai dawang," 9; Feng, "Jiguang shiji," 16. Guan's clients included, among others, China's biggest cigarette companies, British American Tobacco Company and Nanyang Brothers Cigarette Company (Feng, "Jiguang shiji," 16).
12. Luo Yi, "Wo suo zhidao de Hu Wenhu," 52.
13. Laopai, *Hu Wenhu*, 9.
14. For photographs showing Aw's multilingual advertising, see Figure 6.2 and Brandel and Turbeville, *Tiger Balm Gardens*, 26–38.
15. Brandel and Turbeville, *Tiger Balm Gardens*, 30–31, 37.
16. Laopai, *Hu Wenhu*, 17–18; King, *Tiger Balm King*, 252–254; Brandel and Turbeville, *Tiger Balm Gardens*, 27, 36, 38–39.
17. Brandel and Turbeville, *Tiger Balm Gardens*, 17, 56.
18. Ibid., 58–59, 84, 108; Laopai, *Hu Wenhu*, 109–111.
19. Kang, *Hu Wenhu zhuan*, 52, Hu Zhifei, "Hu Wenhu yishi," 11–12; England, "Aws," 14; Chi Zi, "Hu Wenhu," 67–68; Lynn Pan, *Sons of the Yellow Emperor*, 177.
20. Laopai, *Hu Wenhu*, 17–18.

21. Lynn Pan, *Sons of the Yellow Emperor,* 176.
22. Personal communications from three Thai historians, Thak Chaloemtiarana, Kamala Tiyavanich, and Chiranan Prasertkul, February 2001.
23. Wessing, *Soul of Ambiguity,* 53.
24. Steinberg, ed., *In Search of Southeast Asia,* 257.
25. Ibid., 254–261.
26. Shi Jian, "Wei Shaobo," 67–68; Wu Chengluo, "Zhongguo," 128.
27. Kang, *Hu Wenhu zhuan,* 188–189.
28. Zhang Yonghe, *Hu Wenhu,* 54; Ji Dan, *Baoye haomen,* 46–47.
29. Kang, *Hu Wenhu zhuan,* 188–189; Li Fengrui and Wang Dong, *Hu Wenhu pingzhuan,* 46–48.
30. Sng Choon Yee, transcript of interview A000064/48, 1984, 199, 202–210, Singapore Archives; Chen Danxin and Li Fengrui, "Hu Wenhu fengyun lu," 16–17; Zhang Wenqiang, "Hu Wenhu," 9.
31. Kang, *Hu Wenhu zhuan,* 57–59; Ji Dan, *Baoye haomen,* 53. Tan and Aw later became rivals not only as newspaper publishers but also as political activists and philanthropists. On their rivalry in the 1930s and 1940s, see Yong, *Tan Kah-kee,* 183, 189–191, 193, 301–302, and Zheng Liren, "Overseas Chinese Nationalism," 297–293, 304–306, 311–316.
32. Lin Aimin, "Liangnian yilai," jia-5.
33. Ibid.; Laopai, *Hu Wenhu,* 34; Quentin Pan, review.
34. Laopai, *Hu Wenhu,* 34.
35. Lin Aimin, "Benbao guoqu ji jianglai"; Laopai, *Hu Wenhu,* 40.
36. Laopai, *Hu Wenhu,* 48, 51, 53; Hu Zhifei and Chen Danxin, "Hu Wenhu dashiji," 14; Chen Danxin and Li Fengrui, "Hu Wenhu fengyun lu," 17; Li Fengrui, "Hu Wenhu zai kangri zhanzheng shiqi," 3; Li Fengrui and Wang Dong, *Hu Wenhu pingzhuan,* 60–61.
37. Tsang, comp., "Biography of Aw Boon-haw," 25.
38. Leong, "Hakka Chinese," 305.
39. Luo Yi, "Wo suo zhidao de Hu Wenhu," 46–47. See also Kang, *Hu Wenhu zhuan,* 77; Jiang, "Hu Wenhu sanlun," 31; Luo Zhenqing, "Hu Wenhu," 37–43.
40. Luo Zhenqing, "Hu Wenhu," 37–43; Xu Guoren, "Xingxi baoye," 65–66; Zhao Jiaxin, "Fujian de liangjia xingxibao," 81–82.
41. Hu Guanzhong, "Hu Zizhou," 81.
42. Photographs of Aw's factories in Singapore and Shantou show the similarities between the two. See Brandel and Turbeville, *Tiger Balm Gardens,* 31.
43. Zhang Wenqiang, "Sanshi niandai," 40.

44. Hu Guanzhong, "Hu Zizhou," 81–82; Xu Guoren, "Xingxi baoye," 65–66; Zhao Jiaxin, "Fujian de liangjia xingxibao," 81–82.
45. *Xingdao Daily,* August 1, 1938.
46. Lin Aimin, "Liangnian yilai," jia-5, jia-10; Jiang, "Hu Wenhu de baoye," 35; Li Fengrui and Wang Dong, *Hu Wenhu pingzhuan,* 75–76.
47. Chen Danxin and Li Fengrui, "Hu Wenhu fengyun lu," 25. In 1941 Aw gave a similar explanation to Lin Sen, a high official in the Nationalist government. See Hu Yongzhong, "Hu Wenhu," 5–6.
48. Li Fengrui and Wang Dong, *Hu Wenhu pingzhuan,* 64.
49. Laopai, *Hu Wenhu,* 51.
50. Li Fengrui and Wang Dong, *Hu Wenhu pingzhuan,* 156; Kang, *Hu Wenhu zhuan,* 70, 88–89, 200; Laopai, *Hu Wenhu,* 63–65, 69–74, 80; Li Fengrui, "Hu Wenhu zai kangri zhanzheng shiqi," 3; Hong and Kong, "Lun Hu Wenhu," 186–187.
51. Laopai, *Hu Wenhu,* 47–49.
52. Aw's philanthropy was undoubtedly attributable to more than one motivation. On his possible patriotic and philosophical rationales, see Chan, "Exploratory Study."
53. Eastman, *Abortive Revolution,* 91.
54. Li Fengrui, "Hu Wenhu zai kangri zhanzheng shiqi," 5.
55. Both quotations are from Zhu and Chen, "'Wanjinyou da wang' Hu Wenhu," 31.
56. Eastman, *Abortive Revolution,* 92.
57. Fu, ed., *Xingzhou ribao.* Though General Cai and the Nineteenth Route Army were celebrated in the press, they were regarded as rivals by Chiang Kai-shek, who removed them from the public spotlight by transferring them southward from Shanghai to Fujian Province in May 1932. Later Chiang confronted and defeated them in a military battle in January 1934. See Eastman, *Abortive Revolution,* chap. 3, and Coble, *Facing Japan,* 39–55.
58. Luo Tiexian, "Hu Wenhu," 73.
59. Coble, *Facing Japan,* 55, 76–77, 80–89.
60. Aw's newspapers at Xiamen in the 1930s and Fuzhou in the 1940s became particularly well known for their left-wing journalists and their pro-Communist editorial positions. See Hu Guanzhong, "Hu Zizhou," 81, and Zhao Jiaxin, "Fujian de liangjia xingxibao."
61. Chen Danxin and Li Fengrui, "Hu Wenhu fengyun lu," 32; Zhang Wenqiang, "Hu Wenhu," 9, Zhang Wenqiang, "Sanshi niandai," 39–40; Ji Dan, *Baoye haomen,* 107–108.

62. Laopai, *Hu Wenhu*, 76–79; Chen Danxin and Li Fengrui, "Hu Wenhu fengyun lu," 20; Shen Lixin, "Jiwu liqun," 4; Liu Dafu, "Yi tianxia zhi cai," 18–19. For a photograph of one of Aw's schools, see Brandel and Turbeville, *Tiger Balm Gardens*, 201.

63. Hu Zhifei and Chen Danxin, "Hu Wenhu dashiji," 16–17; Li Fengrui, "Hu Wenhu zai kangri zhanzheng shiqi," 7–8.

64. Tsang, comp., "Biography of Aw Boon-haw," 9; King, *Tiger Balm King*, 322.

65. Shen Lixin, "Jiwu liqun," 4; Liu Dafu, "Yi tianxia zhi cai," 18; Hu Yongzhong, "Hu Wenhu," 3–5; Hu Zhifei and Chen Danxin, "Hu Wenhu dashiji," 9; Li Fengrui, "Hu Wenhu zai kangri zhanzheng shiqi," 10.

66. For details on Aw's recovery of authority over his business, see Hong and Kong, "Lun Hu Wenhu," 188; Laopai, *Hu Wenhu*, 66–72; Li Fengrui and Wang Dong, *Hu Wenhu pingzhuan*, 152–153.

67. *Xiangdao ribao*, March 14, 1943.

68. Iriye, *Power and Culture*, 71.

69. Li Fengrui and Wang Dong, *Hu Wenhu pingzhuan*, 132–135; Ji Dan, *Baoye haomen*, 116–117. On the rice gluts in Burma and Thailand and food shortages elsewhere in Asia at this time, see Iriye, *Power and Culture*, 45–46, 98–99, and Stockwell, "Southeast Asia," 335.

70. Ito Takashi, Hirohashi, and Katashima, eds., *Tojo*, 1100–1104.

71. Ibid.

72. Laopai, *Hu Wenhu*, 72–73; Hong and Kong, "Lun Hu Wenhu"; Chen Danxin and Li Fengrui, "Hu Wenhu fengyun lu," 34; Hu Zhifei and Chen Danxin, "Hu Wenhu dashiji," 20; Li Fengrui, "Hu Wenhu zai kangri zhanzheng shiqi," 10–11.

73. Laopai, *Hu Wenhu*, 68–69; Kang, *Hu Wenhu zhuan*, 200; Chen Danxin, "Hu Wenhu zai Xianggang," 25.

74. "Hu Wenhu di Xingjiapo," *Xingdao ribao*, December 14, 1945.

75. Ibid.

76. Laopai, *Hu Wenhu*, 47–48, 80–81, 127.

77. Hu Yongzhong, "Hu Wenhu," 4, 6; Hu Guanzhong, "Hu Zizhou," 81; Zhao Jiaxin, "Fujian de liangjia xingxibao."

78. Chen Danxin and Li Fengrui, "Hu Wenhu fengyun lu," 35; Hu Zhifei and Chen Danxin, "Hu Wenhu dashiji," 21–22; Li Fengrui and Wang Dong, *Hu Wenhu pingzhuan*, 188–189; Li Fengrui, "Hu Wenhu zai kangri zhanzheng shiqi," 10.

79. Li Fengrui, "Hu Wenhu zai kangri zhanzheng shiqi," 10; Chen Danxin and Li Fengrui, "Hu Wenhu fengyun lu," 35–36.

80. Hu Zhitei and Chen Danxin, "Hu Wenhu dashiji," 21–22.
81. Chen Danxin and Li Fengrui, "Hu Wenhu fengyun lu," 17–18; Chen Min, *Minguo huaqiao mingren zhuan,* 157–158.
82. Laopai, *Hu Wenhu,* 51.
83. Temporel, *Branding in Asia,* 19–20.
84. As quoted in Chen Min, *Minguo huaqiao mingren zhuan,* 157–158.
85. Trocki, *Opium and Empire,* 30.
86. Eastman, *Abortive Revolution;* Coble, *Shanghai Capitalists;* Bergère, *Golden Age;* 274; Kirby, "Continuity and Change," 125–132. Their positions are summarized in Chapter 1 in this volume.
87. Coble, *Chinese Capitalists.*
88. Gardner, *"Wu-fan* Campaign"; Vogel, *Canton under Communism.*
89. Nye, *Bound to Lead,* 188.
90. Watson, "Introduction," 36–38.
91. Clunas, "Modernity," 1507.

7. AGENTS OF CONSUMER CULTURE

1. Davis, "Introduction," 2.
2. For the original model, see the classic book by Immanuel Wallerstein, *Modern World System.*
3. Sugihara, "Japan as an Engine," 137.
4. Chandler, *Scale and Scope,* 605–606.
5. The question of why Chinese and other Asian entrepreneurs concentrated on light industry and left heavy industry to Western manufacturers in the first half of the twentieth century has recently been addressed by Sugihara Kaoru. He has argued that whereas Westerners in heavy industry followed a capital-intensive "industrial revolution path," Asians complemented what they did by taking a labor-intensive "industrious revolution path." See his "East Asian Path of Economic Development." For a long-term perspective on this and other divergences, see Pomeranz, *Great Divergence.*
6. Selden, "China, Japan, and the Regional Political Economy of East Asia," 338.
7. On Western businesses' delegation of authority to Chinese networks, see Cochran, *Encountering Chinese Networks,* chaps. 2–3.
8. Rubinfien, "Commodity to Brand"; Huffman, *Creating a Public;* Quataert, "Introduction"; Rowe and Schelling, *Memory and Modernity;* Paz-Soldán and Castillo, eds., *Latin American Literature.*

9. Katzenstein and Shiraishi, "Conclusion," 350.

10. Watson, "Introduction," 37.

11. Ibid., 15, table 2.

12. Link, *Mandarin Ducks,* 204.

13. Recently specialists on politics and culture on the one hand and specialists on society and the economy on the other have called for research on mediators in Chinese history. In political and cultural history, Prasenjit Duara has urged scholars "to seek out cultural negotiators in our sources," and he has done so in his own research on the Concordia Association and redemptive societies in Manchukuo during the 1930s (see his "Response," 33–34, and his *Sovereignty and Authenticity*). In social and economic history, Gary Hamilton and Wei-an Chang have noted that China specialists have neglected to investigate Chinese merchants as merchandisers in late imperial China, and they have argued that these merchants mediated between the production and distribution of goods so decisively that the economy became "buyer driven" rather than "producer driven" (see their "Importance of Commerce").

14. See, for example, Lee, "Cultural Constructions"; Fraser, "Smoking Out the Enemy"; and Gerth, *China Made.*

15. On the size of China's population in the early twentieth century, see Perkins, *Agricultural Development,* 122; Schran, "China's Demographic Evolution," 644; Rawski, *Economic Growth,* 280. It is worth noting that the decade between the mid-1920s and mid-1930s was also a crucial period in the emergence of consumer cultures in the United States and Europe. See Kammen, *American Culture,* 21, and de Grazia, "Mass Culture," 53–70.

16. My calls for widening the temporal and spatial boundaries of consumer culture echo those that have been made by historians of other times and places. Specialists on China have found evidence of it in pre-twentieth-century history, especially during the Ming dynasty (1368–1644) (Hamilton and Lai, "Consumerism without Capitalism"; Clunas, *Superfluous Things;* Brook, *Confusions of Pleasure;* Pomeranz, *Great Divergence*); and historians of Southeast Asia, the Middle East, the United States, continental Europe and England (which has been most intensively studied) have cited parallel developments and speculated that early modern societies in Europe, the Middle East, Southeast Asia, and East Asia were all part of "a shared consumer revolution" (Quartaert, "Introduction" 4). On Southeast Asia, see Reid, *Southeast Asia.* On Europe and especially England, see Brewer and Porter, eds., *Consumption*

and the World of Goods; Brewer and Staves, eds. *Early Modern Conceptions of Property;* and Bermingham and Brewer, eds., *Consumption of Culture.* The influential book that served, arguably, as the point of departure for this entire body of literature is McKendrick, Brewer, and Plumb, *Birth of a Consumer Society.* For perceptive reviews of the growing literature on consumer culture in Western history published in the 1980s and 1990s, see Agnew, "Coming Up for Air," and Clunas, "Modernity."

17. Hanlong Lu, "To Be Relatively Comfortable," 130–131.
18. Kammen, *American Culture,* 21.
19. Ibid., 168.
20. On Tongren Tang, see BJTRTS; on Zhonghua (originally Huang Chujiu's business), *Longteng;* on New Asia, Chen Lizheng and Yuan Enzhen, eds., *Xinya de licheng,* and Chen Lizheng and Yuan Enzhen, eds., *Shanghai Xinya;* on Tiger Balm, *Legend from a Jar.* The one exception, Five Continents, has been the topic of several articles that were published in the 1980s and 1990s and cited in Chapter 4, but as far as I know, its business managers have not commissioned or published a book-length history of the company.
21. Gail Henderson, personal message, May 4, 1998.
22. Henderson, "Competing," 27.
23. Henderson, personal message.
24. Yunxiang Yan, "State Power," 43–44.
25. Yan has identified the four leading agents of consumer culture in contemporary China as transnational companies, the Chinese state, Chinese intellectuals, and Chinese youth (Yan, "State Power," 34–35). Whether he is justified in omitting Chinese entrepreneurs from this list is open to question, especially in light of complaints from businesspeople, such as the one lodged recently by Austin Lally, Procter and Gamble's general manager in China. "China is a very competitive market," Lally observed of the country that is currently the sixth largest consumer of his company's goods. "There are many hundreds of local brands in all of the categories in which we compete" (Fowler, "The Advertising Report").

ARCHIVES

Aw Boon Haw Papers, *Sing Tao Jih Pao* Archives, Hong Kong.

Aw Kow (Datin), transcript of interview, 1984, Singapore Archives and Oral History Department, Singapore National Archives, Singapore.

Liu Dajun Papers, Center for Research on Chinese Business History, Shanghai Academy of Social Sciences, Shanghai.

Peking Union Medical College Papers, Rockefeller Archives, Tarrytown, N.Y.

"Political Development: Aw Boon Haw," a collection of documents from the British Colonial Office, Central Library, National University of Singapore, Singapore.

Shanghai Municipal Police (International Settlement) Files. Microfilms from the U.S. National Archives.

Sng Choon Yee, transcript of interview, 1984, Singapore Archives and Oral History Department, Singapore National Archives, Singapore.

Wuzhou da yaofang (Great Five Continents Drugstores) Papers, Shanghai Municipal Archives, Shanghai.

Xinya huaxue zhiyao gongsi (New Asia Chemical and Medical Company) Papers, Shanghai Municipal Archives, Shanghai.

Adorno, Theodor, and Max Horkheimer. *Dialectic of Enlightenment*. London: Verso, 1979.

Agnew, Jean-Christophe. "Coming Up for Air: Consumer Culture in Historical Perspective." In *Consumption and the World of Goods*, edited by John Brewer and Roy Porter. London: Routledge, 1993.

Ahern, Emily. "Chinese-Style and Western-Style Doctors in Northern Taiwan." In *Culture and Healing in Asian Societies*, edited by Arthur Kleinman. Cambridge, Mass.: Schenkman, 1978.

Alford, William P. *To Steal a Book Is an Elegant Offense: Intellectual Property Law in Chinese Civilization*. Stanford, Calif.: Stanford University Press, 1995.

Alitto, Guy. *The Last Confucian: Liang Shu-ming and the Chinese Dilemma of Modernity*. Berkeley: University of California Press, 1979.

An Guanying. "Dui zi gaizao zhong de daibiao renwu Yue Songsheng" (Yue Songsheng as a representative of the people in the reforms). *Tianjin wenshi ziliao xuanji* (Collected literary and historical materials on Tianjin), ser. 71, 3 (1996): 9–23.

———. "Fazhan zhong de Beijing Tongren Tang" (The development of Tongren Tang in Beijing). In *Zhonghua bainian lao yaopu* (A century of old medicine shops in China), edited by An Guanying and Han Sunfang. Beijing: Zhongguo wenshi chubanshe, 1993.

———. "Tongren Tang chuanren Yue Songsheng" (Yue Songsheng: Heir to Tongren Tang). *Beijing wenshi ziliao* (Literary and historical materials on Beijing) 55 (1997): 125–159.

An Guanying, Han Shufan, and Pan Xichen. "Tongren Tang." In *Zhonghua bainian lao yaopu* (A century of old medicine shops in China). Beijing: Zhongguo wenshi chubanshe, 1993.

Appadurai, Arjun. *Modernity at Large: Cultural Dimensions of Globalization*. Minneapolis: University of Minnesota Press, 1996.

Bacon, C. A. "Pharmacy in Shanghai." *Chinese Economic Journal* (August 1929): 650–661.

Bai Ding. "Tongren Tang laodian xinkai" (A new face for the old shop Tongren Tang). In *Chengdu fengwu* (Chengdu customs), vol. 2. Chengdu: Chengdushi qunzhong yinshuguan, 1981.

Barlow, Tani E. "Theorizing Woman: Funü, Guojia, Jiating." In *Body, Subject, and Power in China,* edited by Angela Zito and Tani E. Barlow. Chicago: University of Chicago Press, 1994.

Barnet, Richard J., and John Cavanagh. *Global Dreams: Imperial Corporations and the New World Order.* New York: Simon and Schuster, 1994.

Beer, John Joseph. *The Emergence of the German Dye Industry.* New York: Arno Press, 1981.

Beijing baike quanshu bianji weiyuanhui (Editorial committee of the Beijing encyclopedia), ed. *Beijing baike quanshu: Cai tu, ditu ji* (Beijing encyclopedia with color illustrations and maps). Beijing: Aolinpike chubanshe, 1991.

Beijing Zhongyiyao laonian baojian yanjiusuo (Beijing research institute on Chinese medicine and pharmacy to prevent senility), ed. "Tongren Tang jianshi" (A brief history of Tongren Tang). In *Beijing Tongren Tang mingyao* (Famous medicines of Beijing's Tongren Tang). Beijing: Zhongyi guji-chubanshe, 1986.

Benson, Carlton. "Consumers Are Also Soldiers: Subversive Songs from Nanjing Road during the New Life Movement." In *Inventing Nanjing Road: Commercial Culture in Shanghai, 1900–1945,* edited by Sherman Cochran. Ithaca, N.Y.: Cornell East Asia Program, 1999.

Bergère, Marie-Claire. *The Golden Age of the Chinese Bourgeoisie, 1911–1937.* Translated by Janet Lloyd. Cambridge: Cambridge University Press, 1989.

Bermingham, Ann, and John Brewer, eds. *The Consumption of Culture, 1600–1800: Image, Object, Text.* London: Routledge, 1995.

Boorman, Howard L., and Richard C. Howard, eds. *Biographical Dictionary of Republican China.* 5 vols. New York: Columbia University Press, 1968.

Brandel, Judith, and Tina Turbeville. *Tiger Balm Gardens: A Chinese Billionaire's Fantasy Environments.* Hong Kong: Aw Boon Haw Foundation, 1998.

Bray, Francesca. *Technology and Gender: Fabrics of Power in Late Imperial China.* Berkeley: University of California Press, 1997.

Brewer, John, and Roy Porter, eds. *Consumption and the World of Goods.* London: Routledge, 1993.

Brewer, John, and Susan Staves, eds. *Early Modern Conceptions of Property.* London: Routledge, 1995.

Brook, Timothy. *Confusions of Pleasure: Commerce and Culture in Ming China.* Berkeley: University of California Press, 1998.

Buji. "Jiefangqian de 'yuefenpai' nianhua shiliao" (Historical materials on pre-liberation New Year's calendar posters). *Meishu yanjiu* (Research on art) 2 (1959): 51–56.

Cahill, James. "The Three Zhangs, Yangzhou Beauties, and the Manchu Court." *Orientations* (January 1996): 59–68.

———. "'Where Did the Nymph Hang?' (Ching Yuan Chai so-shih I)." *Kaikodo Journal* 7 (spring 1998): 8–16.

Cameron, John. "Some Sidelights on Pharmacy in Peking, China." *American Journal of Pharmacy* 97, no. 10 (1925): 665–671.

Cameron, John, and K. K. Chen. "The Old and the New in Pharmacy in China." *Pharmaceutical Journal and Pharmacist* 14 (June 6, 1925): 633–636.

Cao Juren. *Jiuri jinghua* (The capital in olden times). Hong Kong: Nantian shuye gongsi, 1971.

Cartier, Carolyn. "Origins and Evolution of a Geographical Idea: The Macroregion in China." *Modern China* 28, no. 1 (2002): 79–143.

Certeau, Michel de. *The Practice of Everyday Life.* Translated by Steven F. Randall. Berkeley: University of California Press, 1984.

Chan, John S. N. "An Exploratory Study of Aw Boon Haw's Thought." *Journal of the South Seas Society* 52 (August 1998): 22–57.

Chandler, Alfred D., Jr. *Scale and Scope: The Dynamics of Industrial Capitalism.* Cambridge: Harvard University Press, 1990.

Chang Chung-li. *The Chinese Gentry: Studies on Their Role in Nineteenth-Century Chinese Society.* Seattle: University of Washington Press, 1967.

Chang Hao. *Chinese Intellectuals in Crisis: Search for Order and Meaning (1890–1911).* Berkeley: University of California Press, 1987.

Chang Kia-ngau. *The Inflationary Spiral: The Experience in China, 1939–1950.* Cambridge: Technology Press of the Massachusetts Institute of Technology, 1958.

Chang Te-chang. "The Economic Role of the Imperial Household in the Ch'ing Dynasty." *Journal of Asian Studies* 31, no. 2 (1972): 242–273.

Chen Danxin. "Hu Wenhu zai Xianggang lunxian shiqi zhi mi" (What did Aw Boon-haw do during the occupation of Hong Kong?). *Hu Wenhu yanjiu* 2 (1987): 24–28.

Chen Danxin and Li Fengrui. "Hu Wenhu fengyun lu" (The colorful life of Hu Wenhu). *Hu Wenhu yanjiu* 1 (1985): 11–37.

Chen Diexian (Tianxu Wosheng). "Shiyan jiating changshi" (Common sense about family experiments). *Jiankang jiating* 5 (1939).

Chen, Joseph T. *The May Fourth Movement in Shanghai.* Leiden: Brill, 1971.

Chen, K. K. "Chinese Drug Stores." *Annals of Medical History* 7, no. 2 (1925): 103–109.

Chen Lizheng and Yuan Enzhen, eds. *Shanghai Xinya yaoye youxian gongsi zhi* (Annals of Shanghai New Asia Pharmaceuticals Company, Ltd.). Shanghai: Shanghai Xinya yaoye youxian gongsi, Shanghai shehui kexue yuan jingji yanjiu suo, 1996.

———. *Xinya de licheng—Shanghai xinya zhiyaochang de guoqu xianzai he jianglai* (New Asia step by step—Shanghai New Asia Pharmaceutical Company in the past, present, and future). Shanghai: Shanghai shehui kexue yuan chubanshe, 1990.

Chen Min. *Minguo huaqiao mingren zhuan* (Biographies of eminent overseas Chinese during the Republican period). Beijing: Zhongguo huaqiao chuban gongsi, 1990.

Chen Xinqian and Zhang Tianlu. *Zhongguo jindai yaoxue shi* (A history of modern medicine in China). Beijing: Renmin weisheng chubanshe, 1992.

Chi Zehui, Lou Xuexi, and Chen Wenxian. *Beipingshi gongshangye gaikuang* (A survey of industry and business in the city of Beiping). Beiping: Beiping shehui ju, 1932.

Chi Zi. "Hu Wenhu yu yuanlin guji" (Hu Wenhu and his gardens). *Hu Wenhu yanjiu* 2 (1987): 67–69.

Choi Chi-cheung. "Competition among Brothers: The Kin Tye Lung Company and Its Associate Companies." In *Chinese Business Enterprise in Asia*, edited by Rajeswary Ampalavanar Brown. London: Routledge, 1995.

Chuan Anying. "Huiyi Tongren Tang guo yaodian" (Reminiscences about the national medicine store Tongren Tang). *Jiangxi Dingnan wenshi ziliao* (Literary and historical material on Dingnan, Jiangxi Province) 1 (December 1988): 72–74, 22.

Clunas, Craig. "Modernity Global and Local: Consumption and the Rise of the West." *American Historical Review* (December 1999): 1497–1511.

———. *Superfluous Things: Material Culture and Social Status in Early Modern China*. Urbana: University of Illinois Press, 1991.

Coble, Parks M., Jr. *Chinese Capitalists in Japan's New Order: The Occupied Lower Yangzi, 1937–1945*. Berkeley: University of California Press, 2003.

———. *Facing Japan: Chinese Politics and Japanese Imperialism, 1931–1937*. Cambridge: Council on East Asian Studies, Harvard University, 1991.

———. *The Shanghai Capitalists and the Nationalist Government, 1927–1937*. Cambridge: Council on East Asian Studies, Harvard University, 1980.

Cochran, Sherman. *Big Business in China: Sino-Foreign Rivalry in the Cigarette Industry, 1890–1930*. Cambridge: Harvard University Press, 1980.

———. *Encountering Chinese Networks: Western, Japanese, and Chinese Corporations in China, 1880–1937*. Berkeley: University of California Press, 2000.

————. "Marketing Medicine and Advertising Dreams in China, 1900–1950." In *Becoming Chinese: Passages to Modernity and Beyond,* edited by Wen-hsin Yeh. Berkeley: University of California Press, 1999.

————. "Transnational Origins of Advertising in Early Twentieth Century China." In *Inventing Nanjing Road: Commercial Culture in Shanghai, 1900–1945,* edited by Sherman Cochran. Ithaca, N.Y.: Cornell East Asia Program, 1999.

————, ed. *Inventing Nanjing Road: Commercial Culture in Shanghai, 1900–1945.* Ithaca, N.Y.: Cornell East Asia Program, 1999.

Cochran, Sherman, Andrew Hsieh, and Janis Cochran. *One Day in China: May 21, 1936.* New Haven: Yale University Press, 1983.

Cohen, Paul A. *Between Tradition and Modernity: Wang T'ao and Reform in Late Ch'ing China.* Cambridge: Harvard University Press, 1974.

Cole, James H. *Shaohsing: Competition and Cooperation in Nineteenth-Century China.* Tucson: University of Arizona Press, 1986.

Comaroff, Jean, and John L. Comaroff. Introduction to *Modernity and Its Malcontents: Ritual and Power in Postcolonial Africa,* edited by Jean Comaroff and John L. Comaroff. Chicago: University of Chicago Press, 1993.

Corley, T. A. B. "Interactions between the British and American Patent Medicine Industries, 1708–1914." *Business and Economic History,* 2d ser., 16 (1987): 111–129.

Cowen, David L., and William H. Helfand. *Pharmacy: An Illustrated History.* New York: Abrams, 1990.

Croizier, Ralph C. *Art and Revolution in Modern China: The Lingnan (Cantonese) School of Painting, 1906–1951.* Berkeley: University of California Press, 1988.

————. *Traditional Medicine in Modern China: Science, Nationalism, and the Tensions of Cultural Change.* Cambridge: Harvard University Press, 1968.

Crossman, Carl L. *The China Trade: Export Paintings, Furniture, Silver and Other Objects.* Princeton, N.J.: Pyne Press, 1972.

Davis, Deborah S. "Introduction: A Revolution in Consumption." In *The Consumer Revolution in Urban China,* edited by Deborah S. Davis. Berkeley: University of California Press, 2000.

De Grazia, Victoria. "Mass Culture and Sovereignty: The American Challenge to European Cinemas, 1920–1960." *Journal of Modern History* 61 (March 1989): 53–87.

Deng Ming, ed., *Shanghai bainian lueying, 1840s–1940s* (Survey of a century in Shanghai, 1840s–1940s). Shanghai: Shanghai renmin meishu chubanshe, 1996.

Ding Hao. "Ji lao Shanghai guanggao huajiaqun" (On advertising artists in old Shanghai). In *Lao Shanghai guanggao* (Advertising in old Shanghai), edited by Yi Bin. Shanghai: Shanghai huabao chubanshe, 1995.

Ding Wenjiang, Weng Wenhao, and Zeng Shiying, comps. *Zhonghua minguo xin ditu* (New maps of the Republic of China). Shanghai: Shanghai shen-bao guan, 1934.

Dirlik, Arif. *The Origins of Chinese Communism.* New York: Oxford University Press, 1989.

Duara, Prasenjit. "Response to Philip Huang's 'Biculturality in Modern China and Chinese Studies.'" *Modern China* 26, no. 1 (2000): 32–37.

———. *Sovereignty and Authencity: Manchukuo and the East Asia Modern.* Lanham, Md.: Rowman and Littlefield, 2003.

Eastman, Lloyd E. *The Abortive Revolution: China under Nationalist Rule, 1927–1937.* Cambridge: Harvard University Press, 1974.

———. "Facets of an Ambivalent Relationship: Smuggling, Puppets, and Atrocities during the War, 1937–1945." In *The Chinese and the Japanese: Essays in Political and Cultural Interactions,* edited by Akira Iriye. Princeton, N.J.: Princeton University Press, 1980.

———. *Seeds of Destruction: Nationalist China in War and Revolution, 1937–1949.* Stanford, Calif.: Stanford University Press, 1984.

Elman, Benjamin A. *A Cultural History of Civil Examinations in Late Imperial China.* Berkeley: University of California Press, 2000.

Elvin, Mark. "Tales of *Shen* and *Xin*: Body-Person and Heart-Mind in China during the Last 150 Years." *Zone 4,* pt. 2 (1989): 266–349.

"Engineering and Industrial Notes." *China Journal* 12, no. 5 (1930): 101.

England, Vaudine. "The Aws: Remnants of an Empire." *Asia Magazine* (July 28, 1985).

Esherick, Joseph W., ed. *Remaking the Chinese City: Modernity and National Identity, 1900–1950.* Honolulu: University of Hawai'i Press, 2000.

Feldwick, W., ed. *Present Day Impressions of the Far East and Prominent and Progressive Chinese at Home and Abroad.* London: Globe Encyclopedia Company, 1917.

Feng Liming. "Jiguang shiji—Yazhou shiyin ju hua dangnian" (Collecting missing bits—History of the Asiatic Litho Printing Press). In *Xianggang wenhua xilie: Yuefenpai wang—Guan Huinong* (Hong Kong culture series: The art of Guan Huinong—King of the calendar poster), edited by Yan Shufen. Hong Kong: Xianggang yishu zhongxin, 1993.

Fowler, Geoffrey A. "The Advertising Report: China." *Wall Street Journal,* January 21, 2004, B7.

Fraser, David. "Smoking Out the Enemy: The National Goods Movement and the Advertising of Nationalism in China, 1880–1937." Ph.D. diss., University of California, Berkeley, 1999.

Friedman, Thomas L. *The Lexus and the Olive Tree.* New York: Anchor, 2000.

Fruin, W. Mark. *The Japanese Enterprise System: Competitive Strategies and Cooperative Structures.* Oxford: Clarendon Press, 1994.

Fu Wumen, ed. *Xingzhou ribao sizhounian jiniankan: "Xin Fujian"* (*Xingzhou Daily*'s fourth annual yearbook: "New Fujian"). Singapore: *Xingzhou ribao,* 1933.

Furth, Charlotte. *Ting Wen-chiang: Science and China's New Culture.* Cambridge: Harvard University Press, 1970.

Gan Gu, ed. *Shanghai bainian mingchang laodian* (One hundred years of famous factories and old shops in Shanghai). Shanghai: Shanghai wenhua chubanshe, 1987.

Gardner, John. "The *Wu-fan* Campaign in Shanghai: A Study in the Consolidation of Urban Control." In *Chinese Communist Politics in Action,* edited by A. Doak Barnett. Seattle: University of Washington Press, 1969.

Gerth, Karl. *China Made: Consumer Culture and the Creation of the Nation.* Cambridge: Harvard University Asia Center, 2003.

Glosser, Susan L. "The Business of Family: You Huaigao and the Commercialization of a May Fourth Ideal." *Republican China* 20, no. 2 (1995): 80–116.

———. "Milk for Health, Milk for Profit: Shanghai's Chinese Dairy Industry under Japanese Occupation." In *Inventing Nanjing Road: Commercial Culture in Shanghai, 1900–1945,* edited by Sherman Cochran. Ithaca, N.Y.: Cornell East Asia Program, 1999.

Gong Jimin. "Huang Chujiu zhuan" (A biography of Huang Chujiu). Pt. 1. *Zhuanji wenxue* (Biographical literature) 60, no. 2 (February 1992): 53–58.

———. "Huang Chujiu zhuan" (A biography of Huang Chujiu). Pt. 2. *Zhuanji wenxue* (Biographical literature) 60, no. 3 (March 1992): 72–77.

———. "Huang Chujiu zhuan" (A biography of Huang Chujiu). Pt. 3. *Zhuanji wenxue* (Biographical literature) 60, no. 4 (April 1992): 93–99.

———. "Huang Chujiu zhuan" (A biography of Huang Chujiu). Pt. 4. *Zhuanji wenxue* (Biographical literature) 60, no. 5 (May 1992): 105–110.

———. "Huang Chujiu zhuan" (A biography of Huang Chujiu). Conclusion. *Zhuanji wenxue* (Biographical literature) 61, no. 1 (January 1993): 69–73.

Goodman, Bryna. *Native Place, City and Nation: Regional Networks and Identities in Shanghai, 1853–1937.* Berkeley: University of California Press, 1995.

Grieder, Jerome. *Hu Shih and the Chinese Renaissance: Liberalism in the Chinese Revolution, 1917–1937.* Cambridge: Harvard University Press, 1970.

Gu Haojun. "Guan Huinong shengping jianjie" (A brief biography of Guan Huinong). In *Xianggang wenhua xilie: Yuefenpai wang—Guan Huinong* (Hong Kong culture series: The art of Guan Huinong—King of the calendar poster), edited by Yan Shufen. Hong Kong: Xianggang yishu zhongxin, 1993.

Guan Zhichang. "Huang Chujiu." *Zhuanji wenxue* (Biographical literature) 47, no. 3 (1985): 138–140.

Guohuo diaochalu (A record of research on national goods), no. 3 (Shanghai, 1915).

Ha Yi. "Qingdai tai yiyuan" (The Imperial Hospital in the Qing dynasty). *Yandu* (Capital of Yan) 3 (1986): 40.

Haber, L. F. *The Chemical Industry, 1900–1930: International Growth and Technological Change.* Oxford: Clarendon Press, 1971.

Haishang mingren zhuan (Illustrious maritime personages). Shanghai: Wenming shuju, 1930.

Hamashita, Takeshi. "The Intra-Regional System in East Asia in Modern Times." In *Network Power: Japan and Asia,* edited by Peter J. Katzenstein and Takashi Shiraishi. Ithaca, N.Y.: Cornell University Press, 1996.

———. "Tribute and Treaties: Maritime Asia and Treaty Port Networks in the Era of Negotiation, 1800–1900." In *The Resurgence of East Asia,* edited by Giovanni Arrighi, Takeshi Hamashita, and Mark Selden. London: Routledge, 2003.

Hamelink, C. J. *Cultural Autonomy in Global Communications.* New York: Longman, 1983.

Hamilton, Gary G., and Wei-an Chang. "The Importance of Commerce in the Organization of China's Late Imperial Economy." In *The Resurgence of East Asia,* edited by Giovanni Arrighi, Takeshi Hamashita, and Mark Selden. London: Routledge, 2003.

Hamilton, Gary G., and Chi-kong Lai. "Consumerism without Capitalism: Consumption and Brand Names in Late Imperial China." In *The Social Economy of Consumption,* edited by Henry J. Rutz and Benjamin S. Orlove. Lanham, Md.: University Press of America, 1989.

Han Baode. *Jianzhu yu wenhua jinsilu* (Recent reflections on architecture and culture). Taipei: Guoli lishi bowuguan, 1995.

Han Wenwei and Li Xiu. "Tongren Tang." In *Zhonguo laozihao* (Old Chinese shops), vol. 9, edited by Kong Lingren and Li Dezheng. Beijing: Gaodeng jiaoyu chubanshe, 1998.

Hannerz, Ulf. *Transnational Connections: Culture, People, Places.* London: Routledge, 1996.

Hay, John. "The Body Invisible in Chinese Art?" In *Body, Subject, and Power in China,* edited by Angela Zito and Tani E. Barlow. Chicago: University of Chicago Press, 1994.

He Bei. "Tianjin Daren Tang" (Daren Tang in Tianjin). In *Jinmen laozihao* (Old shops in Tianjin), edited by Tianjin wenshi ziliao yanjiuhui (Research group on literary and historical materials in Tianjin). Tianjin: Baihua wenyi chubanshe, 1992.

Henderson, Gail. "Competing for the Antibiotic Market in China: The Case of Cepholsporins." Unpublished manuscript, n.d.

Henriot, Christian, and Wen-hsin Yeh, eds. *In the Shadow of the Rising Sun.* London: Routledge, 2003.

Hirschmeier, Johannes, and Tsunehiko Yui. *The Development of Japanese Business, 1600–1973.* Cambridge: Harvard University Press, 1975.

Ho Ping-ti. "In Defense of Sinicization." *Journal of Asian Studies* 57, no. 1 (1998): 123–152.

———. *The Ladder of Success in Imperial China: Aspects of Social Mobility, 1368–1911.* New York: Da Capo Press, 1962.

Hong Puren and Kong Yongsong. "Lun Hu Wenhu zai Xianggang lunxian qijian de dajie" (Was Aw Boon-haw a collaborator during the Japanese occupation of Hong Kong?). N.p., n.d.

Honig, Emily. *Sisters and Strangers: Women in Shanghai Cotton Mills, 1919–1949.* Stanford, Calif.: Stanford University Press, 1986.

Hou Chi-ming. *Foreign Investment and Economic Development in China, 1840–1937.* Cambridge: Harvard University Press, 1965.

Hou Shiheng. "Tongren Tang." In *Beijing laozihao* (Old Beijing shops), edited by Hou Shiheng. Beijing: Zhongguo huanjing kexue chubanshe, 1991.

Hu Guanzhong. "Hu Zizhou yu *Xingguang ribao*" (Aw Chu-chew and *Xingguang Daily*). *Xiamen wenshi ziliao* (Literary and historical materials on Xiamen) 15 (October 1989): 80–90.

Hu Jiru and Li Baochen. "Puyu shuju yu Wuzhou da yaofang" (Puyu Bookstore and Great Five Continents Drugstores). *Xuzhou wenshi ziliao* (Literary and historical materials on Xuzhou) 7 (1986): 90–95.

"Hu Wenhu xiansheng liushi jinwu shouzhen zhuan" (Special supplement on the sixty-fifth birthday of Mr. Aw Boon-haw), *Xingdao ribao* (Singapore), January 16, 1947, 2.

Hu Yongzhong. "Hu Wenhu zai Chongqing" (Aw Boon-haw in Chongqing). *Hu Wenhu yanjiu* 2 (1987): 3–8.

Hu Zhifei. "Hu Wenhu yishi" (Anecdotes on Aw Boon-haw). *Hu Wenhu yanjiu* 2 (1987): 9–12.

Hu Zhifei and Chen Danxin. "Hu Wenhu dashiji" (A historical record of Aw Boon-haw's life). *Hu Wenhu yanjiu* 2 (1987): 13–23.

Huang Kewu. "Cong *Shenbao* yiyao guanggao kan minchu Shanghai de yiliao wenhua yu shehui shenghuo, 1912–1926" (Medical advertisements in *Shenbao* as reflections of medicine, culture, and social life in early republican Shanghai, 1912–1926). *Zhongyang yanjiu yuan jindai shi yanjiu suo jikan* (Journal of Academia Sinica, Institute of Modern History) 17, pt. 2 (1988): 141–194.

Huffman, James. *Creating a Public: People and Press in Meiji Japan*. Honolulu: University of Hawai'i Press, 1997.

Hung, Chang-tai. *War and Popular Culture: Resistance in Modern China, 1937–1945*. Berkeley: University of California Press, 1994.

Imahori, Seiji. *Peipin shimin no jiji kosei* (The self-governing organizations of the people of Beiping). Tokyo: Bunkyudo, 1947.

Iriye, Akira. *Power and Culture: The Japanese-American War, 1941–1945*. Cambridge: Harvard University Press, 1981.

Ito Takashi, Hirohashi Tadamitsu, and Katashima Norio, eds. *Tojo Naikaku Sori Daijin kimitsu kiroku* (The classified files of Prime Minister Tojo). Tokyo: Tokyo daigaku shuppankai, 1990.

Ito Yoichiro. "Morishita Hiroshi o o shinobu" (Remembering the venerable Morishita Hiroshi). *Keizai jin* 7, no. 1 (1953): 385–395.

Ji Dan. *Baoye haomen: Hu Wenhu, Hu Xian zhuan* (A family of newspaper tycoons: Biographies of Aw Boon-haw and Aw Sian). Guangzhou: Guangzhou chubanshe, 1995.

Ji Shihua. "Tianjin Daren Tang qishiwu nian" (Seventy-five Years at Daren Tang in Tianjin). *Tianjin Hebei wenshi* (Literature and history of the Hebei district of Tianjin) 2 (1988): 99–108.

Jiang Guohua. "Hu Wenhu de baoye yu baoren jingshen" (Aw Boon-haw's newspapers and his attitude toward journalism). *Hu Wenhu yanjiu* 3 (1988): 30–36.

———. "Hu Wenhu sanlun" (A discussion of Aw Boon-haw). *Hu Wenhu yanjiu* 2 (1987): 29–34.

Jiankang jiating (Healthy home). Shanghai, 1937–1945.

"Jintan." *China Medical Journal* 30, no. 2 (1916): 150.

Jintan kara JINTAN e: Morishita Jintan hyakushunen kinenshi (From Jintan [in characters] to JINTAN [in capitalized roman letters]: Commemorating

Morishita Jintan's one hundredth anniversary). (Osaka: Morishita Jintan kabushiki kaisha, 1995.

Jones, Susan Mann. "The Ningpo Pang and Financial Power at Shanghai." In *The Chinese City between Two Worlds,* edited by Mark Elvin and G. William Skinner. Stanford, Calif.: Stanford University Press, 1974.

———. "Trade, Transport, and Taxes: The Decline of a National Medicine Fair in Republican China." In *Select Papers from the Center for Far Eastern Studies,* vol. 4, edited by Tang Tsou. Chicago: University of Chicago, 1979–1980.

Ju Chengmao. "Yueren Tang de jingshang zhidao" (Yueren Tang's way of trading). *Shijiazhuang wenshi ziliao* (Literary and historical materials on Shijiazhuang) 2 (August 1984): 111–116.

Kammen, Michael. *American Culture, American Tastes: Social Change and the 20th Century.* New York: Knopf, 1999.

Kang Jifu. *Hu Wenhu zhuan* (A biography of Aw Boon-haw). Hong Kong: Longmen wenhua shiye youxian gongsi, 1984.

———. "*Hu Wenhu zhuan* buyi" (An addendum to *A Biography of Aw Boon-haw*). *Nanbeiji yuekan* (Nanbeiji monthly) (Hong Kong), January 16, 1987.

Kao, Mayching Margaret. "China's Response to the West in Art: 1898–1937." Ph.D. diss., Stanford University, 1972.

Katzenstein, Peter J., and Takashi Shiraishi. "Conclusion: Regions in World Politics, Japan and Asia—Germany in Europe." In *Network Power: Japan and Asia,* edited by Peter J. Katzenstein and Takashi Shiraishi. Ithaca, N.Y.: Cornell University Press, 1996.

Ke Mu. "Xianggang kewang chengwei Tongren Tang haiwai jidi" (Hong Kong might become Tongren Tang's overseas base). *Guangjiaojing yuekan* (Wide-angled mirror monthly) 12 (December 1999): 97.

Kikuchi Takaharu. *Chugoku minzoku undo no kihon kozo: Taigai boikotto no kenkyu* (The structure of Chinese nationalism: A study of anti-foreign boycotts). Tokyo: Daian, 1966.

King, Sam. *Tiger Balm King: The Life and Times of Aw Boon Haw.* Singapore: Times Books International, 1992.

Kirby, William C. "The Chinese War Economy." In *China's Bitter Victory: The War with Japan, 1937–1945,* edited by James C. Hsiung and Steven I. Levine. Armonk, N.Y.: M. E. Sharpe, 1992.

———. "Continuity and Change in Modern China: Chinese Economic Planning on the Mainland and on Taiwan, 1943–1958." *Australian Journal of Chinese Affairs* 24 (July 1990): 125–132.

Kleinman, Arthur. *Patients and Healers in the Context of Culture.* Berkeley: University of California Press, 1980.

Kong Lingren and Li Dezheng, eds. *Zhongguo jindai qiye de kaituozhe* (Pioneers in modern Chinese enterprises). Vol. 2. Jinan: Shandong renmin chubanshe, 1991.

Kulp, Daniel H. *Country Life in South China: The Sociology of Familism.* New York: Bureau of Publications, Teachers College, Columbia University, 1925.

Kwan Man Bun. *The Salt Merchants of Tianjin: State-Making and Civil Society in Late Imperial China.* Honolulu: University of Hawai'i Press, 2001.

Kwok, D. W. Y. *Scientism in Chinese Thought, 1900–1950.* New Haven, Conn.: Yale University Press, 1965.

Laing, Ellen Johnston. "Chinese Palace-Style Poetry and the Depiction of *A Palace Beauty.*" *Art Bulletin* 72, no. 2 (1990): 284–295.

———. *Selling Happiness: Calendar Posters and Visual Culture in Early Twentieth-Century Shanghai.* Honolulu: University of Hawai'i Press, 2004.

Lao She. "Lao zi hao" (Old shops). In *Lao She wenji* (Collected works of Lao She), vol. 8. Beijing: Renmin wenxue chubanshe, 1984.

Laopai jizhe. *Hu Wenhu fada qushi* (An anecdotal history of Aw Boon-haw's career). Macao: Yuzhou chubanshe, 1960.

Lee, Leo Ou-fan. "The Cultural Construction of Modernity in Urban Shanghai: Some Preliminary Explorations." In *Becoming Chinese: Passages to Modernity and Beyond,* edited by Wen-hsin Yeh. Berkeley: University of California Press, 2000.

Lee, Leo Ou-fan, and Andrew J. Nathan. "The Beginnings of Mass Culture: Journalism and Fiction in the Late Ch'ing and Beyond." In *Popular Culture in Late Imperial China,* edited by David Johnson, Andrew J. Nathan, and Evelyn S. Rawski. Berkeley: University of California Press, 1985.

Legend from a Jar: The Story of Haw Par. Singapore: Haw Par Brothers International, 1994.

Leong, S. T. "The Hakka Chinese of Lingnan: Ethnicity and Social Change in Modern Times." In *Ideal and Reality: Social and Political Change in Modern China, 1860–1949,* edited by David Pong and Edmund S. K. Fung. Lanham, Md.: University Press of America, 1985.

Leung Yuen Sang. "Regional Rivalry in Mid-Nineteenth-Century Shanghai: Cantonese vs. Ningpo Men." *Ch'ing-shih wen-t'i* 4, no. 8 (1982): 29–50.

Li Chunsheng. "Qingdai gongting dang'an yu Beijing Tongren Tang de lishi" (The Qing court archives and the history of Tongren Tang in Beijing). In

Qingdai gongting yihua (Medical consultations at the Qing court), edited by Chen Keji. Beijing: Renmin weisheng chubanshe, 1990.

Li Fengrui. "Hu Wenhu zai kangri zhanzheng shiqi" (Aw Boon-haw in the Sino-Japanese War). *Hu Wenhu yanjiu* 3 (1988): 1–12.

Li Fengrui and Wang Dong. *Hu Wenhu pingzhuan* (A critical biography of Aw Boon-haw). Shanghai: Huadong shifan daxue chubanshe, 1992.

Liang Ssu-ch'eng. *A Pictorial History of Chinese Architecture: A Study of the Development of Its Structural System and the Evolution of Its Types.* Edited by Wilma Fairbank. Cambridge: MIT Press, 1984.

Lin Aimin. "Benbao guoqu ji jianglai" (Our newspaper's past and future). In *Xingzhou ribao sizhounian jiniankan: "Xin Fujian"* (*Xingzhou Daily*'s fourth annual yearbook: "New Fujian"), edited by Fu Jimen. Singapore: *Xingzhou ribao,* 1933.

———. "Liangnian yilai" (The past two years). In *Xingzhou ribao erzhounian jiniankan* (*Xingzhou Daily*'s second annual yearbook). Singapore: *Xingzhou ribao,* 1931.

Lin Yutang. *Moment in Peking: A Novel of Contemporary Chinese Life.* New York: John Day, 1939.

Link, E. Perry, Jr. *Mandarin Ducks and Butterflies: Popular Fiction in Early Twentieth-Century Chinese Cities.* Berkeley: University of California Press, 1981.

Liu Dafu. "Yi tianxia zhi cai, gong tianxia zhi yong" (Using all wealth under heaven to serve the common good). *Hu Wenhu yanjiu* 3 (1988): 13–21.

Liu Haopu and Xu Zisu. "Qizhou miaohui, yaocai shichang gaishu" (The Qizhou medicine fair: A brief account of the medicine market). In *Tianjin wenshi ziliao xuanji* (Collected literary and historical materials on Tianjin), edited by Tianjin zhengxie (Tianjin Political Consultative Council) 20 (1982): 194–213.

Liu Yongcheng and He Zhiqing. "Wanquan Tang de youlai yu fazhan" (Origins and development of Wanquan Tang). In *Zhongguo shehui jingji shi yanjiu* (Research on Chinese social and economic history), edited by Xiamen daxue Zhongguo shehui jingjishi yanjiu bianjibu (Xiamen University's editorial board on Chinese social and economic history). Xiamen: Xiamen daxue chubanshe, 1983.

Liu Zhaoqi. "Daren Tang." In *Zhongguo laozihao* (Old Chinese shops), edited by Kong Lingren and Li Dezheng. Beijing: Gaodeng jiaoyu chubanshe, 1998.

Loeb, Lori. "George Fulford and Victorian Patent Medicines: Quack Mercenaries or Smilesian Entrepreneurs?" *Canadian Bulletin of Medical History* 16 (1999): 125–145.

Longstreth, Richard W. *The Buildings of Main Street: A Guide to American Commercial Architecture*. Washington, D.C.: Preservation Press, 1987.

Lu, Hanchao. "Away from Nanking Road: Small Stores and Neighborhood Life in Modern Shanghai." *Journal of Asian Studies* 54, no. 1 (1995): 93–123.

Lu, Hanlong. "To Be Relatively Comfortable in an Egalitarian Society." In *The Consumer Revolution in Urban China*, edited by Deborah S. Davis. Berkeley: University of California Press, 2000.

Lu Jin. "Yuefenpai dawang Guan Huinong" (Guan Huinong, King of the calendar poster). In *Xianggang wenhua xilie: Yuefenpai wang—Guan Huinong* (Hong Kong culture series: The art of Guan Huinong—King of the calendar poster), edited by Yan Shufen. Hong Kong: Xianggang yishu zhongxin, 1993.

Lu Xun. "Lu Xun zai Zhonghua yishu daxue yanjiang jilu" (Transcript of Lu Xun's lecture at the China College of Art), recorded by Liu Ruli, 21 February 1930. In *Xuexi Lu Xun de meishu sixiang* (Studying Lu Xun's thoughts on art). Beijing: Renmin meishu chubanshe, 1979.

Luo Tiexian. "Hu Wenhu yu Hu Hao" (Aw Boon-haw and Aw Kow). *Hu Wenhu yanjiu* 2 (1987): 73.

Luo Yi. "Wo suo zhidao de Hu Wenhu shengping diandi" (What I know about Aw Boon-haw). *Hu Wenhu yanjiu* 2 (1987): 46–53.

Luo Zhenqing. "Hu Wenhu de xingxibao yu Yongdingji xinwen zhanshi" (Aw Boon-haw's Star newspapers and the journalists from Yongding). *Hu Wenhu yanjiu* 3 (1988): 37–43.

Man'gu Yong'an wuxian gongsi (Wing On Group of Companies, Bangkok), comp. *Nadu Hu Qingcai boshi kangli Tai teji* (Special publication on Dr. Hu Qingcai and his wife in Thailand). Bangkok: Man'gu Yong'an wuxian gongsi, 1964.

Marchand, Roland. *Advertising the American Dream: Making Way for Modernity, 1920–1940*. Berkeley: University of California Press, 1985.

Martin, Brian G. "Resistance and Cooperation: Du Yuesheng and the Politics of the Shanghai United Committee, 1940–1945." In *In the Shadow of the Rising Sun*, edited by Christian Henriot and Wen-hsin Yeh. London: Routledge, 2003.

McKendrick, Neil, John Brewer, and J. H. Plumb. *The Birth of a Consumer Society: The Commercialization of Eighteenth-Century England*. Bloomington: Indiana University Press, 1982.

Meisner, Maurice J. *Li Ta-chao and the Origins of Chinese Marxism*. Cambridge: Harvard University Press, 1967.

Meskill, John. "A Conferral of the Degree of Chin-Shih." *Monumenta Serica* 23 (1964): 351–371.

Murphey, Rhoads. *A History of Asia.* New York: Harper Collins, 1992.

———. "The Treaty Ports and China's Modernization." In *The Chinese City between Two Worlds,* edited by Mark Elvin and G. William Skinner. Stanford, Calif.: Stanford University Press, 1974.

Naquin, Susan. *Peking: Temples and City Life, 1400–1900.* Berkeley: University of California Press, 2000.

Nye, Joseph S., Jr. *Bound to Lead: The Changing Nature of American Power.* New York: Basic Books, 1990.

Pan, Lynn. *Sons of the Yellow Emperor: A History of the Chinese Diaspora.* Boston: Little, Brown, 1990.

Pan, Quentin. Review of *Xingzhou ribao yizhounian jiniankan* (*Xingzhou Daily's* first annual yearbook). *China Critic* 3, no. 22 (1930): 521.

Paz-Soldán, Edmundo, and Debra A. Castillo, eds. *Latin American Literature and Mass Media.* New York: Garland, 2001.

Perkins, Dwight H. *Agricultural Development in China, 1368–1969.* Chicago: Aldine, 1969.

Perry, Elizabeth J. *Shanghai on Strike: The Politics of Chinese Labor.* Stanford, Calif.: Stanford University Press, 1993.

Ping Jinya. "Mantan Huang Chujiu jiqi 'shiye'" (Random remarks on Huang Chujiu and his "industry"). In *Wenshi ziliao xuanji* (Collection of cultural and historical materials). Beijing: Renmin chubanshe, 1963.

Pomeranz, Kenneth. *The Great Divergence: China, Europe, and the Making of the Modern World Economy.* Princeton, N.J.: Princeton University Press, 2000.

Porkert, Manfred. *The Theoretical Foundation of Chinese Medicine: Systems of Correspondence.* Cambridge: MIT Press, 1982.

Potter, Jack M. "Cantonese Shamanism." In *Religion and Ritual in Chinese Society,* edited by Arthur P. Wolf. Stanford, Calif.: Stanford University Press, 1974.

Qi Heming. "Xu Guanqun yu Xinya yaochang" (Xu Guanqun and New Asia Pharmaceutical Mills). *Wujin wenshi* (Literature and history of Wujin) 7 (December 1986).

Qiu Guozhen, ed. *Zhangshu yaosu* (The culture of medicine in Zhangshu). Nanchang: Jiangxi gaoxiao chubanshe, 1996.

"Qixue nianliu" (Years of tears and bloodshed). Television program, Shanghai, 1995.

Quataert, Donald. "Introduction." In *Consumption Studies and the History of the Ottoman Empire, 1550–1922: An Introduction,* edited by Donald Quataert. Albany: State University of New York Press, 2000.

Rawski, Evelyn Sakakida. *Education and Popular Literacy in Ch'ing China*. Ann Arbor: University of Michigan Press, 1979.

———. "Presidential Address: Reenvisioning the Qing." *Journal of Asian Studies* 55, no. 4 (1996): 829–850.

Rawski, Thomas G. *Economic Growth in Prewar China*. Berkeley: University of California Press, 1989.

Reardon-Anderson, James. *The Study of Change: Chemistry in China, 1840–1949*. Cambridge: Cambridge University Press, 1991.

Reid, Anthony. *Southeast Asia in the Age of Commerce, 1450–1680*. New Haven, Conn.: Yale University Press, 1988.

Remer, C. F. *Foreign Investments in China*. New York: Macmillan, 1933.

———. *A Study of Chinese Boycotts with Special Reference to Their Economic Effectiveness*. Baltimore: Johns Hopkins University Press, 1933.

Rogaski, Ruth. *Hygienic Modernity: Meanings of Health and Disease in Treaty-Port China*. Berkeley: University of California Press, 2004.

Rottman, Allison. "Crossing Enemy Lines: Shanghai and the Central China Base." In *In the Shadow of the Rising Sun,* edited by Christian Henriot and Wen-hsin Yeh. London: Routledge, 2003.

Rowe, William, and Vivian Schelling. *Memory and Modernity: Popular Culture in Latin America*. London: Verso, 1991.

Rowe, William T. *Hankow: Commerce and Society in a Chinese City, 1796–1889*. Stanford, Calif.: Stanford University Press, 1984.

Rowe, William T. "The Qingbang and Collaboration under the Japanese, 1939–1945." *Modern China* 8, no. 4 (1982): 491–499.

Rubinfien, Louisa D. "Commodity to Brand: Manufacturers, Merchants, and the Development of the Consumer Market in Interwar Japan." Ph.D. diss., Harvard University, 1995.

Saenz, E. L. "Squibb in Foreign Lands." *Squibb Sales Bulletin* 18, no. 47 (1941): 451–453.

Sammons, Thomas. *Proprietary Medicine and Ointment Trade in China*. Department of Commerce, Bureau of Foreign and Domestic Commerce, Special Consular Report No. 76. Washington, D.C.: Government Printing Office, 1917.

Sanger, J. W. *Advertising Methods in Japan, China, and the Philippines*. U.S. Department of Commerce, Special Agent Series no. 209. Washington, D.C.: Government Printing Office, 1921.

Schiller, H. I. *Communication and Cultural Domination*. Armonk, N.Y.: M. E. Sharpe, 1976.

Schran, Peter. "China's Demographic Evolution 1850–1953 Reconsidered." *China Quarterly* 75 (1978): 638–646.

Schwarcz, Vera. *The Chinese Enlightenment: Intellectuals and the Legacy of the May Fourth Movement of 1919.* Berkeley: University of California Press, 1986.

Scientific Terminology Association, comp. *A Dictionary of Anatomical Terms Approved by the Ministry of Education.* N.p.: Scientific Terminology Association, 1927.

Selden, Mark. "China, Japan, and the Regional Political Economy of East Asia, 1945–1995." In *Network Power: Japan and Asia,* edited by Peter J. Katzenstein and Takashi Shiraishi. Ithaca, N.Y.: Cornell University Press, 1996.

Shanghai shehui kexue yuan jingji yanjiu suo (Shanghai Academy of Social Sciences, Institute of Economics). *Longteng huyao bashi nian: Shanghai Zhonghua zhiyaochang chang shi* (Eighty years of the dragon soaring and the tiger leaping: A factory history of the Zhonghua medicine factory of Shanghai). Shanghai: Shanghai renmin chubanshe, 1991.

———. *Shanghai jindai xiyao hangye shi* (A history of the modern medicine trade in Shanghai). Shanghai: Shanghai shehui kexue yuan chubanshe, 1988.

———. *Zhongxi yaochang bainian shi* (A history of one hundred years at the China and the West Medicine Factory). Shanghai: Shanghai shehui kexue yuan chubanshe, 1990.

Shen Hongxian. "Qiantan Tongren Tang de wan san gao dan" (Brief remarks on Tongren Tang's big pills, powders, plasters, and small pills). In *Qinian hua cangsang* (Old men's chats on history), edited by Zhang Changbing, Ning Yuhuan, and Zhang Yonglin. Shanghai: Shanghai shudian, 1993.

Shen Lixin. "Jiwu liqun, aiguo aixiang" (Philanthropist and patriotic localist). *Hu Wenhu yanjiu* 1 (1985): 3–7.

Shen Zuwei. "Xiang Songmao, diyige Kangri xunnan di qiyejia" (Xiang Songmao, the first entrepreneur to be martyred in the War of Resistance against Japan). In *Guonan zhong de qiyejia* (Chinese entrepreneurs during the national crisis), edited by Shen Zuwei and Du Xuncheng. Shanghai: Shanghai shehui kexueyuan chubanshe, 1996.

Shi Chuan. "Tongren Tang de zhenbian" (Great changes at Tongren Tang). *Guangjiaojing yuekan* (Wide-angled mirror monthly) 12 (December 1999): 94–96.

Shi Jian. "Wei Shaobo yu Ertianyou" (Wei Shaobo and Two Heavens Oil). *Foshan wenshi* no. 7 (Literature and history of Foshan) (1987): 67–68.

Shiba Yoshinobu. "Ningpo and Its Hinterland." In *The City in Late Imperial China,* edited by G. William Skinner. Stanford, Calif.: Stanford University Press, 1977.

Sivin, Nathan. *Chinese Alchemy: Preliminary Studies.* Cambridge: Harvard University Press, 1968.

———. *Traditional Medicine in Contemporary China.* Ann Arbor: Center for Chinese Studies, University of Michigan, 1987.

Skinner, G. William. "Chinese Cities: The Difference a Century Makes." In *Cosmopolitan Capitalists: Hong Kong and the Diaspora at the End of the Twentieth Century,* edited by Gary G. Hamilton. Seattle: University of Washington Press, 1999.

———. "Introduction: Urban Social Structure in Ch'ing China." In *The City in Late Imperial China,* edited by G. William Skinner. Stanford, Calif.: Stanford University Press, 1977.

———. "Mobility Strategies in Late Imperial China: A Regional Systems Analysis." In *Regional Analysis,* vol. 1 of *Economic Systems,* edited by Carol A. Smith. New York: Academic Press, 1976.

———. "Presidential Address: The Structure of Chinese History." *Journal of Asian Studies* 44, no. 2 (1985): 271–292.

———. "Regional Urbanization in Nineteenth-Century China." In *The City in Late Imperial China,* edited by G. William Skinner. Stanford, Calif.: Stanford University Press, 1977.

———, ed., *The City in Late Imperial China.* Stanford, Calif.: Stanford University Press, 1977.

Spence, Jonathan D. *The Gate of Heavenly Peace: The Chinese and Their Revolution, 1895–1980.* New York: Viking Press, 1981.

———. *The Search for Modern China.* New York: W. W. Norton, 1999.

Starr, Paul. *The Social Transformation of American Medicine.* New York: Basic Books, 1982.

Steinberg, David Joel, ed. *In Search of Southeast Asia.* Honolulu: University of Hawaii Press, 1987.

Stockwell, A. J. "Southeast Asia in War and Peace: The End of European Colonial Empires." In *The Cambridge History of Southeast Asia,* vol. 2, edited by Nicholas Tarling. New York: Cambridge University Press, 1992.

Sugihara Kaoru. "The East Asian Path of Economic Development: A Long-term Perspective." In *The Resurgence of East Asia,* edited by Giovanni Arrighi, Takeshi Hamashita, and Mark Selden. London: Routledge, 2003.

———. "Japan as an Engine of the Asian International Economy, c. 1880–1936." *Japan Forum* 2, no. 1 (1990): 127–145.

Sun Dexiang. "Xiang Songmao." In *Minguo renwu zhuan* (Biographies of figures from the Republican period), edited by Zhu Xinguan and Yang Ruping. Vol. 4. Beijing: Zhonghua shuju, 1984.

Tan Yulin. "Wuzhou yaochang bashi nian lai hua cangsang" (A talk about eighty years of vicissitudes at Five Continents Medicine Plants). *Changning wenshi ziliao* (Literary and historical material on Changning) (Shanghai) 5 (1989).

———. "Xu Guanqun." In *Minguo renwu zhuan* (Biographies of figures from the Republican period), edited by Zhu Xinquan and Yan Ruping. Vol. 4. Beijing: Zhonghua shuju, 1984.

Tatsukawa Shoji. *Meiji iji orai*. Tokyo: Shinchosha, 1986.

Temporel, Paul. *Branding in Asia*. Singapore: John Wiley and Sons, 2000.

Thomson, John. *Through China with a Camera*. Westminster, Eng.: Constable, 1898.

"Tianjin chengshi jianshe" congshu bian weihui "Tianjin jindai jianzhu" bian xie zu (Series editorial committee for "Tianjin City reconstructs" and editorial writing group for "Architecture of modern Tianjin"), comps. *Tianjin jindai jianzhu* (Architecture in modern Tianjin). Tianjin: Tianjin kexue jishu chubanshe, 1990.

Tien Hung-mao. *Government and Politics in Kuomintang China, 1927–1937*. Stanford, Calif.: Stanford University Press, 1972.

Tiersten, Lisa. "Redefining Consumer Culture: Recent Literature on Consumption and the Bourgeoisie in Western Europe." *Radical History Review* 57 (1993): 116–159.

Tomlinson, John. *Cultural Imperialism: A Critical Introduction*. Baltimore: Johns Hopkins University Press, 1991.

Trocki, Carl A. *Opium and Empire: Chinese Society in Colonial Singapore, 1880–1910*. Ithaca, N.Y.: Cornell University Press, 1990.

Tsang, Sharon, comp. "The Biography of Aw Boon-haw (1882–1954)." Hong Kong, 1990.

Tsin, Michael. "Canton Remapped." In *Remaking the Chinese City*, edited by Joseph W. Esherick. Honolulu: University of Hawai'i Press, 2000.

Tsuien kinencho (A commemorative album in honor of the ancestors). Osaka: Morishita Jintan kabushiki kaisha, 1959.

Vogel, Ezra. F. *Canton under Communism: Programs and Politics in a Provincial Capital, 1949–1968*. New York: Harper and Row, 1971.

Waara, Carrie. "Invention, Industry, Art: The Commercialization of Culture in Republican Art Magazines." In *Inventing Nanjing Road: Commercial Culture in Shanghai, 1900–1945*, edited by Sherman Cochran. Ithaca, N.Y.: Cornell East Asia Program, 1999.

Wakeman, Frederic, Jr. *Policing Shanghai, 1927–1937*. Berkeley: University of California Press, 1995.

———. "Shanghai Smuggling." In *In the Shadow of the Rising Sun,* edited by Christian Henriot and Wen-hsin Yeh. London: Routledge, 2003.

Wakeman, Frederic, Jr., and Wen-hsin Yeh, eds. *Shanghai Sojourners.* Berkeley: University of California Institute of East Asian Studies, 1992.

Wallerstein, Immanuel. *The Modern World System.* New York: Academic Press, 1974.

Wang Duyuan. "Baowei yaohuang shimo" (Burroughs Wellcome Medicine Company from beginning to end). *Shanghai wenshi ziliao xuanji* (Collected literary and historical materials on Shanghai) 55 (February 1987): 251–269.

Wang Gungwu. "The Limits of Nanyang Chinese Nationalism." In *Southeast Asian History and Historiography,* edited by C. D. Cowan and O. W. Wolters. Ithaca, N.Y.: Cornell University Press, 1976.

Wang Jinyuan. "'Tongren' yao fang shimo" ("Tongren" Medicine Shop from beginning to end). *Yi xian wenshi ziliao* (Literary and historical materials on Yi county) 4 (1987): 201–207.

Wang Ke-wen. "Collaborators and Capitalists: The Politics of 'Material Control' in Wartime Shanghai." *Chinese Studies in History* 26, no. 1 (1992): 42–62.

Wang Liping. "Tourism and Spatial Change in Hangzhou, 1911–1927." In *Remaking the Chinese City,* edited by Joseph W. Escherick. Honolulu: University of Hawai'i Press, 2000.

Wang Renze. "Kangri xunshen de aiguo qiyejia Xiang Songmao" (Martyr of the War of Resistance against Japan: The patriotic entrepreneur Xiang Songmao). *Zhejiang wenshi ziliao xuanji* (Literary and cultural materials on Zhejiang) 39 (1989).

Wang Yingkui. "Chutan Tianjin shangbiao" (Interesting anecdotes about trademarks in Tianjin). *Tianjin wenshi ziliao xuanji* (Collected literary and historical materials on Tianjin), ser. 67, 3 (1995): 130–141.

Wang Ziran. "Xinyu zhuozhu de Yueren Tang Zhongyao dian" (Yueren Tang, a respected Chinese medicine shop). *Taiyuan wenshi ziliao* (Literary and historical materials on Taiyuan) 1 (September 1984): 118–126.

Watson, James L. "China's Big Mac Attack." *Foreign Affairs* 79, no. 3 (2000): 120–134.

Watson, James L. "Introduction: Transnationalism, Localization, and Fast Foods in East Asia." In *Golden Arches East,* edited by James L. Watson. Stanford, Calif.: Stanford University Press, 1997.

Weidner, Marsha. "Women in the History of Chinese Painting." In *Views from Jade Terrace: Chinese Women Artists, 1300–1912*, edited by Marsha Weidner et al. Indianapolis and New York: Indianapolis Museum of Art and Rizzoli, 1988.

Wessing, Robert. *The Soul of Ambiguity: The Tiger in Southeast Asia*. [DeKalb, Ill.]: Northern Illinois University Center for Southeast Asian Studies, 1986.

Wilkins, Mira. *The Emergence of Multinational Enterprise: American Business Abroad from the Colonial Era to 1914*. Cambridge: Harvard University Press, 1970.

Wilson, G. L. "Architecture, Interior Decoration, and Building in Shanghai Twenty Years Ago and Today." *China Journal* 12, no. 5 (1930): 248–252.

Wright, Arnold. *Twentieth Century Impressions of Hongkong, Shanghai, and Other Treaty Ports of China: Their History, People, Commerce, Industries, and Resources*. 3 vols. London: Lloyd's Greater Britain Publishing Company, 1908.

Wu Chengluo. "Zhongguo zhi huaxue yaopin ji huaxue yuanliao gongye" (China's pharmaceutical industry and chemical raw-materials industry). *Jingji jianshe jikan* 1, no. 4 (1943): 127–139.

Wu Hao, Zhuo Botang, Huang Ying, and Lu Wanwen. *Duhui modeng: Yuefenpai, 1910s–1930s* (Calendar posters of the modern Chinese woman). Hong Kong: Sanlian shudian youxian gongsi chubanshe, 1994.

Wu Hong and Wu Tingkai. "Xia'er wenming de Daren Tang yaodian" (The famous Daren Tang Medicine Shop). *Wuhan wenshi ziliao* (Literary and historical materials on Wuhan) 4 (December 1989): 67–69.

Wu Tsu-hsiang. "Fan Village." In *Modern Chinese Stories and Novellas, 1919–1949*, edited by Joseph S. M. Lau, C. T. Hsia, and Leo Ou-fan Lee. New York: Columbia University Press, 1981.

Wuzhou da yaofang sanshi zhounian jinian kan (A commemorative volume on the thirtieth anniversary of Great Five Continents drugstores). Shanghai, 1936.

Xiamenshi tudi zhi bianzuan weiyuanhui (Committee for the compilation of the Xiamen City local gazetteer). *Xiamen shi tudi zhi* (Xiamen City local gazetteer). Xiamen: Lujiang chubanshe, 1996.

Xiandai Shanghai dashiji (Great events in modern Shanghai). Shanghai: Shanghai cishu chubanshe, 1996.

Xiang Zenan. "Wuzhou guben feizao he xiangmao feizao de jingxiao jingguo" (The rivalry between Five Continents' Guben Soap and Xiangmao Soap). *Wenshi ziliao xuanji* (Collected literary and historical materials) (Shanghai) 16 (1964).

————. "Wuzhou zaochang yu Yingshang de jingzheng yiji dui Ridi de dou-zheng" (Five Continents' rivalry with British merchants in the struggle against Japanese imperialism), *Yangpu wenshi ziliao* (Literary and histori-cal materials on Yangpu) 1 (1987).

Xiang Zenan and Tan Yulin. "Aiguo shiyejia Xiang Songmao yunan jingguo" (The murder of the patriotic entrepreneur Xiang Songmao). *Shanghai shi ziliao xuanji* (Collected materials on Shanghai history) 50 (1985).

Xie Mu and Wu Yongliang. *Zhongguo de laozihao* (China's old stores). 2 vols. Beijing: Jingji ribao chubanshe, 1988.

Xu Guanqun. "Fumujie yougan" (Some thoughts on Parents' Day). *Jiankang jiating* 5, no. 4 (1944).

————. "Women de yuanwang yu nuli—xie zai benkan gexinhao zhiqian (Our goals and plans—a few words on our magazine's new format and style). *Jiankang jiating* 2, no. 8 (1940).

————. "Xinya yaochang sanshinian laide huigu" (Reflections on my thirty years at New Asia Pharmaceutical Company). 1964. (The original copy of this unpublished manuscript is in the office of the New Asia Pharma-ceutical Company, Shanghai.)

Xu Guoren. "Xingxi baoye yu Xiamen Xingguang ribao" (The Star chain of newspapers and Xiamen's *Xingguang Daily*). *Xiamen wenshi ziliao* no. 10 (September 1986): 64–70.

Xu, Xiaoqun. *Chinese Professionals and the Republican State: The Rise of Profes-sional Associations in Shanghai, 1912–1937.* Cambridge: Cambridge Uni-versity Press, 2001.

Yamamoto Taketoshi. *Kokoku no shakai shi* (A social history of advertising). Tokyo: Hosei dagaku shuppan kyoku, 1984.

Yan Shufen. "Guanshi jiazu shilue" (Guan's family). In *Xianggang wenhua xilie: Yuefenpai wang—Guan Huinong* (Hong Kong culture series: The art of Guan Huinong—King of the calendar poster), edited by Yan Shufen. Hong Kong: Xianggang yishu zhongxin, 1993.

————, ed. *Xianggang wenhua xilie: Yuefenpai wang—Guan Huinong* (Hong Kong culture series: The art of Guan Huinong—King of the calendar poster). Hong Kong: Xianggang yishu zhongxin, 1993.

Yan, Yunxiang. "State Power and Cultural Transition in China." In *Many Glob-alizations: Cultural Diversity in the Contemporary World,* edited by Peter L. Berger and Samuel P. Huntington. Oxford: Oxford University Press, 2002.

Yang, Simon, and L. K. Tao. *A Study of the Standard of Living of Working Fami-lies in Shanghai.* Peiping: Institute of Social Research, 1931.

Yeh, Wen-hsin. "Progressive Journalism and Shanghai's Petty Urbanites: Zou Taofen and the *Shenghuo Weekly*, 1926–1945." In *Shanghai Sojourners*, edited by Frederic Wakeman Jr. and Wen-hsin Yeh. Berkeley: University of California Institute of East Asian Studies, 1992.

Yong, C. F. *Tan Kah-kee: The Making of an Overseas Chinese Legend*. Singapore: Oxford University Press, 1987.

Young, Arthur N. *China and the Helping Hand, 1937–1945*. Cambridge: Harvard University Press, 1963.

Young, James Harvey. *Pure Food: Securing the Federal Food and Drug Act of 1906*. Princeton, N.J.: Princeton University Press, 1989.

———. *The Toadstool Millionaires: A Social History of Patent Medicines in America before Federal Regulation*. Princeton, N.J.: Princeton University Press, 1961.

Yu Yue and Wu Liyue, eds. *Jiangxi minsu wenhua xulun* (Collected essays on Jiangxi's popular culture). Beijing: Guangming ribao chubanshe, 1995.

Yuan Shude. "Beijing Tongren Tang sanbai nian cangsang" (Three hundred years of changes at Tongren Tang). *Chunqiu* 35 (spring and autumn 1985): 59–63.

Yuan Yuquan. "Rikou jiaqiang luedou huazhong zhanlue wuzi paozhi shangtonghui jingguo" (How the Japanese established the Commercial Control Committee to take control of strategic materials in central China). *Dang'an yu lishi* (Archives and history) 4 (1986): 82–87, 75.

Yue Songsheng. "Beijing Tongren Tang de huigu yu zhanwang (The past and future of Tongren Tang in Beijing). *Wenshi ziliao xuanji* (Collected literary and historical materials) 11 (1960): 132–148.

Zeng Guangfang. "Kexue yu jiating" (Science and the family). *Jiankang jiating* 1 (1939).

Zhang Baohao and Fan Nengchuan. *Shanghai luyou wenhua* (The culture of Shanghai tourism). Shanghai: Shanghai shudian, 1992.

Zhang Bingxin. "Tongren Tang Yuejia laopu" (The Yue family's old shop Tongren Tang). In *Zhuming jinghua de laozihao* (Famous old businesses in the capital), edited by Zhongguo renmin zhengzhi xie shang huiyi Beijingshi weiyuanhui wenshi ziliao yanjiu weiyuanhui (Chinese people's political consultative council on reminisences, Committee for research on cultural and historical materials). Beijing: Wenshi ziliao chubanshe, 1986.

Zhang Muhan. "Cong meiren hua kan nüxing mei" (The ideal of feminine beauty as reflected in paintings of classical beauties). In *Lidai meiren huaxuan* (Selected paintings of beauties through the ages). Taipei: Yishu tushu gongsi, 1984.

Zhang Weihan. "Wo suo zhidao de Tianjin Daren Tang" (What I know about Daren Tang in Tianjin). *Tianjin wenshi ziliao xuanji* (Collected literary and historical materials on Tianjin) 34 (January 1986): 143–148.

Zhang Wenqiang. "Hu Wenhu weihe rezhong yu banbao" (Why was Aw Boon-haw interested in publishing his own newspaper?). *Hu Wenhu yanjiu* 1 (1985): 8–10.

———. "Sanshi niandai de Shantou *Xinghua ribao*" (Shantou's *Xinghua Daily* in the 1930s). *Hu Wenhu yanjiu* 1 (July 1985): 39–50.

Zhang Yanfeng. *Lao yuefenpai: Guanggao hua* (Old calendar posters: Advertising paintings). 2 vols. Special issue of *Han sheng zazhi* (Echo magazine) (Taipei), no. 61 (1994).

Zhang Yonghe. *Hu Wenhu zhuan* (Biography of Aw Boon-haw). Singapore: Congwen chubanshe, 1993.

Zhang Zhiyu. "Tongren Tang yaopu shimo" (Tongren Tang Medicine Shop from beginning to end). *Bengbu gongshang shiliao* (Historical materials on industry and commerce in Bengbu) 9 (1987): 202–205.

Zhang Zhongli, ed. *Jindai Shanghai chengshi yanjiu* (Urban studies on modern Shanghai). Shanghai: Shanghai shehui kexue yuan, 1990.

Zhao Hongjun. *Jindai Zhongxiyi lunzhengshi* (History of the rivalry between Chinese and Western medicine). Hefei: Anhui renmin chubanshe, 1989.

Zhao Jiaxin. "Fujian de liangjia xingxibao—Xiamen *Xingguang ribao* yu Fuzhou *Xingmin ribao*" (Fujian's two newspapers in the Star chain—Xiamen's *Xingguang Daily* and Fuzhou's *Xingmin Daily*). *Fuzhou wenshi ziliao* no. 23 (July 1990): 81–90.

Zheng Liren. "Overseas Chinese Nationalism in British Malaya, 1894–1941." Ph.D. diss., Cornell University, 1997.

Zheng Tianting. "Zheng Tianting jiaoshou xu" (Professor Zheng Tianting's preface). In *Cixi Guangxu yifang xuanyi* (Selected comments on recipes used for Cixi and Guangxu), edited by Chen Keji. Beijing: Zhonghua shuju, 1990.

Zhongguo minzhu jianguo hui Beijingshi weiyuanhui, Beijingshi gong shangye lianhehui wenshi gongzuo weiyuanhui (Beijing committee on reconstruction of the Chinese people, Association of Beijing's industry and commerce, Working committee on literature and history). "Tongren Tang." In *Beijing gong shang shihua* (History of industry and commerce in Beijing), edited by Zhongguo minzhu jianguo hui Beijingshi

weiyuanhui, Beijingshi gong shangye lianhehui wenshi gongzuo weiyuanhui. Beijing: Zhongguo shangye chubanshe, 1987.

Zhongguo Tongren Tang jituan gongsi Beijing Tongren Tangshi bianweihui
(Editorial Committee for the History of Tongren Tang from the Tongren Tang Group of Companies of China), ed. *Beijing Tongren Tangshi*
(The history of Tongren Tang in Beijing). Beijing: Renmin ribao chubanshe, 1993.

Zhou Jianduan. *Jinghua ganjiu lu* (Reminiscences about the capital). Hong
Kong: Nanyue chubanshe, 1987.

Zhu Zonghai and Chen Danxin. "'Wanjinyou da wang' Hu Wenhu" (Tiger
Balm king Aw Boon-haw). In *Zhongguo qiyejia liezhuan* (Biographies of
Chinese entrepreneurs), vol. 3, edited by Xu Dixin. Beijing: Jingji ribao
chubanshe, 1989.

Zhuang Xinru. "Rijun qiangkou xia de jushang fuzi" (Two generations of
commercial giants facing the guns of the Japanese army). *Shanghai tan* 8
(1993).

Zhuo Botang. "Guan Huinong yu Zhongguo zaoqi de shangpin haibao"
(Guan Huinong and early commercial newspapers on the China coast).
In *Xianggang wenhua xilie: Yuefenpai wang—Guan Huinong* (Hong Kong
culture series: The art of Guan Huinong—King of the calendar poster),
edited by Yan Shufen. Hong Kong: Xianggang yishu zhongxin, 1993.

Zhuo Nansheng, ed. *Cong Xingzhou ribao kan Xingzhou wushinian, 1929–1979*
(Xingzhou's fifty years, 1929–1979, from *Xingzhou Daily*). Singapore:
Xingzhou ribao, 1980.

2.1. Beijing in the eighteenth century. Tongren Tang's store was built in the circled area just to the left of the great road that led up to the massive Front Gate—as close to the imperial court as it could officially be. Beijing baike quanshu bianji weiyuanhui, *Beijing beike quanshu: Cai he, ditu ji* (Beijing: Aolinpike chubanshe, 1991), 28.

2.2. A catalogue of Tongren Tang's medicines. The first edition was published in the early eighteenth century, and the edition shown here, which listed 495 medicines, was published in the late nineteenth century. Zhonggua Tongren Tang, *Beijing Tongren Targshi* (Beijing : Renmin ribao, 1993).

2.3. The Yue family in the 1890s, under the leadership of Xu Shi (in the middle of the next-to-last row), widow of Yue Pingquan. Zhongguo Tongren Tang, *Beijing Tongren Targshi* (Beijing: Renmin ribao, 1993).

2.4. Yue Daren with his wife (seated) and children, ca. 1933. Courtesy of Yue Daren's son, John Yueh, who is in the front row, second from left.

2.5. Tongren Tang's unpretentious and dimly lit building in 1925. Constructed in Beijing in 1900, it served as Tongren Tang's store in the early twentieth century. K. K. Chen, "Chinese Drug Stores," *Annals of Medical History* 7, no. 2 (1925), 104.

2.6. Architectural drawings of Daren Tang's main store in Tianjin. Built in 1914, it stretched from one street to another (as shown on the street map). The doors on its front gate (in the upper drawing) opened into an entryway that led through a second set of doors (in the lower drawing) and from there into its salesroom. "Tianjin chengshi jianshe," comps., *Tianjin jindai jianzhu,* (Tianjin: Tianjin kexue jishu chubanshe, 1990), 119–120.

3.1. Huang Chujiu, the Chinese founder and head of China-France Drugstores, who had no experience or connection with France or any other Western country. *Haishang mingren zhuan* (Sharghai: Wenming shuju, 1930), 62.

3.2. Ailuo Brain Tonic with "Dr. T. C. Yales" printed in English on the bottle's wrapper. Zhang Yanfeng, *Lao yuefenpai Guanggao hua* (Taipei: 1994), 2:34.

3.3. Huang's letterhead, shop sign, and other promotional materials listed its Chinese name, "China-France Drugstore of Shanghai," above its English name. Zhang Yanfeng, *Lao yuefenpai Guanggao hua* (Taippei: 1994), 1:41.

3.4. A large billboard in North China near Tianjin in the late 1910s featuring Japanese-owned Humane Elixir's trademark: the company's name below a bust of a man wearing a "Humane Elixir mustache." Photo in J. W. Sanger, *Advertising Methods, in Japan, China, and the Philippines* (Washington, D.C.: Government Printing Office, 1921), opposite 74.

3.5. A parade of sandwich board carriers promoting Humane Elixir in the Middle Yangzi region outside the city wall of Hanyang in 1914. *Tsuien Kinensho* (Osaka: Morishita Jintan Kabushiki Kaisha, 1959).

3.6. The trademark for Chinese-owned Human Elixir with the nationalistic slogan "Chinese National Goods" in four circles at the top and the traditional Daoist pairing of the dragon and tiger at opposite corners. Zhang Yanfeng, *Lao yuefenpai Guanggao hua* (Taipei, 1994), 2:47.

3.7. A calendar poster by Hang Zhiying using the "one bare breast" motif to advertise Ailuo Brain Tonic, Human Elixir, and Huang Chujiu's other medicines (shown around the border). Zhang Yanfeng, *Lao yuefenpai Guanggao hua* (Taipei, 1994), 1:29.

3.8. The Great World amusement hall was built by Huang Chujiu in 1917 and is shown here in the 1930s. Deng Ming ed., *Shanghai bainian lueying 1840–1940s* (Shanghai: Shanghai renmin meishu chubanshe, 1996), 203.

4.1. Xiang Songmao, head of Five Continents Drugstores, 1911–1931. *Wuzhou da yaofang sanshi zhounian jinian kan* (Shanghai, 1936), 90.

4.2. Five Continents' headquarters at its opening in Shanghai in 1913, with Xiang Songmao posed in front (at the spot marked "X"). *Wuzhou da yaofang sanshi zhounian jinian kan* (Shanghai, 1936), 103.

4.3. Five Continents' most popular product, Man-Made Blood. Its Western-style glass bottle is labeled entirely in Chinese. Zhang Yanfeng, *Lao yuefenpai Guanggao hua* (Taipei, 1994), 2:32.

4.4. Shops in traditional-style Chinese architecture in South China at Guangzhou in the 1890s. Photo in John Thomson, *Through China with a Camera* (Westminster, Eng.: Constable, 1898), opposite 66.

4.5. Five Continents' branch stores in Western-style architecture in the North China cities of Jinan (top left, built in 1930), Tianjin (right, 1928), and Beijing (bottom left, 1931). Like all Five Continents' branches, they bore the store's name and had its globe trademark plastered high on their facades. *Wuzhou da yaofang sanshi zhounian jinian kan* (Shanghai, 1936), 118.

4.6. Five Continents' branch stores in the Middle Yangzi region at Hankou (top, built in 1926) and Jiujiang (bottom, 1930) featured "Western" columns of the Chinese builders' own creation and Chinese-style floral motifs. *Wuzhou da yaofang sanshi zhounian jinian kan* (Shanghai, 1936), 120.

4.7. Five Continents' branch store (built in 1932) in Southeast China at Xiamen was given an arcade to make it resemble other shops in the city (see Figure 4.8). *Wuzhou da yaofang sanshi zhounian jinian kan* (Shanghai, 1936), 122.

4.8. This commercial district, built in Xiamen in the 1920s, set an architectural pattern that Five Continents followed when it constructed its local branch in the 1930s (see Figure 4.7). Xiamenshi tudi zhi bianzuan weiyuanhui, *Xiamenshi tudi zhi* (Xiamen: Lujiang chubanshe, 1996).

4.9. Five Continents' ten-story headquarters at Shanghai (built in 1936) in Art Deco style, with its display windows twelve feet wide and twenty-four feet high. (Contrast this with its smaller and more modest predecessor, shown in Figure 4.2). *Wuzhou da yaofang sanshi zhounian jinian kan* (Shanghai, 1936), 107.

4.10. Five Continents' Shanghai headquarters glittering at night in 1936. *Wuzhou da yaofang sanshi zhounian jinian kan* (Shanghai, 1936), 182.

4.11. Five Continents' brightly lit sales room on the ground floor of its Shanghai headquarters in 1936. *Wuzhou da yaofang sanshi zhounian jinian kan* (Shanghai, 1936), 108.

4.12. The Xiang Songmao Memorial Hall, designed in traditional Chinese style, on the third floor of Five Continents' Shanghai headquarters, 1936. *Wuzhou da yaofang sanshi zhounian jinian kan* (Shanghai, 1936), 201.

4.13. A poster advertising Man-Made Blood, with space left for each branch to fill in the name of its locality. From right to left the line at the top says, "[Blank] Great Five Continents Drugstores." Zhang Yanfeng, *Lao yuefenpai: Guanggao hua* (Taipei, 1994), 1:75.

5.1. Xu Guanqun, founder and head of New Asia Pharmaceutical Company. Chen Lizheng and Yuan Enzhen, eds., *Shanghai Xinya yaoye youxian gongsi zhi* (Shanghai Xinya yaoye youxian gongsi, 1996).

5.2. New Asia Pharmaceutical Company's trademark with a star (pronounced *xing* in Mandarin) as a pun on "New" (xin), and with the character for "Asia" (ya) colored red on the inside. Chen Lizheng and Yuan Enzhen, eds., *Xinya de licheng—Shanghai xinya zhiyaochang de guoqu xianzai he jianglai* (Shanghai: Shanghai shehui kexue yuan chubanshe, 1990).

5.3. *A Child's Growth to Manhood* on the cover of *Healthy Home* shows how, under scientific parenting, a child advances stage by stage in a linear progression. *Jiankang jiating* (Shanghai), August 30, 1941.

5.4. This cover of *Healthy Home* illustrates the compatibility of traditional grandparents and their modern children and grandchildren living together in a Chinese family. (The illustration is untitled.) *Jiankang jiating* (Shanghai), December 1942.

5.5. A *Healthy Home* cartoon, "Nonscientific Doctors of the Masses," mocks the deficiencies of "superstitious remedies" and "nonscientific medicine," thus implying that New Asia's scientific products were superior. *Jiankang jiating* 8 (Shanghai, 1939).

6.1. Aw Boon-haw, manufacturer and promoter of Tiger Balm. Aw Boon Haw Papers. Used with permission.

6.2. The springing tiger, shown here on an early twentieth-century tin of Tiger Balm, was originally designed by Aw Boon-haw himself. Judith Brandel and Tina Turbeville, *Tiger Balm Gardens: A Chinese Billionaire's Fantasy Environments* (Hong Kong: Aw Boon Haw Foundation, 1998), 26. Used with permission.

6.3. Guan Huinong, a commercial artist who painted advertisements for Tiger Balm in the early twentieth century. Yan Shufen, ed., *Xianggang wenhua xilie: Yue fenpai wang—Guan Huinong* (Hong Kong: Xianggang yishu zhongxin, 1993).

6.4. *Roaring Tiger* (1908) by Gao Qifeng, a political revolutionary with whom Guan worked before becoming a commercial artist.

6.5. A tiger on the cover of the magazine that was founded by Guan, Gao, and their fellow painters in support of the revolution of 1911.

6.6. Guan Huinong's poster of a modern woman and a springing tiger for Tiger Balm. The company's name was given in English and Thai as well as Chinese characters and romanized Chinese, thereby conveying a transnational and transcultural message rather than a nationalistic one. Yan Shufen, "Guanshi jiazu shilue," in *Xianggang wenhua xilie: Yuefenpai wang—Guan Huinong,* Yan Shufen, ed. (Hong Kong: Xianggang yishi zhongxin, 1993), 28.

6.7. Tiger Balm Garden in Hong Kong, with Aw Boon-haw's residence in the foreground. Man'gu Yong'an, comp., *Nadu Hu Qingcai boshi kangli Tai teji* (Bangkok: Man'gu Yong'an wuxian gongsi, 1964).

6.8. Aw Boon-haw shaking hands with Chiang Kai-shek at Chiang's wartime capital of Chongqing in 1941. "Hu Wenhu xiansheng liushi jinwu shouzhen zhuan," *Xingdao ribao* (Singapore), January 16, 1947, 2.

DATE DUE